Understanding Race, Ethnicity, and Power

Understanding Race, Ethnicity, and Power

THE KEY TO EFFICACY IN CLINICAL PRACTICE

Elaine Pinderhughes

THE FREE PRESS
A Division of Macmillan, Inc.
NEW YORK

Maxwell Macmillan Canada
TORONTO

Maxwell Macmillan International
NEW YORK   OXFORD   SINGAPORE   SYDNEY

The Free Press
A Division of Macmillan, Inc.
866 Third Avenue, New York, N. Y. 10022

Maxwell Macmillan Canada, Inc.
1200 Eglinton Avenue East
Suite 200
Don Mills, Ontario M3C 3N1

Macmillan, Inc. is part of the Maxwell Communication
Group of Companies.

Printed in the United States of America

printing number
5   6   7   8   9   10

Library of Congress Cataloging-in-Publication Data

Pinderhughes, Elaine.
    Understanding race, ethnicity, and power.

    Bibliography: p.
    Includes index.
    1. Human services—United States. 2. Social service
and race relations—United States. 3. Social work with
minorities—United States. 4. Minorities—Education—
United States. I. Title.
HV95.P55 1989   362.8'4'00973   88–33554
ISBN 0–02–925341–1

To Charles,
Whose enduring support and unfailing candor
have always meant so much, and
To Our Children

Contents

Foreword

Understanding Race, Ethnicity, and Power is a much-needed and long-overdue book. Elaine Pinderhughes addresses cross-cultural problems in the delivery of human services, one of the most neglected and unstudied dynamics in client-practitioner interactions. She does this in a work that is original, offering unique insights and much-needed integration of the fragmentation that besets this area of practice.

As a psychiatrist who has supervised and consulted with trainees in all the mental health disciplines, I wished on many occasions that just such an invaluable resource had been available. The biases and ignorance of ethnocentric or culturally one-dimensional therapists have not only hindered treatment but have, all too often, harmed clients. Clinicians who evince their unrealized prejudices or view their clients stereotypically as members of a particular ethnic group can unwittingly abuse their patients, rendering them powerless to cope with the practitioner's consciously or unconsciously expressed superiority.

Unfortunately, these problems are not limited to persons who are ethnocentric, ignorant, or prejudiced. Each of us is biased by our prior life experiences, which offer the only basis available to us for understanding and interpreting the present. Professor Pinderhughes' use of practitioner experiences dramatically illustrates this issue, engaging the reader in a self-reflective process. In this scholarly and dynamic presentation, she accurately and thoroughly demonstrates the complexities involved in understanding cultural differences. At the same time, she provides an opportunity for everyone to enrich his or her own experiential base for understanding and interpreting the behavior of others who are different. The author's focus on the critical power issues in ethnicity and service delivery is a major contribution to the mental health field.

The chapters are so well written and the many quotes and illustrations so effectively, clearly, and graphically presented that this book will prove of substantial benefit not only to practitioners in mental health, but to scholars and professionals in education and the social sciences. Although it is clear that we are living in an increasingly complex multicultural society, we are doing very little to prepare our young people to prosper in it. I believe this volume should become required reading for all who aspire to careers in the field of human services.

ALVIN F. POUSSAINT, M.D.
Associate Professor of Psychiatry
Harvard Medical School
January 25, 1989

Preface

A FOCUS ON THE PERCEPTIONS, ATTITUDES, AND BELIEFS which people bring to the cross-cultural treatment encounter, particularly those of the clinician, is an idea whose time has come. In the rapidly proliferating field of practice with culturally different populations, experts unfailingly emphasize the importance of the professional's own cultural identity and awareness of the biases he or she may harbor which significantly impact the work. At the same time it remains clear that Americans, accustomed as they are to "limited amounts of interaction according to well-defined roles . . . are somewhat inept at accepting people from other cultures as equals with a viewpoint worthy of attention" (Brislin 1980, p. 30). This is a handicap that must be transcended for effective interaction in the increasingly interdependent world of today. Treatment and training for effectiveness must now be considered incomplete if practitioners have been unable to integrate their culture of origin with their current life-style (Spiegel 1984, p. 2).

The content presented here was derived from the efforts of practitioners to develop such integration and to use their cultural self-understanding as a backdrop for examining general principles about cultural dynamics as they affect human functioning and clinical practice. The data that is examined illustrates the rich variety of people's experiences that can be used as a vehicle for such learning. It was gathered from classes in schools of social work, from seminars, workshops, and institutes which took place at professional conferences, in social agencies, mental health centers, corporations, and educational institutions, both public and private, from elementary to graduate levels.

Because of my work as chief social worker in a child guidance agency and a large mental health center, both of which served large inner-city populations, I began to receive requests for consultation and teaching relative to intervention with Afro-American clients and patients. The organizations requesting assistance were struggling with staff conflict concerning differing perceptions of Black clients and of interventions that were appropriate. The earliest attempts involved setting up single meetings where people could discuss their concerns with some comfort and freedom, avoiding as much as possible polarization and destructive behavior. This soon evolved into a series format where the goal became that of understanding and better managing bias in the interest of better cross-cultural work. As a part of the process, participants were asked to identify their feelings about their racial identity. Many Whites insisted that they did not think of themselves in terms of race but, rather, in terms of national origin, religion, or locality. Since I was at that time not knowledgeable about the dynamics of systemic process and the significance of ethnicity in human functioning, I questioned whether this behavior constituted an effort to avoid the self-confrontation necessary for controlling and changing racial bias. However, in an effort to involve participants at a level that was safe and meaningful to them, I changed the procedure to begin the exploration with ethnicity. The immediate gratification experienced by nearly everyone made it abundantly clear that ethnicity had great significance. Even those who seemed ambivalent or negative were clearly involved in the process and found the discussions helpful. For nearly all, it was a more comfortable subject, and I began to see it as a mechanism for building the trust that was necessary for the more painful work on race which followed. It was only later that I discovered the deeper implications of the ethnic exploration.

The shift to begin the process with an understanding of ethnicity and its impact on clinical work, while facilitating involvement, nevertheless did not lend significant clarity to the enigma of race, nor substantially alter the resistance surrounding the subject. On one occasion, in searching for a mechanism to illustrate logically the complex dynamics behind the conflicts that develop as a result of discussing racial issues, I constructed a

chart with lists of feelings and behaviors related to the experience of being White or Black. The lists grew as Whites spoke of
feeling lucky, comfortable, and superior, but also guilty, confused, and afraid. Blacks identified feeling frustrated, angry,
trapped, at times hopeless, but proud of their ability to cope. Several Jewish participants objected to the chart, one exclaiming,
"I'm White, but I belong on both of those lists." In the long and
heated discussion which followed, some Whites insisted they had
often experienced the feelings and behaviors we had identified
as Black, while some of the Blacks suggested that many of their
feelings and behaviors more approximated those we had labeled
White. Eventually, it became clear that everyone had experiences
which placed them on both sides of the chart. This all made sense
when we changed the column headings from White and Black
to power and non-power (pp. 130–133). This shift added even more
clarity, for power is a primary issue in racial dynamics and a
focus on power assures attention to those aspects of race that
can remain hidden even in the racial exploration. In addition, it
immediately calls into play experiences, feelings, and perceptions related to other areas of social functioning that are affected
by power. Therefore, the focus eventually became expanded to
include, in addition to ethnicity and race, experiences related to
class identity, sexual identity, or other experiences where power
had been significant. The constellation of feelings and perceptions which people identified in relation to their experiences with
power or lack of power became known as one's "power gestalt"
(Pinderhughes 1979). Finally modifications were made to include
(1) more focused discussion on feelings of difference, both early
memories and current experiences, and (2) delineation of values
emphasized in one's family in childhood and in one's current
life. An ongoing effort was made to relate the content of the ex-
plorations to practice.

Originally the format combined group process with educational procedures which had worked well in classroom format.
At the consulting sites, the lectures proved troublesome as there
was more interest in experiential approaches. Moreover, the shift
back and forth from cognitive to affective modes bothered some
participants who felt a sense of discontinuity. The activity and
directiveness of the leader when lecturing appeared to spill over
into the experiential process, interfering with sharing and self-
disclosure. And the lecture format tended to seduce some group

members into intellectualizing the strong feelings that were mobilized by the highly charged material, thus defeating the goal of self-confrontation. In the interest of facilitating the experiential process and eliminating the discontinuity and provocation to resistance, the lecture format was dropped. Nevertheless, information that places the personal sharing of participants in a conceptual framework remains an important aspect of the process.

The voluminous data which emerged from these varied cross-cultural training endeavors has been carefully studied and organized. Included here are excerpts from the process along with observations, generalizations, guidelines, and principles that have proved valuable in understanding ethnicity, race, and power issues in clinical work.

This book, it is hoped, will prove useful to all service providers, especially to those who may not have access to in-depth experiential cross-cultural training. In offering them an opportunity to appreciate vicariously others' exploration of experiences in relation to ethnicity, race, and power, it may prompt them to work toward cultural self-understanding for themselves and facilitate application of new insights to their clinical work.

Acknowledgments

To Boston College, where for the past thirteen years its scholarly environment has fostered growth and creativity for me, enabling integration of my clinical identity with an academic one

To Putnam Children's Center, where the ideas on which this book is based first took root

To the Department of Psychiatry, Boston University School of Medicine, where for seven years I conducted yearlong seminars on developing cultural sensitivity for residents and other trainees

To the American Orthopsychiatric Association, where for the last several years I led an all-day institute on cultural self-awareness

To the administrators and planners in these and many other institutions who welcomed me as consultant and valued my ideas

To the hundreds who have participated in the seminars, work-shops, and institutes, making them exciting, growth-producing experiences

To my students, whose growth in the struggle to understand cultural identity and meaning always encouraged my own

To Amalia Johnson-Tournas, whose doctoral research at Bos-ton College on prejudice, maturity, and developmental theory played an important role in the germination of my ideas on difference and will make a significant contribution to the field

To Robbie Tourse, whose work with me at Ortho and on other occasions helped to perfect the consultation model

To Velma Hoover, Elmer Freeman, Jorge Reyes, and Pat Se-dina, who also were colleagues in this venture

To Carole DiFabio, who willingly prepared countless versions of the manuscript; to Mary Kelly, who also helped; and to Tod Nordhal, our teaching assistant, who performed many un-interesting but necessary tasks

To June Gary Hopps, whose model of hard work, demand for excellence from her faculty, and support for their productivity played a significant role in making this book possible

To Leon Williams, Monica McGoldrick, Alvin Poussaint, Gretchen Franklin; and to my son, Howard, and especially my husband, Charles, who took the time from their busy schedules to review the manuscript while it was in preparation.

To these and countless others who have provided encourage-ment through their acceptance of my work, I offer my deepest appreciation.

1

Introduction

I BRING TO THE THERAPEUTIC INTERFACE a growing and at
times painful acceptance of the sorrowful part of my Irish
ethnicity and an appreciation of the value placed on giving,
humor, hard work, religious faith, family independence, and
an increasing expression of feeling. I also bring a working-
middle-class orientation to my work; an orientation that tries
to fight against my father's bigoted message that people-of-
color were not to be trusted or liked. To feel powerful, he
needed to ridicule, a response defined by his Irishness and
his fear. I am still grappling with the ways in which this has
affected me in my work, whether I do have power and feel
powerful, and how I can use this to help my clients.

So wrote a social work student as she struggled to complete a
written assignment on the significance of her cultural background to her effectiveness in cross-cultural practice.

Experiences related to cultural differences can cause people to
develop negative, ambivalent, or confused perceptions, feelings,
and attitudes about themselves and others. Such internalizations
can prompt one to behave in unhelpful ways toward others and
thus can compromise the ability of the practitioner to demonstrate the competencies that are necessary for effective assistance to the client. At the same time, these internalizations can
also cause clients to misperceive or distort the intentions and
interventions of practitioners. This book addresses the need for
attention to these issues in its focus on what professionals as well
as clients bring to the cross-cultural treatment encounter. It ex-

1

amines how cultural perceptions and experiences related to ethnicity, race, and power affect people's sense of themselves as well as others, their feelings and attitudes, and the behavior they manifest in ways that show up in service delivery.

For generations in America diverse, often opposing, values and beliefs have interacted dynamically. Democratic principles supporting the equality of people before the law and tolerance for diversity and pluralism have found expression in religious, philosophical, and political writings and in the Constitution. However, in the competitive sociopolitical and economic process that also influences behavior and culture, power and resources determine which persons, ideas, values, and traditions prevail. Forces pressing for equality and for discrimination, for rights and privileges for all and for men only, for democracy and for slavery have interacted dynamically with the superior resources and power of the most influential—middle-class White Anglo-Saxon Protestants—often determining the outcome. Rewards and positive value came to diverse people who adopted the behaviors, customs, and language of this influential cultural group. The blending process and "melting pot" ethic at times prevailed over forces favoring separate though equal cultural and ethnic identities.

Native Americans, descendants of slaves, and immigrants all learned in countless ways that the individuals viewed as having the most value and power in the United States were those who embraced the homogenization of the melting pot. From the time of the Civil War through the era of the expansion of the West, and subsequently during the growth of urbanization and industrialization, this thrust toward homogenization urged would-be adherents to give up their ethnicities and abandon their pre-American cultures. To belong and to be embraced, people were encouraged to change their names; disavow old-country values, beliefs, and language; relinquish familiar cultural practices; and become generally ashamed of any identity that was less than "100 percent red-blooded American." "The proponents of the melting pot theory could be terribly cruel to ethnics who would not melt" (Solomon 1976, p. 176).

The pressures to adopt this sameness existed on every level of the American social system, remaining strong until the 1960s. In the field of education as in all other areas of American life this ideology reigned supreme, for the task of the public school system was conceptualized as teaching American democracy and English to the children of immigrants (Cafferty and Chestang 1976, xii). History, literature, art, music, as well as the sciences endorsed the value of cultural assimilation and provided no reference point for the culturally different except in depicting their culture as inferior and inadequate. Contributions of the unmelted were largely ignored.

In human services, the cultural blindness of the melting pot perspective was also the guiding ethic. In the fields of health, mental health, and social services, the needs and problems identified as significant to White middle-class persons were assumed to be the appropriate yardsticks for understanding and delivering services to everyone. The definition of problems, i.e., what is pathological and deviant, the theoretical constructs that determine assessment and intervention methods, the strategies devised, the programming of services, and even the evaluation of outcomes had been developed in terms of what seemed appropriate for the White American middle class.

For generations Blacks along with other people-of-color sought acceptance into this melting pot. Their hopes, brightened by the civil rights movement, were dashed when the White backlash showed them that they would continue to be excluded because they could not change their skin color. Realizing that the role and acceptance of a people are related to the resources, influence, and advocacy of its members, Blacks launched a determined effort to change the negative identity that Americans had forced upon them which had been used as a basis for their exclusion. In this undertaking, they struggled to develop pride, power, and a positive sense of identity based on their present attributes. That effort sparked the desire of other people-of-color and other excluded people to do the same.

Responding to the demands of Blacks and other people-of-color that they be viewed in terms of their strengths, coping efforts, and cultural adaptations rather than via projections and stereotypes, White ethnics also insisted on such recognition. Their claim to power and their movement toward reaffirmation of cultural identity was more than simply the cry of oppressed or minority groups; it became for many a method to achieve political aspirations (Fieldstein and Giordano, 1976). Now recognized as a significant source of group identification and an important factor in the values, family patterns, life-styles, and behaviors that have persisted over generations, ethnicity has become identified as a vital force in America.

> There is increasing evidence that ethnic values and identification are retained for many generations after immigration . . . and play a significant role in family life and personal development throughout the life cycle. . . . Second, third and even fourth generation Americans, as well as immigrants, differ from the dominant culture in values, lifestyles and behavior. (McGoldrick 1983, p. 4)

Such awareness has signaled to many that America is at last set on the course of pluralism, the original intention of the Founding Fathers (Papajohn and Spiegel 1976; Cafferty and Chestang 1976, p. xi). Its rediscovery is hailed as a sign that the country is at last beginning "to come to terms with the religious, racial, ethnic and geographic diversity that exists within its boundaries" (Greeley 1976, p. 6). Pluralism has also brought recognition of the high psychological costs exacted by the melting pot ethic. For many—including those who chose to melt, those who did not, as well as those who could not—the price has been too high. Cut off from cultural roots and reference groups, they experience political powerlessness and a personal sense of isolation and become vulnerable to cultural ambiguity, negative identity, and psychological conflict. Many have sought relief from confusion, depression, alienation, and self-hatred in alcohol and drugs. Such consequences of cultural ambiguity have been dramatized by several novelists including Ralph Ellison (*Invisible Man*), Theodore Dreiser (*Sister Carrie*), and Abraham Cahan (*Rise of David Levinsky*).

Pluralism is now recognized as a welcome antidote for the sense of powerlessness, impotence, and rootlessness that pervaded American life for those who tried to melt (Fieldstein and Giordano 1976). Its validation of a group connectedness and positive cultural identity for everyone can bestow meaning and identity in a society grown complex and impersonal (Sanders 1975). An appreciation of pluralism nourishes attributes urgently needed in people today: psychological security, capacity for understanding, and appreciation of difference.

Recently the significance of pluralism and the importance of appreciating cultural difference have been further reinforced by the influx of immigrants and refugees from Southeast Asia, Central America, South America, and the Caribbean. In fact, the United States is now rapidly becoming "the most ethnically diverse society in the world" (Comas-Diaz and Griffith 1988, p. 2).

In the human service professions of health, mental health, social services, and education, the thrust toward pluralism in America has led to profound changes. Hospitals, health and mental health settings, and social agencies are now attempting to structure services that are sensitive to the cultural preferences of patients and clients. In the field of education, schools are now pressed to offer multicultural education and to include in the curriculum content on a variety of ethnic and racial groups.

Preparing teachers and practitioners to meet these challenges has involved the acquisition of knowledge about specific cultural groups and of skills for working with them. The ability to become comfortable with culturally different others and to recognize the relativity of one's own values are critical elements in professional training but are extremely difficult to develop. The development of cultural sensitivity requires first an awareness and understanding of one's own cultural background and its meaning and significance for one's interactions with others.

This book seeks to develop such an awareness by examining individual, racial, and ethnic identification and the psychological and social dynamics of interactions among individuals from diverse backgrounds. It will draw upon the experiences of people engaged in the search for cultural self-awareness and consider the implications for what happens and what should happen at the cross-cultural helping interface. Using this data the following chapters will examine the dynamics of ethnicity, race, and power, and show how they emerge in practice. It will demonstrate that the work involved in helping people may require changes on a variety of levels: in social structures, in people's definition of others and/or themselves, as well as changes in their behavior on different levels. And most importantly, it will demonstrate that the changes which are needed may well need to occur in the practitioner as well as in the client.

Culture and Human Functioning

The concept of culture is a complex one. The province of anthropologists, sociologists, psychologists, and other social scientists, it has been a topic of disagreement among scholars who have gotten entangled in the intricacies of the systemic processes characterizing it. One approach to understanding is the perspective of open systems, which emphasizes the interdependence of the many areas of human functioning that affect and are affected by culture. Thus, in order to understand individual behavior or emotion one must consider the relationships among the individual, the family, and the social system; the value orientations of the individual, family, subgroup, and social system; the geographical setting; and the interpenetration of all these systems and processes that operate in a reverberating and reciprocal manner. All of these factors influence and are influenced by each other, and they must all be taken into account in any understanding of culture (Papajohn and Spiegel 1976).

Culture may be defined as the sum total of ways of living developed by a group of human beings to meet biological and psychosocial needs. It refers to elements such as values, norms, beliefs, attitudes, folkways, behavior styles, and traditions that are linked together to form an integrated whole that functions to preserve the society (Leighton 1982). Ethnicity refers to connectedness based on commonalities (such as religion, nationality, region, etc.) where specific aspects of cultural patterns are shared and where transmission over time creates a common history. Race, while a biological term, takes on ethnic meaning when and if members of that biological group have evolved specific ways of living. An illustration of its having acquired a cultural meaning is seen in the use of the term White Anglo-Saxon Protestant. Ethnic values and practices foster the survival of the group and of the individuals within. They also contribute to the formation and cohesiveness of the group and to both group and individual identity.

The survival of the group and its members is best assured when the environment (defined as all that is external to the individual and family including the neighborhood, peer group affiliations, church, school or employment, governmental and economic institutions) provides appropriate resources at the appropriate time in an appropriate way (Germain 1979). Necessary resources, defined as protection, security, support, and supplies, ensure biological, cognitive, emotional, and social development. Lack, distortion, or excess in these environmental nutrients cause stress and conflict resulting in disorganization and malfunctioning on individual, group, and societal levels (Germain 1979). The interaction of the environment, whether depriving or nourishing, with the group, family, and individual is mediated by culture. On each of these levels culture contributes to the existence of environmental lacks and sufficiencies and to people's responses to these conditions.

The mediation function of culture is best understood through the concept of social role, which links the individual with family, group, and society via the culturally patterned behaviors that transact these various levels of functioning. Roles program individuals to adopt behavior that is complementary to that of other persons in these systems, while also satisfying inner needs and drives. Personality and ego functioning develop—the self evolves—through the unfolding of internal processes as stimulated by the environment. Key among environmental stimuli for a given individual are surrounding persons who enact these culturally programmed roles. The degree of reciprocity and complementarity in these roles helps determine the degree of conflict within the family, the group, and other parts of the social system. On these various levels of human functioning, culture via social roles acts as a mediator, determining life-cycle tasks and the criteria for appropriate mastery of them. These tasks include the development of trust; the acquisition of language; the management of psychological aspects of puberty; negotiating young adulthood; marriage and child rearing; and the management of middle age and old age.

Environmental phenomena such as immigration, urbanization, industrialization, and other systemic processes can change the interaction of the cultural group with its environment, jeopardizing the established reciprocity and complementarity in culturally programmed roles. Pressing people to take on different values and roles in order to cope, these shifts can threaten the balance that has existed in role function, jeopardizing both family and individual functioning.

As a result of these complex, interactive processes people of different cultures perceive the world and each other vastly differently. The perception of difference in others, whether based on beliefs, language and behavior, or appearance, impels each person to categorize himself and others as "we" and "they" (Bochner 1982). This categorization becomes the basis for stereotyping and discrimination. Stereotyping has been explained by social psychologists in various ways: (1) as a generic norm of behavior; (2) as a result of competition for scarce resources; (3) as a result of the process of de-individuation, i.e., when people are not known or not visible, they are not seen as individuals; and (4) as a result of the violation of laws of interpersonal distance. Prejudice has been explained as having the purpose of (1) easing adjustment because it is rewarded by one's group; (2) defending the personality against harsh realities concerning the self and thus protecting self-esteem; (3) providing a vehicle for reaffirming prized values related to religion, and society; and (4) providing a mechanism for organizing many confusing stimuli (Brislin 1981). Social systems, declare some social scientists, maintain stability by identifying certain persons or behaviors as deviant. In defining what is not acceptable, the system uses deviance to separate the normal from the abnormal, thus reinforcing boundaries within systems. All of these societal processes—stereotyping, discrimination, prejudice, labeling—employ projection upon another.

Psychiatrists have also offered explanations. The "we"–"they" categorization that characterizes prejudice has been explained as having a basis in physiological functioning (C. Pinderhughes and E. Pinderhughes 1982) and early psychological development (May 1976). As a result of psychophysiological processes, people come to aggrandize one mental representation while denigrating another (e.g., the good Whites and the bad Blacks) and then behave in accordance with these perceptions and cognitions.

There is little agreement among experts as to whether the relationship between individuals who are culturally different determines or is determined by the existence and content of the stereotypes held. The process is probably one in which stereotypes function in both capacities (Klineberg 1982). Scholars also disagree as to whether conflict between people of different cultures is inevitable or whether intimacy and getting to know the culturally different will usually undermine bias. While it is easy to find examples of intercultural conflict, it is also worth noting that multicultural societies do exist in which persons of culturally different groups live in relative harmony (Bochner 1982; Klineberg 1982).

In addition to playing a key role in the relationships which develop between persons who are culturally different, stereotypes can also influence which differences determine minority or majority status. For, in combination with the mechanism of stratification, stereotypes aid in creating structures in the social system that circumscribe people's life changes and life-styles and thus their cultural responses (Berger and Federico 1982). In this situation, a dominant group uses biological, psychological, or cultural characteristics to differentiate others from itself. The group puts the differentiated in a subordinate position, isolating them and barring access to necessary resources, thus reinforcing dominance for themselves as the differentiating and categorizing group. This stratification is institutionalized into social structures so that the expectations generated by the dominant group concerning tasks and functions appropriate for the subordinate group influence the latter's behavior and self-esteem, fostering a sense of relative powerlessness. Power thus becomes a factor in these dynamics. At the same time, the subordinates may tend to take on the definition of the dominant group as part of their identity.

> The sad truth is that in any system based on suppression, exclusion and exploitation, the suppressed, excluded and exploited unconsciously accept the evil image they are made to represent by those who are dominant. (Erikson 1967)

Thus, the assignment of people to dominant and subordinate groups, in part based on culture, is erected and maintained by social structures that help determine how people are viewed, how they view themselves, their access to resources, and their response to these conditions.

Race takes on a cultural significance as a result of the social processes that sustain majority—minority status. (1) The subordinate status assigned to persons with given physical (racial) traits and the projections made upon them are used to justify exclusion or inclusion within the society; in this sense race takes on the meaning of caste; (2) the responses of both those who are dominant, and therefore exclude, and the victims who are subordinate, and therefore are excluded, become part of their cultural adaptation. The meaning assigned to class status as well as racial categorization is determined by the dynamics of stratification and to some degree stereotyping. Hopps (1982) suggests that true understanding of minority status requires understanding of the various levels of oppression endured by the group. While discrimination and exclusion have existed in this country for persons from a number of groups who may be classified as minorities, oppression has been the most severe, deeply rooted, persistent, and intractable for people-of-color (Hopps 1982). Afro-Americans, American Indians, Native Alaskans, Mexican Americans, and Puerto Ricans constitute groups who "by any social, economic or political indicators" have been the most severely disadvantaged (Longres 1982, p. 8). The key issue, no matter the level of oppression and who is identified as minority or majority, appears to be that of dominance and subordination. Power, thus, becomes a primary factor in the cultural process. Stereotypes can be considered rationalizations to maintain the status quo and justify domination and immoral behavior on the part of persons in power.

For both the dominant and subordinate groups, class status, which is based on economic resources, as well as racial categorization can determine life chances, coping responses, and lifestyles. Work identity, degree of wealth, and the values placed on these are consequences of class structure and are factors that mediate ethnic identity and behavior (DeVore and Schlesinger 1987). Cultural background thus can be seen to embrace racial categorization, ethnic belonging, social class, and minority-majority group status (Brislin 1981).

On an individual level, cultural belonging has implications far beyond that of uniqueness based on shared religion, national origin, geography, or race. It involves processes, both conscious and unconscious, that satisfy a deep psychological need for a sense of historical continuity, security, and identity (Giordano and Levine 1975). Cultural belonging refers to a sense of connectedness with the world that can be seen as both vertical and horizontal, external and internal. Vertical connectedness refers to one's linkage with time and history, one's continuity that is "based on a preconscious recognition of traditionally held patterns of thinking, feeling and behaving" (Arce 1982, p. 137). Horizontal connectedness involves present linkage to others who share these same ways of thinking and belonging in the world. It thus constitutes a bridge to all that is external. Via these vertical and horizontal linkages, cultural identity guards against emotional cutoff from the past and psychological abandonment in the present.

A cultural sense of self is key to healthy self-esteem, for culture forms part of an individual's own self-representation and contributes to the sense of cohesiveness, sameness, and continuity that is the essence of psychological integrity (Erikson 1968, Gehrie 1979). Moreover, culture facilitates separation (from parental figures) because the cultural value system functions as a substitute for early transitional objects (Winicott 1971). There is a direct relationship between how one feels about one's ethnic or cultural background and how one feels about oneself, for a positive sense of ethnicity can be an important factor in one's emotional stability (News from the Committee 1980). Being secure in one's own cultural identity enables one to act with greater freedom, flexibility, and openness to others of different background (McGoldrick 1983).

In summary, culture is a factor in the interactive processes between individuals, their families, their groups, and their environment; in the assignment of people's opportunities and life-styles by their place in the social structures; in the cohesiveness and solidarity of groups and their manner of survival; in the structure and process of family dynamics; in the development of personality and ego functioning, including the sense of cohesiveness and the stability of the self; in the coping mechanisms evolved and the identity achieved; in how people are viewed and how they view themselves; and in how people view and behave toward culturally different others.

2

Culture, Social Interaction, and the Human Services

Culture as an Aspect of Service Delivery

Culture-free service delivery is nonexistent (Navarro 1980). The differences between client and practitioner in values, norms, beliefs, lifestyles, and life opportunities extend to every aspect of the health, mental health, and social services delivery system, which is itself a cultural phenomenon. The programming of service delivery, the structuring of services for people, the engagement of patients and clients in the help-giving process, the degree to which people use services, the assessment and treatment of problems, and the evaluation of outcomes are all in some way influenced by cultural values and traditions. For clients and patients, culture determines what they see as a problem, how they express it (i.e., whether it is somatic, behavioral, or affective; what specific symptoms they use), whom they seek out for help, what they regard as helpful, and the treatment strategies they prefer (McGoldrick 1983). For practitioners, culture also defines what is seen as a problem, how this is expressed, who can provide help, and what treatment options may be considered.

Recently, many have criticized the degree to which such concerns have been traditionally ignored, so that the needs and problems identified as significant to White middle-class persons have been assumed to be the norm for understanding and delivering services to everyone. The medical model, long the basis of many forms of service delivery, has reinforced this norm in its emphasis on diagnosis and cure as fixed entities not dependent on the

13

individual's perception of what is wrong and what needs fixing. Traditional mental health philosophy, moreover, has valued directive approaches, individual responsibility, looking inward, self-understanding and insight, personal growth and change, resolution of dependency needs, verbal and emotional expressiveness and thinking problems through. This philosophy differs from that of non–White, non–middle-class cultures that may value directive approaches, change efforts directed toward the environment, working with extended family and other relationships and systems toward increasing interdependence, giving advice, and hands-on approaches from a powerful clinician (Ivey 1981; Sundberg 1981). The use of the White middle-class yardstick has resulted in inappropriate and even destructive service delivery to persons of certain backgrounds. Among the dangers of not knowing the culture and thus misunderstanding the client's behavior is that of "confusing a client's appropriate cultural response with neurotic transference" (Brislin and Pedersen 1976, p. 145). The view of many counselors and psychologists that "YAVIS" persons (youthful, attractive, verbal, intelligent, successful) are more acceptable for psychotherapy than QUOID persons (quiet, ugly, old, indigent, and culturally dissimilar) (Shofield 1964) is now well-known. As a result ethnic applicants are excluded not only because they are dissimilar, but because they themselves very often will refuse to seek services, perceiving them as inappropriate to their needs and inconsistent with their cultural practices. These impediments to mental health care force families and communities to compensate for the inadequacy in services, often overburdening them (Valdez and Gallegos 1982).

Even when services have been sought and ethnic persons accepted for treatment, premature termination is often common. Fifty percent of Asian-Americans, Blacks, Chicanos, and Native Americans ended counseling after the first interview (Ivey 1981). The cultural insensitivity marked by the persistence of the White middle-class model has been labeled not only inappropriate but problematic, dysfunctional, disrespectful, unethical, and a sign of the incompetence of the service deliverer or clinician (Draguns 1981; Leighton 1982; Sue 1978).

The use of this model has reinforced ignorance of cultural variations in people. Moreover, it has also encouraged failure to assess the impact of environmental forces on functioning and a disinclination to direct intervention to external as well as internal systems. Social workers have long lamented this state of affairs in their struggle to give dignity to their work and in their recognition of its significance.

In fact the significance of external factors in the life of minorities has received such recognition that psychiatry and other disciplines now espouse what social workers have always known: that attending to reality problems is basic to effective treatment. (Bragg 1982, p. 183)

Other disciplines have begun to echo this concern and helpers who fail to use a framework that assigns significance to systemic factors have been accused of being oppressive to patients and clients and practicing symbolic violence and cultural imperialism (Ivey 1981). Approaches based on this failure, it is claimed, are designed to help clients feel better about being powerless vis-à-vis systemic influences, and thus constitute a form of social control that supports the system status quo.

On the other hand, the focus during and after the 1960s upon poverty and low socioeconomic status as critical in people's functioning was an attempt to assign some importance to these forces and to structure services accordingly. Until the recent push toward cultural sensitivity, the major emphasis had been on class determinants. As far back as 1975, Giordano and Levine identified ethnic as well as class determinants as significant in service delivery. They argued that the physical health, mental health, and social service needs of large numbers of Americans would best be met by organizing services within the natural and structural systems of working-class ethnic communities. Nevertheless even the focus on the "culture of poverty" did direct more attention to the level of support that existed for people to interact effectively with mainstream culture. However, this focus tended to stress the negative and dysfunctional and ignored the positive aspects of culture as a response to systemic factors (DeVore and Schlesinger 1987).

Effective service delivery now gives consideration to these factors. It embraces the notion that the state of being mentally healthy is facilitated by a positive sense of connectedness with one's own cultural group (Gary 1978; Gomez 1982). It sets goals to validate, preserve, and enhance clients' chosen cultural identity in order to facilitate healthy relationships and group interaction; accords respect to the client's belief system as a link between him and his cultural group and as a way of providing meaning to his individual experience; enables clients to gain some control over their environment and to establish a society for themselves that maintains self-esteem (Gomez 1982; Monteil and Wong 1983; Padilla 1981).

Validation of the client's cultural identity demands that the service provider understand the variations that exist within a culture and the way in which cultures shift and change, providing strength, connectedness, and a sense of identity, but also producing conflict and stress. Enhancing the client's *chosen* cultural identity means that services will be structured so that clients have choices in terms of their degree of acculturation or assimilation (DeVore and Schlesinger 1987; Gomez 1982). Levine and Giordano (1978) advocate programs that are fine-tuned enough to offer choices in preferred forms of help, i.e., matching programs with people in different ethnic, social, and economic circumstances. Other possibilities include the existence of three models of services delivery: (1) regular mental health services based on American models; (2) independent services based on traditional ethnic practices; and (3) new types of strategies and institutions (Sundberg 1981).

The location of services, the choice of staff, the scheduling of activities, and the intervention strategies used will all be consistent with these goals, which validate clients' cultural identity and reinforce their sense of value as individuals and as persons connected with worthwhile, competent groups. Such structuring should be based on equal respect for all groups, equal attention from government, a commitment to social change by funding agencies, community input into service delivery and, where necessary, the utilization of bicultural staff (Cafferty and Chestang 1976; Jenkins 1981; Valdez and Gallegos 1982). Assessment and intervention must take into account people's strengths and coping styles; the reciprocal interaction between people, their groups, neighborhoods, and the larger social system; and the mediating role of culture in this ecological process. To accomplish this, counselors need to consider the interaction of class, language and culture on communication, to act on understanding not only their clients' conditioning but their own, to be cognizant of their own part in the functioning of the sociopolitical system and how their values concerning locus of control and locus of responsibility compare to those of the client (Sue 1978). Also, it is important that social workers give attention to the variables necessary for understanding the community, its needs, and services; know how to intervene in various environmental systems on behalf of clients; become able to adapt interventive efforts to the tenets of the culture vis-à-vis privacy, self-disclosure, and the context of service delivery; and develop the flexibility to pace intervention appropriately (DeVore and Schlesinger 1981). Social workers are cautioned about the necessity of being particularly sensitive to the referral route as an indication of the degree of powerlessness being experienced by the ethnic client in his situation and need for services (DeVore and Schlesinger 1981; Gary 1978; E. Pinderhughes 1983; Solomon 1976).

In assessing and treating psychopathology, clinicians must recognize that cultural differences are not deviances. While delusions are false beliefs, the criteria of false must be culturally appropriate to the heritage and experience of the patient rather than to those of the clinician. Therapists also need the self-awareness to permit effective handling of transference and countertransference phenomena (Leighton 1982; Spurlock 1982).

Family therapists are counseled to learn well the role of cultural broker, i.e., how to help family members recognize their cultural values and to resolve value conflicts that emanate from perceptions and experiences that differ within the family, between the family and the community, or in larger social milieus of which the family is a part.

Validating the client's cultural identity and providing effective cross-cultural service delivery also entail attention to the environmental factors that influence individual functioning and family process. For many persons who do not belong to the White middle class problems are related in part to conditions stemming from social and economic inequality and especially those connected with racial categorization or class status. For example, Chicanos' experience of racial discrimination and poverty produces stress that causes high rates of delinquency, school dropouts, and conflicts in personal and cultural identity (Valdez and Gallegos 1982). The impact on self-image is evident: Chicanos born in this country have a more negative self-image than those who are foreign-born, while the self-image of those foreign-born who have lived much longer in the United States approximates that of the American-born, i.e., it becomes more negative over time (Wilkerson 1982). Most disciplines now call for work on all levels of the system from counseling individuals on issues within themselves and their families to strategies for coping actively with racism and discrimination (DeVore and Schlesinger 1987; Jenkins 1981; Padilla 1981; E. Pinderhughes 1982; Sue 1978). Activities long recognized as the province of social workers are now demanded by other disciplines: service providers are encouraged to expand their roles, functioning not only as counselor or therapist but as broker, mediator, and advocate (Brislin and Pedersen 1981; DeVore and Schlesinger 1982; Levine and Giordano 1978; Spiegel 1984).

Cross-cultural practitioners must understand the importance of determining the degree to which cultural conflict constitutes a major source of difficulty. Some experience stress as a consequence of being in "the ambiguous position in which the client feels inadequate to deal with the majority culture and disappointed with minority culture" (Padilla 1981, p. 204). Others feel more strongly the stress of biculturalism and having to live in two worlds without the option of cultural integration (Chestang 1976; Papajohn and Spiegel 1976; E. Pinderhughes 1982; Valdez and Gallegos 1982). Intervention should permit clients to set their own goals, to choose the identities they desire, and to resolve these conflicts.

In both individual and group intervention, cultural identity itself may be the focus of intervention (Klein 1976; E. Pinderhughes 1984). A focus on cultural identity offers an opportunity for clients to strengthen a positive sense of self and thus to enhance psychological integration.

Research demonstrating the effectiveness of a group treatment approach that focuses exclusively on cultural identity has been developed. The method evolved as an outgrowth of the researcher's experience with Price Cobbs, a Black psychiatrist who examined the significance of cultural identity and self-esteem via a group technique called "ethnotherapy." As a part of this experience, Black and White group members examined their feelings toward one another including their ideas of their own and each other's ethnic identities (Klein 1980). Adapting this technique to Jewish groups, Klein found that American Jews have experienced an ongoing social dilemma in the pressures to assimilate and the pressures toward Jewish group solidarity. Responses to this conflict have included an internalization of negative Jewish stereotypes, negative identifications, and self-hate. Her adaptation of ethnotherapy aimed to help "Jewish people overcome conflicts in identity, change negative identity, and increase positive feelings of Jewish group belongingness" (Klein 1976, p. 4).

The Cultural Identity of the Practitioner

When patient/client and practitioner meet in the cross-cultural treatment encounter, each brings these multidimensional aspects of their respective cultural identities. All that has been said regarding a sense of connectedness to the past and the present, and the relationship between cultural identity and self-esteem applies to practitioners as well as clients. When practitioners are clear and positive concerning their cultural identities, they are more able to help their clients to be so also. It is not possible to assist clients to examine issues concerning cultural identity and self-esteem if helpers have not done this work for themselves.

Competencies Needed for Effectiveness

Effective service delivery requires practitioners to develop cultural sensitivity that is characterized by flexibility, openness, warmth, and empathy. These qualities, necessary for any healthy interpersonal functioning, signal a way of thinking that is marked by a tolerance and acceptance of difference, and they are mandatory for the human service professional. One who uses this kind of thinking will automatically give consideration to the systemic process and multicausality operative in the dynamics of any single issue. For example, to understand the hyperactivity of a Black child in a predominantly White school, the observer must decide whether this problem is due to physical factors such as neurological problems, to environmental factors such as poor schools and discouraging teachers, whether it is a symptom choice stemming from intrapsychic dynamics, or whether it represents an interpretation based on bias in the observer (Spurlock 1982). Since any of these factors may influence and be influenced by each other, more than one may be operative at any one time. Practitioners must be able to understand such complexities. Cultural sensitivity also involves openness to variability in cultural identity and practices between and within groups and to the relativity of one's own values. It is marked by a willingness to learn from others, using their perceptual categories rather than imposing formulas or points of view.

Awareness of one's own values, assumptions, and behaviors is necessary for developing the skills that facilitate empathic interaction with clients and appreciation of culturally different others. Blocked receptivity and nonempathic interaction can be triggered by lack of familiarity and learned distortions. The anxiety mobilized by difference is reduced when one is aware of and can hold in check disabling attitudes, perceptions, and behaviors. Awareness of one's attitudes and behavior becomes a critical component of preparation to remove barriers to effective cross-cultural interaction. Such awareness means identifying distortions born of cultural indoctrination as well as psychological need, and it requires an in-depth understanding of one's own cultural background and its meaning.

A variety of strategies have been devised for creating self-awareness (see Appendix). Most involve some personal exploration of experiences to identify the attitudes, perceptions, and behaviors that derive from cultural meaning and influence people's interactions with others. Exploration of these aspects of one's cultural identity can clarify the significance of that identity and connectedness for a given individual, its similarity to and difference from that of others both inside and outside of one's cultural group, and the effect of these upon behavior with those who are culturally different. Moreover, analysis of the content of people's exploration can validate some of the general principles about cultural dynamics cited earlier and therefore can add to conceptual as well as emotional understanding.

3

Understanding Difference

HOW ONE RESPONDS TO BEING DIFFERENT from others and what it means are issues that are rarely given attention in preparing people for cross-cultural work. Yet the experience of the self as different from another is important for both practitioner and client in the cross-cultural encounter. And the feelings, attitudes, perceptions, and behaviors that are mobilized can play a prominent part in the work they do. Because these responses are more frequently than not negative and driven by anxiety, they can interfere with successful therapeutic outcome. "The greater the difference between the therapist and the patient, the more likely the therapist would be to ward off his or her own bad self by a variety of unconscious distancing and defensive maneuvers" (Bradshaw 1978, p. 1521). Unconscious distancing and defensive maneuvers are only a few of the unhelpful responses practitioners as well as clients may manifest in relation to perceptions of themselves as different from one another.

Unhelpful responses can be avoided when practitioners can examine their own reactions and are able to explore early or significant experiences which they have had with people seen as different. Such self-knowledge can provide an opportunity to control or resolve unfavorable reactions and can also produce greater sensitivity to client responses that may be triggered by perceptions of difference.

The Sources of People's Experience with Difference

Cultural values can influence the meaning of being different from others and also our responses to that meaning. American values emphasize competition, winning, and being number one. They promote the stance of better than, comparisons, ranking, and stratifying, and do not encourage respect for uniqueness or difference except in the sense of being "the best." "American" thus not only symbolizes power in the sense of all ethnocentric bias (where the dynamic of pseudospecies prompts perceptions of one's own group as better than others) but in the sense that the *values themselves* carry the meaning of "better than" and thus emphasize power.

Originating as protective responses to difference that may then be reinforced by cultural values, biases in terms of better than or less than are taught in the socialization process. Whereas difference based on cultural values is most often identified in relation to self and persons outside of the family, it may also be experienced inside the family. Physical appearance is a frequently cited source of this experience. It is most commonly mentioned in relation to skin color, as in this example:

> In my Cuban family where my father was blonde and fair and my mother dark, I watched as my mother would literally display my fair-skinned brother. I wished desperately to look more like him.

Skin color difference is not an issue that presents problems only to people-of-color:

> Looking more like my black Irish father, I felt different from all the rest of my siblings, mother and friends. It was painful. I felt isolated and rejected.

> I'm the oldest of four kids. I had dark hair and skin while the others were blonde. I thought I was adopted. I refused to believe my parents when they said that wasn't so. I felt alienated and isolated.

> I remember being with my family friends who looked very blonde. We went to visit an Indian reservation. I suddenly became aware that they saw me as very dark when they joked about my being Indian. I felt very lonely and scared.

When such difference exists between mother and child it can be quite threatening. For the child may perceive that difference as a threat to the mother's acceptance of him or her and to the closeness between them.

Some people strive to control the bias and stereotype that is associated with others who are different by a stance of "we are all human and we are all alike." Often well meaning, it is calculated to stop the misperception and misunderstanding of others. It also represents an attempt to avoid experiencing or inflicting on others the pain that is associated with being distanced from. But this stance pushes them to deny that difference in people exists at all:

> It was a sin in our family to talk about differences from other people, especially other religions. And yet I got the clear message that we Protestants were superior to ignorant, narrow-minded Baptists.

A Black psychologist described how her family's attempt to deal with the prejudice toward dark-skinned people involved a rule whereby it was forbidden to identify people by skin color or to even mention such differences:

> Although people in our family were different colors from dark to very fair, we were forbidden to identify people this way. It was a bad thing to say "that light-skinned girl" or that "dark-skinned man." I think that made the differences even more loaded instead of less so.

These well-intentioned efforts to deal with prejudice and its negative attributions conveyed the message that realistic differences could never be acknowledged, resulting in denial of even the existence of differences and thus emphasizing them even more. When a Black mother used denial and avoidance to protect her son from rejection by his peers due to their negative perception of his differentness, this only created more problems for him and their relationship:

> When my friends first called me a "nigger," I was confused. I asked my mother for an explanation and she protected me. She really lied. I didn't find out till later what it really meant. And then, of course, I was furious at her.

So while a stance of nondifference and "all people are alike" may seem to diminish anxiety related to differentness, it also creates problems in that real differences cannot be acknowledged, sameness may be overemphasized, and distortion and misunderstanding may be reinforced rather than avoided.

However to focus on difference without attention to similarities can also be anxiety-provoking and defeat the goal of understanding. A psychiatrist objected to an exploration of his experiences in being different from others because he felt it emphasized stereotypes. He complained that identifying differences increased lack of understanding rather than reinforcing what people have in common. He also complained that such a focus prevented people from deriving an awareness of the way in which people's values "are uniquely their own and they don't identify with a particular ethnic or racial group." Indeed, it is also important to pay attention to the way people, irrespective of differences, are also alike. Empathy, which is such a critical component of clinical process, depends on it. The frequent conflicts that arise around difference when experiences of oppression and victimization are examined also illustrate the importance of acknowledging the commonalities of human experience as well as the differences. This conflict often occurs because one individual's experience is considered to have been more than or less than another's. When resolution to this conflict is sought in a retreat to "the same as" and "everyone is the same," individuals who feel their experience has been different are offended. On occasion Whites have insisted that their own personal experiences have involved as much or more suffering than those of their colleagues who happen to be people-of-color and vice versa.

The historical oppression of Blacks and Jews has been compared in a similar way. Effective resolution of these polarized positions shifts the focus to a consideration of the ways in which victimization of both parties has been similar and the ways in which it was different. This perspective avoids the struggles embodied in either stance of "they are the same" or "they are not the same." With this expanded perspective comes the recognition that responses to difference must be understood and properly managed, and at the same time, similarity to others must also be accepted but not overemphasized, avoided, or feared.

Self-understanding as well as understanding of cultural dynamics requires the ability to consider both the commonalities and the differences between oneself and others. By respecting

people's connectedness without lumping them together care-
lessly, we recognize our own uniqueness and how it emerges
from our connection to others both inside and outside of our cultural group. A focus on difference as an aspect of cultural dynamics forwards this flexibility in thinking that can be key to
effectiveness in cross-cultural work.

A variety of human attributes and conditions can cause people
to experience themselves as different from others. Cultural
sources are not the only ones. In fact the sources vary widely,
ranging from biological to psychological to sociocultural as illustrated by the following list:

Sources of Difference

Race	Behavior Style
Religion	Sex
Ideology	Age
Nationality	Size
Ethnicity	Family Constellation
Appearance	Occupation
Body Structure	Socioeconomic Class

Each item in the list can be broken down into more specific items
which constitute sources of difference. For instance, appearance
may be subdivided into color, texture, and structure of skin; hair;
features; body parts; clothing; and other observable characteristics. Sex may be subdivided into gender, sexual identity, sexual
role, sexual preferences and various sexual behaviors as potential sources of difference. Practitioners in groups openly exploring attitudes about difference encounter all of the above listed
sources of difference and many others.

While behavior and physical appearance constitute the primary manifestations of the differences that people are able to
identify, those most commonly cited have been connected to ethnicity (especially religion and nationality), race, and class. One
psychiatrist's significant early experience with difference related
to her ethnic pronunciation and ethnic food:

At school after Christmas we were discussing the foods we
ate during the holidays. When I told the White teacher we
had chitlins and hoghead cheese, she acted as though it was
something weird. She asked me to say it again, she turned to
the class and said, "You mean chit-ter-lings." She put the

word on the board and spelled it and then said, "Class, repeat after me, Chit-ter-lings." I was embarrassed beyond belief and I dealt with it by joking with my family. When I went home I told them that they didn't know what they were eating because they couldn't pronounce it right.

Class, too, can be a source of pain—whether one is rich or poor—if it sets one apart from those one cares about. For example, a social worker recalled an early sense of difference within her family that stemmed from comparison with her poorer relatives:

My aunt's family was very poor although we were fairly well-off. Her children were always dirty and poorly cared for and the house was a mess. My mother stayed angry and disgusted at her sister. But somehow I felt guilty about what we had; it was so different from what they had. I remember also that I was often angry at my mother for her attitude.

A psychiatric resident whose earliest recollection of difference centered on rejection based on his upper-class status remembered the pain he had felt when a classmate whom he "adored" told him she could never like him because he "was a snob and lived in a big house."

Responses to Being Different

While the sources of difference are varied, there is even greater variation in people's responses to experiences in which they perceive themselves or others as different. Most common are feelings such as confusion, hurt, pain, anger, and fear. Confusion is a common response to cultural differences associated with race and skin color.

I remember that when I was about three years old I was having a conversation with my mother who was usually a loving, caring person. I used the term Negro lady and my mother said, "Never say Negro lady, say Negro woman; only Whites are called ladies." Even when I grew older that confused me.

In the Polish community where I grew up (Iowa), I went to a parochial school and we were taught that we had the Way. So I was confused about how the parishioners treated a Black family that attended: it was so hypocritical.

People were always surprised that I belonged to my mother because she was so dark and I was so light. This caused a lot of confusion and pain for me not just with others but with my brothers and sisters too.

Often the feelings which people identify give a clue to some specific meaning that people have attached to the experience. For example, some responses indicated that being different from another meant that something was wrong or something was intrinsically missing in one's own situation. When differences have such a meaning people tended to identify feelings such as embarrassment, humiliation, deprivation, disappointment, being misunderstood, stupid, and so forth. This is illustrated in these examples where difference concerned physical defect, dialect, and skin color:

> I was different because I had a German accent. Sometimes the boys teased me by calling me Miss Hitler. My parents suffered a lot from being isolated and rejected in their world. There were a lot of barriers that held them back.

> I remember being teased about my West Indian accent. I hated it, of course. People said they thought I sounded arrogant. I worked very hard to speak and sound just like my classmates.

> I was embarrassed at school that my parents both had cerebral palsy and were not like other children's parents.

> I never got used to being stared at when I was with my mother because she looked White and I was so much darker. When she came to visit at school, people didn't believe she was my mother.

In such situations, envy was also a response:

> I longed to celebrate Christmas too and I loved the Christmas tree. I still remember that when I put a bulb on the Christmas tree in the school ceremony I broke the bulb. Gee, did I feel guilty.

When differences had the meaning that something was wrong or missing in the situation of the other or that one had something which the other did not have, a common response was guilt. Guilt is cited most often in relation to race by Whites. It is also frequently mentioned in relation to class differences (middle or upper class versus poor). Experiencing the situation of the other as "less than" also gives rise to pity or sympathy. People rarely identify empathy among the reactions they have to difference from others. Other feelings that people mentioned when difference had the meaning of having something that others didn't were feeling unique, special, privileged, and superior. When being different is perceived as having consequences with which one could not cope, people feel overwhelmed, helpless, or hopeless. These feelings when associated with cultural experiences are most often connected with race, and they are mentioned by Whites but not by people-of-color.

As would be expected the intensity of the associated feelings varies from mild (confusion, hurt) to intense (rage, horror). Feelings tend to be strong when the source of the difference is an emotionally loaded issue, for example revulsion and disgust as in these examples related to sexual matters:

> The realization that I was gay and different from straight people caused me a lot of pain and suffering because people were revolted by me. I didn't feel disgusting but that's what people said I was: a pervert.

> I felt revulsion in a locker room at school when I saw an uncircumcised penis: it was not neat.

But feelings such as shock and horror also emerge when people feel themselves to be greatly distanced from the other. For example, a social worker noted the horror she felt in discovering the abject poverty that could exist for people. This was a condition far removed from her upper middle-class world. People reported responses of disbelief and bewilderment in situations where new information has created that sense of difference:

> My first experience was realizing that my grandfather, to whom I was very close, was really an Indian. It had never been talked about and I felt shocked to learn that this man whom I thought of as Black really was not.

In situations where people felt extremely distanced from others, they reported feelings of loneliness, isolation, rejection, and abandonment:

> I recall being very distressed because all the other White children ostracized me. This was in Oklahoma and my

parents' views of racial acceptance meant that we were often criticized and excluded. I felt singled out and very lonely.

In my dark-skinned family I always felt ambivalent over being the only one who was light-skinned. I was favored over my darker siblings and it made me lonely. I felt distanced from them and I know it was a source of some of the conflict we had. At school I was favored by the teachers and sometimes not liked by my peers. I remember sometimes trying to be bad to get accepted.

Preponderance of the Negative

People's first remembered or significant experiences with difference are rarely recalled with an unmixed sense of pleasure or gratification. If pleasure existed at all, there was also discomfort and even pain as in this example:

I know there was an earlier experience but the one that comes to my mind occurred when I was in a program that planned experiences for Black inner-city kids and those in suburbs. My family lived in a Boston housing project and I remember visiting a pleasant family in Lincoln, Mass. My memory is about being in church with them one Sunday. As the only Black in that church, I felt surrounded and overwhelmed.

When a teacher first became aware of difference as meaning that she and her family were special, she felt conflicted:

I don't really remember feeling different very clearly except that my parents told me that we were German Jews. My grandparents were born here and their parents were born here. My parents felt that made us better. I lived with that a very long time—really feeling better than other Jews because we had been here a long time. What were my feelings? I suppose pride mixed with embarrassment. I also wondered, am I really better?

A social worker who was the daughter of a missionary recalled growing up in China at the end of the colonial period. Her feelings of difference from the Chinese servants involved a sense of superiority and being powerful, which later gave way to a sense of embarrassment and unfairness.

In the following example, the feeling of gratification in relation to difference represented a strategy to cope with initial discomfort:

> My first memory of difference was of feeling little and powerless in relation to adults but discovering the joy of peer relationships, sharing secrets and baseball cards. It was like a language I and my friends spoke that my parents did not understand. There was a feeling of pleasure associated with the power I felt.

Pleasure in this psychiatric trainee's experience was connected with finding a way to outwit parents whose difference from him had embodied a sense of powerlessness.

Feelings of differentness evoke a sense of aloneness, isolation, and abandonment for they signify absence of connection or relationship to others. They can also threaten the sense of psychological wholeness and intactness that people need. This happens because the experience of differentness triggers feelings that have been internalized related to a sense of not being included which frustrates a child's natural sense of grandiosity and perfection (Gehrie 1976). Difference has usually been pivotal in this experience of exclusion, of not being positively mirrored by those one loved and with whom one was struggling to identify. Such an experience constitutes an original narcissistic injury and the feelings related to it are exactly the opposite of what was most fervently desired and needed. A sense of injury that magnifies anxiety about differentness develops as a consequence of being unable to acquire that needed sense of belonging, inclusion, and value.

Kept out of awareness, feelings related to this original narcissistic injury are well defended against by a variety of maneuvers which people use throughout life. These feelings may remain hidden but can be mobilized whenever later experiences involve a sense of difference from others (Gehrie 1976, p. 435). Those feelings often are characterized by hostility toward others who are perceived as hostile and rejecting of one's differentness. These perceptions are believed to justify the anger and the subsequent prejudicial attacks which develop. Prejudice that results from externalizing this anger is thus triggered by differentness and represents a wish to see others uncomfortable also. "It is easier to see rage in others and other groups than be saddled with it as a member of a depreciated group" (Gehrie 1976, p. 436). According to this view then prejudice and negative feelings are defensive responses when there is mobilization of the anxiety and anger about differentness that had developed in relation to early narcissistic injury. They represent a wish to see others uncomfortable.

Another hypothesis contends that the origin of this negative meaning of difference may lie in feelings internalized as a result of the young child's struggle to develop separateness and to master the task of separation–individuation. The struggle that marks this universal task begins with painful awareness that the child is different and therefore separate from the mother. Successful mastery of this stage requires that the child be able to form a mental image of a separate self. The struggle to separate is marked by anxiety, rage, a sense of helplessness, and intense ambivalence, which diminish when mastery is achieved and there is comfort with the self as separate and therefore different (Mahler 1975). Some of the feelings may remain unresolved depending on the degree of intensity that marked the process. This hypothesis posits that the negative feelings connected with this struggle for psychological separateness exists in a greater or lesser degree for everyone. Anxiety, thus, plays a prominent role in how people respond to difference. "What might seem like intense prejudice and discrimination to an onlooker, then, may be simply a reflection of people's preference for what is comfortable and non-stressful" (Brislin 1981, p. 48).

Another factor in the perception of difference as negative may be the tendency for the meaning of "different from" to imply comparison. Although it may be inaccurate, comparison conveys a meaning of inequality, a meaning that the items compared are not equal, one being better than or less than the other. Commenting that "it is difficult to say different without saying better or worse," Carol Gilligan (1982, p. 14) notes how this tendency for comparison to imply greater or lesser value has significantly influenced the way in which female development has been viewed. Since the yardstick of health has been male development, the fact that females develop differently has meant that female development has been seen as deviant rather than merely different. Thus, when people examine their earliest or most significant experience with difference, there is this influence of comparison with another party and in this comparison both parties are *never* equally valued. It is a stance that appears to symbolize "I'm O.K., you're not O.K.," or "I'm not O.K., you're O.K." The nurse who as a child saw difference between her poor cousins' economic circumstances and those of her own affluent family certainly viewed the other as lesser and poverty as far more uncomfortable than her own circumstances. For this social worker an early experience conveyed that being different and female entails limitation and means "not as free as":

> I was four or five years old and playing in the backyard with friends. And I am clearly in the leadership position—in fact I'm Tarzan. Mother comes out and makes me come inside and put on a T-shirt saying "Little girls don't run around without T-shirts." But Tarzan didn't wear T-shirts! Now I couldn't be Tarzan anymore, I had to be Jane or some other peripheral figure—not the powerful individual swinging through the trees. It made me angry and I felt limited.

In conveying the meaning of unequal value, of being more than or less than, differentness thus evokes the notion of power. This becomes particularly clear when one party in the comparison comes to symbolize "good" and the other "bad," pushing the comparison toward a more polarized meaning.

Erikson's notion of pseudospecies (1968) also invokes the notion of power.[1] Groups and individuals reinforce the illusion of being the chosen ones, of being superior to other individuals or groups in order to build unity within the group or to neutralize negative individual identity. These strategies are commonly used in relation to ethnic and racial individual and group identity as will be demonstrated. Power again becomes an issue in cultural dynamics and can be observed as operative in the involvement of inner psychological life and the coping mechanisms people use to deal with differences from others. However, while the stance of "better than" may serve as a solution to pain stemming from differentness, for some this solution can, itself, become a source of distress. A social worker described her sense of embarrassment, guilt, and fear at having been programmed as a wealthy Anglo-Saxon, "to feel superior to everybody." Breaking away, she had become involved with activist movements, but continued to feel excruciatingly alone and different. In her view the distance between herself and others, which had stemmed from this sense of superiority, had immobilized her until she was able to master not only her fear of difference but her fear of sameness.

As a result of this mastery she became more comfortable with her own cultural identity and could feel some connection with her Anglo-Saxon peers.

Fear of sameness is the flip side of fear of difference. It also can be driven by trauma related to early experience. For it is based on a fundamental fear that is associated with intimacy, with merging with another, with fusing, or being trapped and engulfed. While the negative responses that are associated with difference may seem to imply that sameness and similarity are less anxiety-provoking, it must be remembered that the opposite may also be true for the fears associated with sameness, merging, and non-existence spring from an even more primary source. And both may exist, even feeding each other, as fundamental factors driving people's behavior in relation to interaction with others.

While difference as "more than" or "less than" may carry a negative meaning and embody intense discomfort, it may also be actively embraced and even preferred in certain situations. A teacher described her intense dislike in childhood of being the shortest among her peers, and therefore different. Only when an even shorter child joined the class, did she realize that this resented identity had accorded her special status. She became resentful when deprived of her special, if negative, status. When difference has meant being special, and sameness has meant being insignificant, this invokes the threat of nonexistence and non-being and it may represent an even more intensely feared event and be accompanied by pain and discomfort, which then must be warded off. People with this psychological makeup who may feel comfortable being in situations where cultural difference is emphasized tend to be few in number.

Potency of Responses: Current or Past

Both present and past experiences are the source of people's responses to difference. An individual's initial response to experiences with difference may or may not persist into the present. Developmental process or other experience may cause the meaning attached to the source of difference, or even the meaning of differentness itself, to change:

> My first thought about differences is how I felt when my
> father joined the Muslim Church and our life changed. I was

in the second grade and I had to dress in a shirt and tie for school and my sisters had their heads covered. The food we ate was different and there were so many restrictions. It was very strange. I remember resenting the fact that I was so different from my neighborhood friends. I was confused, too, about the hate I felt was being preached in the name of religion. Later I learned to feel pride that I had a real identity and a place where I felt I belonged where there were rituals that told you how to behave.

However, for many people, the feelings and attitudes still persist and may even emerge in the recall of the experience. Tears accompanied the psychiatrist's description of humiliation when her White teacher gave the class the lesson on chitterlings. The reaction of a Japanese-American who described the meaning of Hiroshima was the same. Anger was readily apparent when a Vietnamese described her experience of racism in America.

The persistence into the present of confusion and pain is illustrated in this social worker's description of her struggle to cope with being the child of Irish and Italian parents:

I felt a keen sense of difference, being fair-haired, blue-eyed and living in an Italian neighborhood with my father who was Irish and my mother who was Italian. My father was somewhat cut off from his family but we were very close to my mother's family . . . I've already talked about how my grandfather used to try to get my brother and me to choose which we wanted to be. Sometimes I thought I was adopted. I've spent my whole life struggling against this—feeling different among Italians, feeling rejected, not a part of them and in conflict.

The strength of these feelings and attitudes even when latent exerts its influence on behavior. For example, a Filipino nurse grew up so strongly identified with being White middle class that she became alienated from her identity as Filipino; at age 11 she had looked at herself in the mirror and thought "who is that Chinese girl?" When called upon to explore her feelings about being different (i.e., not White American) she began to have headaches.

A psychiatric trainee identified his most significant experience with difference as related to his gay identity. While the intense discomfort about being gay was now under control, in the past he had found it unmanageable. Indulged, adored, and fully accepted as a human being in his family, he had found himself ill-prepared for being seen as a revolting pervert.

Despite the many situations in which recognition of differences has been managed poorly, it must be pointed out that there are situations where difference has been acknowledged and respected. For example, a Puerto Rican social worker described her family's approach to skin color difference:

> From the moment I was aware of who I was I knew that we [Puerto Ricans] were supposed to be all different colors because that was my family. And yet there was this subtle thing about "Oh, well, I'm lighter than you are." My father was very dark and my mother was very light. And it was like how much Indian is in you and how much Black African and how much . . . so color was something that we all talked about.

A Jewish teacher's description of a community effort to manage difference was recalled with intense pleasure. Her family and other families had joined together for the school's joint celebration of Christmas and Chanukah. Her experience was "one of prideful difference, that I was a part of a community that could do that."

Clients' responses to differences between themselves and practitioners, practitioners' responses to these differences, and their responses to their clients' perceptions of these differences all influence their work. A client may seek to ease his discomfort over difference by resisting involvement in the treatment. A practitioner may react to similar discomfort by devaluing, ignoring, or misperceiving the cultural identity and values of the client. And these responses may be compounded when the source of discomfort lies in early developmental struggles. For example, the distress of a social worker about the macho values of her Latina client's husband were to some degree based on a sensitivity to powerlessness that had grown out of her own developmental struggles to become a separate and assertive person.

One's responses to another's definition of oneself as different may also impede the helping process. Practitioners need to respond appropriately whether the client invokes difference when one sees none or denies difference when one recognizes it clearly. An Anglo-Saxon social worker whose heritage included five different ethnic groups and who identified with none felt threatened by the strong and positive sense of ethnic identity articulated by her Jewish, Black, and Italian colleagues. She objected strongly to the significance they assigned to cultural identity and meaning for themselves. She claimed that "emphasizing differences like that keeps people apart and creates conflict." Insisting on a "we're all human" perspective, she resisted greatly any indication that her situation might be different from theirs. An ordinarily sensitive person, she acknowledged her discomfort in a nervously articulated statement that she wished to be able to respect the wishes of her colleagues about how they want to be identified but this made her very uncomfortable. This reaction took on greater significance when it was revealed that many of this worker's clients were people-of-color for whom cultural identity is often a pivotal issue. In both classes and workshops people have reported great distress, feelings of rejection, and sense of threat in situations where their own devaluation of cultural difference or their own sense of cultural uniqueness has been seen by colleagues as a handicap and possible threat to effectiveness in cross-cultural work. Respecting a client's cultural background, helping him or her to resolve negative conflict or ambivalent identity requires that one be able to manage the uncomfortable feelings that may surface when one's own perspective about cultural identity happens to be different.

It can be critical that the helper understand how and why the other's perception of her may be different from that which she prefers and which makes her most comfortable. A Jewish psychiatric resident fought to be identified as Jewish and *not White* by his Black colleagues because White carried a more negative meaning to Blacks. He could not understand that White had more meaning in the experience of his Black patients than Jewish. This too carried over in his work where his eagerness to avoid identity as White had prompted avoidance of the race issue entirely.

A Black social worker objected to his Korean colleague's identification of him as American rather than Black American. Said he:

> That's a real shock to me—that you lump me with White people. When you were talking about the role of the U.S. in dividing up your country and how you resented that, I

wanted to say, hey, I'm different from them. I, as a Black,
did not participate in the decision about that war. Blacks
have been powerless in this country. We wouldn't have been
over there if Blacks had anything to do with it.

Difference from others within one's own group who do not embrace the same beliefs and values can prompt people to reject the
perceptions of the others about their cultural identity. Clarity and
resolution of ambivalence concerning one's own beliefs and feelings about cultural identity are critical. They will facilitate managing feelings about connection to others in one's own group and
to those outside who believe and feel differently. They also
reinforce the ability to manage feelings when others invoke such
differences. A White social worker experienced a sense of deep
frustration and entrapment as one of two White staff members
in a predominantly Black agency. Being different caused her serious discomfort and great pain since she found herself sometimes
excluded from their interactions. Her sense of pain and loneliness was compounded by the fact that she believed she should
not feel angry about this situation because she felt Blacks had a
right to exclude her based on their political need for unity. Anger
in this situation meant to her that she was a racist instead of a
sensitive, caring White person. What was at issue here was her
sense of White as different and bad. Only when she was able to
develop a more positive meaning for her identity as White (which
involved a change in her behavior with other Whites and in her
approach to racism) could she feel comfortable with behavior on
the part of her Black colleagues that confronted her with her
differentness as a White person. When people are clear and
mainly positive about their own identity and its meaning, difference then becomes less of a threat.

4

Understanding Ethnicity

THE CULTURAL UNIQUENESS embodied in ethnicity is a consequence of complex, interactional dynamics that involve individual functioning as well as family and group behavior. The sense of commonality with others and the individual ethnic meaning that people develop as a result of their experiences have implications far beyond those of shared religion, national origin, geography, or race. Involving individual psychological dynamics and socially inherited definitions of the self, ethnicity is connected to processes, both conscious and unconscious, that satisfy a fundamental need for historical continuity and security (Giordano and Levine 1975; Klein 1976). It thus embraces notions of both the group and the self that are, in turn, influenced by the value society places on the group. Societal definition and assigned value, among other factors, help determine whether ethnic meaning for a given group or individual becomes positive, ambivalent, or negative, which then has great significance for how they behave. While reflected automatically in the feelings, thoughts, perceptions, expectations, and actions of people toward others, ethnic meaning may remain hidden and outside of awareness. Nevertheless, although the experiences which have shaped it may be long forgotten, ethnic meaning is an ever-present influence that is readily mobilized in human interaction. Therefore, all helping professionals must understand the dynamics of ethnicity as these affect themselves as well as their clients, in order to ensure effectiveness in their work together.

The significance of ethnicity is demonstrated in the strong

emotional reaction that people display when they examine ethnic meaning and experiences related to their own ethnic backgrounds. For some, this significance is reflected in a sense of interest, excitement, and liveliness. For others it is manifest in confusion and a sense of uncertainty, while still others react with reluctance, avoidance, and even a direct refusal to engage in exploration.

How one feels about one's ethnic background very often is a reflection of how one feels about oneself. A clear predominantly positive ethnic connection can facilitate a sense of freedom, security and comfort, flexibility in behavior, and a capacity for openness with others who are different (McGoldrick 1983). A positive sense of ethnic identity is reflected in the following statements made by a social worker and a teacher.

> I was reared in an Irish Catholic, working-class community in Boston, and as a result I have always felt more Irish than American. I learned Irish songs, took Irish-step dancing lessons with my sisters and friends. It felt good to be Irish and to be in an atmosphere where almost everybody else was of Irish heritage. . . . I sometimes thought that to be American was almost the same as being Irish. This was the way my friends and brothers and sisters felt too.

> My family is WASP and has been in this country for many generations. I am proud of my family for many worked hard to create open-mindedness and to fight prejudice. My husband and I have worked in many communities: a one-room schoolhouse in New Hampshire, a French-Canadian community in Maine and an inner-city school. I have enjoyed all of it.

Practitioners who value their ethnicity are in a better position to value that of their clients, more ready to help clients learn to value themselves and to use ethnic identity as yet another avenue for building self-esteem.

However, the achievement of that positive and integrated sense of identity, which is so essential to people's mental health and significant in helpers' preparation, may be jeopardized by a number of factors. Ethnic identity for most people involves some ambivalence—some things they do not like about their ethnic connection (Giordano 1988). When that ambivalence is extreme, it can interfere with the attainment of clarity and the necessary sense of value, creating instead vulnerability to negative identity and poor self-esteem. People must strive actively to understand what their ethnicity means to them and to identify what makes them confused and ambivalent. This will enable them to work toward resolution of ambivalence or at least to diminish some of their vulnerability to its costly consequences.

Consequences of Negative, Ambivalent, Confused Ethnic Identity

When people internalize negative societal definitions of themselves and their ethnic group, they experience insecurity, anxiety, and psychological conflict. The self-definitions of these social workers are illustrations:

> I'm Syrian and Italian—pure on each side. To belong to both of these ethnic groups where I grew up meant being inferior. I have mixed feelings about my ethnic background because Italians are associated not only with food but with the underground and I have had to be connected with that emotionally. In the Syrian aspect of my life, they have not had a good historical reputation and are considered sort of sleazy—so you might say I come from a kind of underground sleaze.

> I now realize my father taught us to hate being Black. We couldn't go out of the house until we straightened our hair— he was ashamed of being Black, and I used to envy kids whose fathers taught them to feel proud. I have to work hard to overcome this—even now.

Membership in a group considered to be a "despised minority" makes "integration of self-image difficult and dissociation more compelling" (Klein 1976). Minority children may find it especially difficult to resolve ambivalence and integrate good and bad images because of the socially shared devaluation of objects of identification. One Afro-American social worker stated that as a child in Rochester, New York, she "never realized that Blacks had strengths." But low status assignment and societal denigration of one's ethnic group are not the only contributors to an individual's sense of negative identity.

Negative identity in individuals can stem from a people's history not only as victim but victimizer of others. Without fail, persons of German descent have articulated a pervasive sense of shame related to Germany's history as a purveyor of destruction. One social worker reflected on the meaning to her of having been born on Hitler's birthday, "a reminder that I cannot escape." In several instances, persons of German descent who have married Jews have pondered a connection here. Others have shared their sense of responsibility for the Holocaust, their own very real persecution by others in this country, and despair about being able to carve out any positiveness in relation to being German. Still others who have worked more at this goal have been able to focus on the many contributions Germans have made to Western civilization in literature, music, and art. They too, however, have felt burdened by that identity. A Japanese-American social work student wept as she described the "nightmare" of Pearl Harbor, her family's loyalty to this country as demonstrated by her father's enlistment in the armed services, the internment of some extended family members and friends in concentration camps in the West, and the devastation of others in Hiroshima. She and her family had struggled hard to manage the ongoing sense of shame, entrapment, and rage that were the consequence of belonging to a group considered to have committed a shameful act and itself the victim of another shameful act.

A Filipino psychiatric resident, who complained of having headaches on the day of her cross-cultural seminar and who recognized that on several occasions she had tried to schedule her patients and other activities in the time slot of the seminar, made this comment:

> My parents are from the Philippines. Both are Spanish and
> Filipino. I think my parents were ashamed of being
> Filipino—a country that had allowed itself to be dominated
> by the West, and I came to think of myself as American.

How a group is valued in the larger society in comparison to other groups also shapes the personal meaning of ethnicity. An individual from a Polish-Russian farming background described being taught not to mix with non-Polish neighbors who looked down on them. A French Canadian who grew up among her ethnic peers reported never experiencing the prejudice often directed at her group but learning to look down on Italians and Poles. A Northern Irish Protestant was taught to believe she and her family were superior to their Irish Catholic neighbors. In describing her experience in Canada, a Jewish psychiatric resident explained:

The WASPs put down the French who put down the Jews. I'm most afraid of the French.

Complexities: An Obstacle to Understanding

Not only is there variation in the degree to which ethnicity is viewed as significant but the variations and inconsistencies involved in the notion of ethnicity itself can make the tasks of definition and of understanding meaning more complicated. While ethnicity refers in some groups to nationality and country of origin, for others the reference point is religion. For example, Jewish people focus less on geographical origin than other Europeans, emphasizing instead Jewish religion, peoplehood or associated values. Many Irish people have closer affinity to Catholicism than Irishness. In New England, Irish Catholic has become virtually one word.

Religious denomination is also a source of meaning for persons who have renounced nationality of origin for the ethnicity of the melting pot. They consider themselves American by nationality, but their primary source of cultural meaning has evolved in connection with this smaller collectivity. An Australian psychologist described the situation as similar in his country of origin: "There," he said, "it was more important whether you were Methodist or Presbyterian rather than ethnic." Some Americans derive meaning from regional identification as a midwesterner or westerner, New England Yankee, etc. A social worker explains how region became the basis of ethnic meaning for her family:

I grew up on a farm in southwestern Oklahoma. Our family was middle class, anti-Catholic, and bigoted. I don't know the country of origin of my ancestors—they may have been Scottish or English, but I feel more southwestern than WASP.

Some persons seek their identity not in their ethnic background but in being "human." As noted above, some persons are firmly entrenched in the belief that "all people are alike" and seek a sense of meaning in identity as "human." This has been a solution for some whose identity stems from multiple groups and has also been a position taken by people wishing to put an end to the negative consequences of stereotyping and ethnocentrism. Unfortunately, it can lead to the mistaken notion that perceiving any difference between oneself and others is a prejudiced act and therefore to be avoided. A social worker whose ethnic roots involved five identities—Jewish, Polish, Russian, Irish, and Italian—had little difficulty articulating her values and the meaning of her ethnicity. Prominent among her family's values was the belief that people are the same. Her family had stressed the importance of not judging others on the basis of race, ethnicity, or other badges of difference. To her, acknowledgement of difference was racism, since "a race trait was seen as a stereotype, not a truth," and indicated ignorance. Reflecting on a teenage episode in which she dated a Black, enjoying people's reactions (such as "that takes guts" or "you must not be prejudiced"), she struggled to understand what had been her motivation. She learned that not only had she intended to hold the family accountable for its announced liberal values, but she could now admit that this behavior had helped her deny the fact that differences in people can cause anxiety and discomfort. This to her would have meant being prejudiced. The stance—that all people are alike—protects those holding it from awareness of their ignorance of others and the necessity of exerting the energy and effort to understand and bridge the differences. This social worker admitted that her attitude had defended against the necessity of learning about her Black clients cultural background "instead of pretending my experience explained theirs." She also acknowledged that this attitude limited supporting professional behavior to "see what the clients see" and "feel what they feel." In her work with an Irish Catholic client, the stance had been a particular handicap. The family of her pregnant teenaged client was embattled in a struggle over the girl's keeping the baby or having an abortion. Failing to consider the significance of ethnicity, she lost an opportunity to help her client understand the cultural context of the family's polarization as well as an opportunity to demonstrate empathy and understanding. Her "human" orientation had not only blinded her to her own responses to clients, which had been inappropriate, but also had pushed her to leave out the cultural dimension entirely.

A student who also wished to proclaim his human identity

stated that he had renounced his Irish roots and wished to be seen as an *individual*, i.e., someone not connected to any ethnic identity, "not even the melting pot and definitely not American." A Jewish student, who also viewed her identity as human and nonethnic, announced her belief that a "focus on ethnicity is ethnocentric and biased against others." Said she, "You can't be focused on ethnicity and not get into that superior–inferior thing, being chosen people and putting others down." This stance is often a reaction to ethnocentrism. Such persons embrace what Erikson (1966) has called a "wider identity" and thus reject the stance he calls "pseudospecies," the tendency of ethnic groups to view their own cultural groups as special. In Erikson's view, although this facilitates cohesiveness *within* a group, it also can build up conflict *between* groups. "Wider identity" refers to identity that transcends small collectivity boundaries and centers on identity as a world citizen. Erikson considers such identity characteristic of the highest level of functioning. In my experience persons who embrace this orientation must be firmly anchored in some personal sense of uniqueness and self-value. Otherwise, although they feel a meaningful connection with others, they may fail to appreciate the uniqueness of other people. Also the choice requires a high degree of self-differentiation. A social work student suggests that despite her sense of ethnic ambiguity (she is Anglo-Saxon), she feels comfortable because she has developed just such a strong sense of individual uniqueness:

> It is very, very difficult to address the issue of my ethnic identity because I don't have answers. Somehow, I feel like I've taken a piece from here, a piece from there, and I am still waiting for the final image to emerge. I don't quite see where I "fit into the picture" ethnically. Yet I don't feel lost. I do have a very strong personal identity. It is my place right now to search for meaning and to try to find ways to effect change aimed at increasing social justice.

Using personal identity as a substitute for a strong, integrated sense of ethnicity can be risky. People can and do seek personal meaning in a variety of sources that can be used to substitute for ethnic meaning. Such sources include one's profession, one's talent, religious group, or gay identity. But these choices must offer a sense of meaning that grows out of a connection to others. Otherwise the individual may fall prey to uncertainty about belongingness, which can be costly in terms of self-hate and psychological conflict (Klein 1976).

Another factor that complicates understanding ethnic identity and its meaning is the fact that how an individual defines himself and his group often differs from how he is defined by others. Although this is more clearly seen in relation to racial definition, it also obtains with regard to ethnicity. Helpers must be careful to understand ethnic meaning from the client's perspective and the significance of these differences for the client. A female client described her feelings about such a difference and her reaction to what she perceived as being forced to embrace an ethnic identity that she did not wish to assume:

> I am Jewish but was not raised religious, and I don't identify much. I resent being the resident Jew, to explain how Jews feel, to plan Chanukah celebrations, etc. I wasn't taught those things and it would be a problem for me to identify now. I would feel very uncomfortable.

Inconsistency in the use of race is another area of confusion. As a marker of biological commonality and similarity in genetic traits, race has also taken on an ethnic connotation and has become an important element in ethnic meaning. This is most obvious in the case of Afro-Americans, whose race is always a factor in societal definition, in contrast to Euro-Americans, for whom race is usually not considered at all, or other people-of-color, for whom race is less pivotal in the meaning assigned. These issues make it harder for people to recognize the cultural baggage they bring to encounters with others and thus to the cross-cultural interface. As a southern Afro-American social worker put it, "My race is my ethnicity." For a few, segregation and the outcasting of Blacks have led to a perception of the world primarily in racial rather than ethnic terms, so race has become a source of cultural meaning for them as well. For example, in a workshop at Howard University several Whites who had grown up in Washington, D.C., listed their ethnicity as "White." A Black social worker said:

> I call myself "Afro-American" but that's only since I grew up and realized that there are other ethnic groups within the Black race. When I grew up there were only two things: Black people and White people. So it was always race for me in terms of ethnicity.

Another social worker attempted to cope with this confusion by identifying herself as African-American, because it was a "more clear reference to my heritage and culture, as opposed to Black which describes my skin color."

The situation of Afro-Americans is peculiar in that they are uniquely defined by race while at the same time more completely disconnected from their ethnic roots than any other group. An experiential exercise at a conference for teachers of psychiatry dramatically illustrated how ignorance of origin and separation from the original ethnic group is true for Afro-Americans to a more profound degree than other groups of Americans.

> Everyone in the group was asked to rise; those who were White were directed to the left side of the room, those who were Black to the right and all others to the rear. There were present 30 Whites, 30 Blacks and 9 Asians. All who knew their country of origin, language, and religion of ancestors were asked to sit down. All 9 Asians sat down, 28 of 30 Whites sat down, 4 of 30 Blacks sat down. Two of the 4 Blacks who sat down were from Africa and the Caribbean. The other two were descendants of the Vaughn family which has traced its roots to Africa. Of the 2 Whites who remained standing, 1 had been born out-of-wedlock and the other had been orphaned.

While race may not be the defining factor in the sense of ethnicity held by other people-of-color, it is always interwined with it. Members of this group never fail to note the primary attribution of race that pervades others' perception and treatment of them in America. A Cape Verdean social worker's exploration shows why race became a part of ethnic meaning:

> People wonder why Cape Verdeans are so insular. Well, there are very good reasons. Outside of our community it has not been pleasant. We have had to fight racism every day. When I was in middle school, I couldn't be a cheerleader, which I wanted to very much (tears). Our parents had to fight for us to be on the basketball team or do anything in school. We were routinely sent to the vocational school and a lot of kids, especially boys, dropped out. The White boys were always insulting us girls, but if you told the teacher, nothing happened. In the restaurants you got passed over, and with these insults you couldn't prove anything. In the South, you

knew what you were dealing with but with us we never
knew, we always wondered. So we stayed in our community
where our close-knit families and friends gave us strength
and kept us sane.

For immigrants of color, this situation is especially enigmatic,
because in their countries of origin definition by race was less
rigid and compelling. In the United States, the meaning of the
designation "person-of-color" or "non-White" beomes a trau-
matic reality for them. Three West Indian immigrants discuss the
struggles this has created within themselves and between them
and Afro-Americans.

Sometimes there appear to be many barriers between us. I
have sometimes felt as an intruder who didn't belong. West
Indians get blamed because they tend to form friendships
with Whites more easily. Where I come from (Trinidad) we
are not as suspicious of Whites as Blacks are here. Race is
not a major issue and friendships are not formed based on
race.

As a child, I never understood why my father insisted on
identifying himself as Haitian whenever the issue of race
came up. Later, I understood that he wanted us to dissociate
ourselves from Black Americans. We did everything to this
end—lived in White neighborhoods and socialized with
Whites, because we believed the myth that Blacks will pull
you down if you are struggling to get up. So it wasn't until I
was grown that I began to understand Black history and the
plight of Black Americans and their many struggles.

I am gradually crystallizing my identity as a Black into
something more positive. When I came here as a young
teenager, I knew I was Jamaican and was proud of it. But I
found the issue of being Black is very mixed up. Clearly,
West Indians do not want to be associated with Black
Americans and the stereotypes of them as lazy, not
ambitious, not smart. West Indians feel they can do better
and there is that pressure to excel. When I got to college I
was stunned when a Black American asked me if I was
Black. What she meant was that to her West Indians present
themselves as more like and more close to Whites. As I grow
older and try to connect with my African roots, I am looking
to be closer to Black Americans.

The significance of race as a factor in ethnicity is also illustrated in the experiences of Latinos. Latino individuals have reported being defined by others as people-of-color when the criterion of definition is language, not race. They often find themselves automatically lumped with people-of-color although only some are descended from Indians and/or Africans. In addition, the variety of skin tones in families that are descended from Africans and Indians means that some family members are seen as White and others as people-of-color. This splitting of group and family members according to race threatens cohesion and thus is resented as inconsistent and whimsical. At the same time, however, definition by language alone does not prepare individuals to cope with the issue of race. A White Latino, when invited, joined a people-of-color group on her college campus while others refused to be so labeled. A Cuban student of Spanish and African descent who defined herself as "Afro-Cuban" described her struggles to reach a meaningful definition. Earlier in an all-White high school, she had identified herself only as Cuban, denying her African connection because of its denigrated value. But this solution did not provide the hoped-for protection against pain, for she found that her feelings about her Black identity were constantly being touched off by the racism she found everywhere, in course content and in teacher and student attitudes.

These responses can have great significance for clinical work. A Mexican American psychologist resented intensely any reference to herself as minority or as a person-of-color. She was incensed upon discovering that her assignment to an inner-city mental health center had been predicated on the assumption that she would be empathic and effective with the Black and Mexican clients there. She viewed this assignment as an inferior one and had great difficulty with clients who saw race or ethnicity as a common bond with her.

An East Indian who accepted the frequent designation of himself by others as Black because he viewed Black as a catch-all designation for people-of-color found that this angered several of his colleagues: an Afro-American female, a White female, and another Indian male. The White female accused him of not being clear about his Indian identity, of failing to identify himself as elite and professional, which would allow him to be considered an exception to the rule (and thus a "special" person-of-color, i.e., closer to White). The Afro-American female objected to his identifying himself as Black when he knew little of the culture and people, and the Indian male interpreted his response not only as diagnostic of his sense of confusion and low self-value but also as desertion of his numerically small East Indian group for a more politically powerful one.

Bureaucratic process compounds this inbuilt societal inconsistency in the confused and ambiguous nature of census forms and other data forms used to identify people. One man's response to this ambiguity and inconsistency was reflected in his letter to *The New York Times*.[1] Acknowledging his confusion, he protested being asked on his census form to identify his race/national origin by choosing from among the categories of "white, black, Japanese, Chinese, Korean, etc." He pointed out that if the request was intended to get statistics on race, such a request was not implied in the differentiation between Japanese and Chinese, who are from the same race. While Japanese and Chinese respondents were asked to differentiate themselves by national origin, Whites and Blacks were not. Moreover, since he himself was of mixed Chinese ethnicity (half Manchu and half Han) while his wife was White (Dutch, English, German, and Irish), he questioned how his children would respond to such a request. He found such behavior on the part of the U.S. government disappointing and reflective of ignorance or possibly even racism.

Some of the misunderstanding that occurs in cross-cultural encounters is due to such societal inconsistencies. Sometimes people are expected to identify themselves primarily by race: White, non-White. At other times they are expected to identify themselves by ethnicity, i.e., religion or national origin—except in the case of Blacks, who are always expected to identify themselves by race. This inconsistency is compounded in situations where, at one and the same time, some people are asked to identify themselves by ethnicity and others by race. Moreover, it is further complicated by the fact that when people are descended from more than one ethnic group, they are forced to choose among them.

Societal inconsistency and confusion can breed ambiguity and lack of clarity in the ethnic meanings that people develop. Thus, they place at risk the identity that people, and especially practitioners, need. This ambiguity occurs not only in response to societal confusion about definition; it can also arise when people have ancestral connections to several groups but feel little or no relationship to any of them. A social worker described her predicament:

It is hard when you're Scottish, English, Irish, Luxembourgian, and Canadian for a couple of generations like I am. There is no clear identity when I can say I'm really different from them and this is what I'm like and I can really get behind that. There isn't that experience so I admire in some ways, even long for, the clearcut identity that some of you talk about, because that's not there for me. I guess there are some positives that sink into the background.

Many times, such individuals have come from families who have given up their ethnic connections or lost them over time in the effort to become a part of the melting pot. In addition to confusion, they feel "lost in the shuffle," "amorphous," and "envy for those who know who they are." Some report "experiencing a sense of deprivation" and "wanting a strong culture." For these people, a sense of integration has been elusive.

Melting pot identity creates lack of clarity not only because it has been the source of majority ethnic identity but also because its adoption represents in many instances loss of previous non-American identity and connections. People's descriptions of ethnic denial and of family isolation from old country ties in the effort to embrace the melting pot are often tinged with sadness. Many people know that their family name has been changed "because it didn't sound American enough," and some have reported never discussing the matter and not even knowing what their name was changed from. Recently in Boston, a television commentator expressed with obvious sadness his sense of regret at having given up his Polish old country name and connection in order to cement this melting pot identity. He did this because he believed that a successful career would be more possible for him with the name he had chosen from a telephone book.[2] Many who have embraced the melting pot had found value in the dominance and status it represents, only to realize later that this has entailed a loss for them, particularly in light of the new societal thrust toward pluralism and respect for cultural difference. As one student commented:

The new focus on ethnicity means WASP isn't valued as much. I feel sad about this.

When people have connections to more than one ethnic group they often feel forced to make a choice in order to reduce psychological conflict in themselves and interpersonal conflict with others. A social worker described how this had been an issue for her:

> I've spent my whole life struggling with being Irish (my
> father) and Italian (my mother). I'm fair and I don't look
> Italian, so I always felt very different in Italian groups—
> rejected, isolated and conflicted. When my mother walked
> down the street with my brother and me, people thought we
> were adopted. Also, people used to pit my brother and me
> against each other—he would always say "I want to be
> Italian" and I'd say Irish. My grandfather (maternal) got in
> on it too—he'd ask what would you rather be: Irish or
> Italian, and he'd give you a cookie if you said Italian. Well, I
> wanted to say Italian sometimes, but I was so stubborn that I
> always said Irish.

The conflict experienced as a result of forced choice is especially keen for some individuals from denigrated groups. While Afro-Americans of mixed descent have felt compelled to deny their non-African roots (E. Pinderhughes 1982), Native Americans whose descent involves White or European roots have more often felt compelled to deny their Native American connection (Warner 1987). A psychologist described her experience:

> Hearing people name all the sources of their diverse heritage
> makes me think about the fact that as an Afro-American I
> don't acknowledge all of mine. My family is Black, Indian
> and White, but I don't think of myself as these various
> combinations, only Black. And looking at that it's still not
> ethnic; it's racial.

A Black American psychology trainee wept as she described her high school experience in writing an essay on her family background. She remembered becoming very nervous because her family had always maintained that it was descended from a well-known historical figure who was White. She had carefully avoided any mention of this to her friends, believing that the Black ones would think she was "trying to be White" and the White ones would not believe her. When her mother had encouraged her to include this in her essay, she had responded angrily that she would not because it was a lie. Her tears indicated her remorse over her behavior toward her mother and her distress at

being unable to claim all of her identity and therefore fragment-
ing it.

Despite the vulnerability to negative self-definition, many
members of groups denigrated by society are able to develop a
positive sense of themselves and their group, as evidenced by the
following statements:

> For me, being Afro-American has been a challenge. Being
> able to define myself as I wish to be defined despite how
> others see me and my group has kept me strong and
> flexible—I don't accept the negatives directed at me—that's
> their problem, not mine. And I feel that I can live in two
> worlds—mine and theirs.

> I never had a problem with self-esteem. I grew up in the
> South where there was plenty of support for feeling good
> about being Black. My problem is that I'm not allowed to be
> all that I can be. I don't dislike my group because so many
> people are not ambitious and don't want to learn or achieve.
> I just feel sad.

These examples give a hint at the circumstances under which
people despite membership in a denigrated group are able to
achieve the state of positive ethnic- and self-value that is seen as
critical to mental health. They suggest that a strong connection
to family and group can make the difference. They also show the
difference that can exist between societal definition and personal
ethnic meaning—a factor of pivotal importance in cross-cultural
work. Clinicians must be aware not only of societal definitions
and their potency for people but of the personal sense of ethnic
meaning that people can and do develop and how it can become
positive. While denigrated identity does have the potential for
causing self-hate and conflict, these consequences are much
more closely associated with marginality and uncertainty about
belongingness (Klein 1976). Thus, absence of connection can be
even more critical than connection to a negatively valued group.

Devalued societal status is not the only potential contributor to
negative identity. Persons from high-status societal groups, like
WASPs, manifest negative identity, too. They express pain and a
sense of shame concerning much that is negative in American
history: the suppression of Native Americans, enslavement and
oppression of Blacks, the ethic of the White man's burden. Oth-

ers have expressed feeling guilt, shame, and a sense of unfairness and embarrassment over the unearned privilege that is connected to their ethnic status. This teacher articulated her discomfort:

> I'm a WASP and I'm still trying to figure out what it's meant to be a part of this so-called privileged group. I know we're seen as condescending. In growing up, I was protected and I had little contact with other groups that weren't WASP. I was taught that everyone deserves respect, but I had no experiences in putting this into action. I find that I am now guarded in my struggles to be compassionate without seeming condescending.

A sheltered upbringing has ill-prepared some for life outside the cloistered boundaries of their protected environments, breeding fear and a sense of ignorance. An Anglo-Saxon college professor described the naivete that has resulted from such protection, which she felt put her at a disadvantage in helping her students manage cultural issues in their work. Said she, "Many of them can pick up cultural material that escapes me; others will ask questions about complexities I don't understand."

Some Whites have expressed envy of what they see as a benefit of minority status. To them the vicissitudes that minorities face and the battles they wage against vulnerability to poor self-esteem and fragmented and conflicted identity appear to force them to hammer out a clear, unambiguous ethnic self-definition. A male social worker teased his female colleague who had just made such a statement, saying, "There is always gender." Could this explain the attraction of so many White American women to the women's movement, she wondered? Her thoughtful response raised the question of whether the interest of so many White American middle-class women in the women's movement might have had some relationship to the tendency to view majority identity (i.e., melting pot) as negative or inconsequential.

Anglo-Saxons have commonly expressed confusion and negativism when asked to explore ethnic identity. Some describe feeling insecure, uncertain and scared, saying they don't know what Anglo-Saxon means. An Anglo-Saxon social work student whose biological heritage connected her to the "proper and wealthy few, the true British-American," discussed her attempt to deal with her sense of confusion. Acknowledging a strong pull toward the individualistic, competitive values that characterized her Anglo-Saxon heritage and which conflicted with strong beliefs she had embraced concerning spirituality and social justice, she commented:

My Anglo-Saxon cultural heritage is in conflict with my personal sense of identity. I have in part resolved this conflict by becoming aware of the roots of these contradictory value systems. However, I believe that I am still searching for the meaning that I have not found in any well-defined ethnic identity.

In explaining her general discomfort and confusion, one woman confessed that she has "wished to be Italian or something else because they have fascinating rituals and family times seem so important." By comparison, being Anglo-Saxon to her seemed "normal and boring." Another described himself as "ethnically monochromatic." Ironically this unappreciated Anglo-Saxon identity most closely approximates what has come to signify American identity and the melting pot.[3] However, precisely because it is the identity most valued by the majority, there has been less felt need to be aware of Anglo-Saxon ethnicity and its meaning. It has been, after all, the identity toward which everyone should aspire.

The discomfort that is experienced when ethnic identity is unclear, fragmented, ambivalent, or negative is an essential dynamic to be recognized in the therapeutic process. A psychologist described her adolescent identity struggle that was compounded by the fact that she was the daughter of an Anglo-Saxon mother and a Native American father. In college, this conflict became entangled in her struggle with adolescent identity, causing problems in academic performance with which she sought assistance from the college counselor. When she identified her ethnic background, the counselor's response, "But how much Indian are you?", meant to her that she could "only be a touch Indian." Unable to handle what she experienced as the counselor's invitation to deny her Native American connection (and her father) she never went back. The counselor's insensitivity to her painful identity conflict compounded by conflict around ethnicity drove her away.

The insecurity and psychological conflict that people suffer when their sense of identity is negative, fragmented, or conflicted can drive them to behave in defensive ways. These defensive strategies are attempts to relieve the attendant fear, frustration, anxiety, anger, and sadness.

Denial and avoidance are the most common mechanisms that people use to manage their discomfort. In the following example where they were used as coping strategies, their cost becomes obvious. A Portuguese social work student had grown up with few connections to Portuguese culture. She had attended an Ivy League college graduating with distinction but could not complete her assignment on identifying salient issues related to her ethnic identity and consider their significance for cross-cultural treatment. Her fragmented and negative identity as Portuguese, which she had successfully controlled and avoided up to then, now immobilized her, so that she was unable to even begin the paper. She described confusion and a sense of entrapment that were unfamiliar to her. She was only able to tackle her assignment after several months of therapy with a clinician familiar with Portuguese culture.

Denial and avoidance are common strategies for managing ethnic identity conflict, but they leave people unprepared to manage the feelings mobilized by situations where understanding of ethnic meaning is critical. In this example, the effort needed to complete her assignment broke down her defense of denial. Overwhelmed by the feelings she had so carefully avoided, she could not function. Furthermore, while denial eases the pain of conflict and negative identity, it entails distance from the cultural group and vulnerability to loneliness and isolation. Unconnected to other members of one's ethnic group, one has fewer opportunities to change negative attitudes and develop a sense of group identity or the comfort of an integrated personal identity, which marks healthy functioning.

One social work student, who denied her Afro-American heritage, claiming only a Native American one, found herself isolated from and frightened by other Afro-American students. Her fears and reluctance to learn about Black culture and Black people were extensive. At the same time, others' consistent identification of her as Afro-American continually reminded her of what she was trying to forget. She was even assigned a field placement working with Afro-American clients on the assumption that she was well-equipped to work with them! Her battle to cope with the feelings that were constantly being mobilized left her over-whelmed, depressed, and exhausted. She sought treatment when she feared a breakdown.

A psychologist grew up in a large eastern city. Her family, she believed, was Anglo-Saxon in origin. In actuality her mother's family was Jewish but this was unacknowledged until she was a teenager. At that time her mother reported that her grandparents had changed their names and moved west to hide their Jewish identity, believing that such action was necessary to take advantage of educational opportunities. The news had deeply disturbed her not only because it contradicted her understanding of who she was, but also because she harbored negative stereotypes about Jews. She had nightmares and began to avoid Jewish friends, which she had never done before, finding herself frightened that they could somehow look at her and tell her secret. Unclear about what it meant to be Anglo-Saxon or Jewish, she reported feeling a greater connection to Black culture. This was because she and her siblings had been cared for throughout childhood by an Afro-American housekeeper. Her parents had divorced when she was ten, after which her mother travelled widely, leaving her children behind. Often they stayed with the housekeeper and her family in the Black community. As an adult she had sought employment in an inner city agency, becoming "passionately dedicated" to work-ing with Afro-American clients. In a workshop on cultural sensi-tivity she acknowledged that her over determined efforts to help Afro Americans served to protect her from confronting her own discomfort about her Jewish identity, and that this conflict was seriously undermining her well intended efforts.

As noted in the examination of difference, this maneuver, which creates a sense of distance and isolation from others who may be seen as unlike oneself or one's group, is a potential source of disharmony and conflict. Another response that may cause these same difficulties is that of distrust and avoidance of all but one's own ethnic group. A Jewish psychiatric resident reflected on his distrust of all non-Jews: "I just plain do not trust them." Recognizing that this contributed to his sense of being an out-sider in American life, he reasoned that "there was really no ra-tionale for me to hold onto Jewishness. the way I do." Maladaptive for his role as clinician, this distrust, he discovered, lay at the bottom of his expectations that his non-Jewish patients felt the same way about him. When exaggerated, distrust and avoidance of outsiders can create additional problems such as isolation and loneliness. A Jewish social worker who remembered the pain of being isolated and not invited to play with non-Jewish children noted that her parents' response was to cut her off completely and to teach her to avoid all non-Jews. Thus, the protection from rejection that they sought for her bred isolation and a tendency to view the world in narrow terms as Jewish and non-Jewish.

Efforts to cope with denigrated identity and its consequences can also reinforce an intolerance of difference *within* as well as outside of the ethnic group. In responding to the denigration and in struggling to change negative meaning, people feel compelled to identify and require others to identify in a prescribed way. Others who do not demand the same level of loyalty and intensity of passion are viewed as traitors. Such people may develop a rigid need for sameness and a narrow definition of the ethnic connection. They may also behave in a highly ethnocentric manner.

A psychologist's story demonstrated how intolerance to differences within the Jewish group became a problematic solution to denigrated identity and ethnic identity conflict. Her father, who was the son of Holocaust victims, had attempted valiantly to rescue his parents only to fail at the last minute. She had reacted intensely to her father's perpetual depression with a keen sense of pain and mourning, defended against by a zealous embracing of Jewish identity and the conviction that Jewish unity must become the highest priority for every Jew. Her bitterness and demand for such commitment on the part of all Jewish people promoted an immutable conflict with a male colleague, product of Southern Anglo-Saxon and Jewish roots who identified himself primarily as Unitarian and WASP. She did not believe that her position affected her clinical work since there were no Jews in her caseload. However, she was surprised to find evidence of intolerance, irritation, and lack of empathy in her work with two Latina clients who clearly had distanced themselves from their ethnic group and were experiencing value conflict.

What appears as narrowness, bigotry, or intolerance of difference can sometimes also be seen in another light. It may represent the universal wish for survival and the fear of disappearance, which drives our natural proclivity toward family and group continuity:

> I have always believed in religious tolerance and being open to all people. I didn't mind when my Jewish son married a Catholic girl, but I am now upset at myself because I find myself insisting that they raise their child in the Jewish faith.

No longer viewing her mother's wish for a red-haired grandson as symbolic of pathological connection to her own father, an Irish social worker now saw it as an indication of her mother's wish for ethnic survival. Not only did this understanding facilitate more insight into her value conflict with her mother, but it also facilitated empathy with clients who had ethnocentric perspectives. In such instances she no longer reacted with irritation and impatience. Fear of ethnic disappearance and the wish for continuity are powerful forces driving ethnocentric behavior. These imperatives represent serious dilemmas for people who wish to emphasize values of equality and acceptance of differences. Clinicians must manage these dilemmas in their personal and professional lives. While recognizing the benefit of ethnocentrism in terms of ethnic preservation and survival, they must also recognize the costs in terms of the potential it creates for prejudiced, bigoted behavior that blocks growth and the ability to value differences in others. Resolution lies in being vigilant about developing appreciation for differences in people. This means that when one honors this wish for continuity, one makes sure that it is not driven by fear of difference or by developmental traumas. While the belief that "we are the best" provides a sense of cohesiveness and group value, it also limits one's ability to see value and strengths in other groups.

People can use specialness as a defense in relationship to persons *within* the group as well as outside. The use of specialness as a defense was illustrated in the example of an Afro-American teacher who described her family's efforts to perceive and be perceived as elite, aristocratic, and special: "It was as though special Black meant non-Black." Akin to the psychological defense of identifying with the aggressor, this coping mechanism can also be costly in its consequences of ambivalence, confusion, and even self-hatred as seen in this example:

My ancestors were wealthy German Jews. My paternal grandfather fancied himself an English country gentleman. And my mother, who is Austrian, had little Jewish identity. I have always been confused about how the family was proud of itself and also anti-Semitic. It seems that being Jewish is dangerous. My confusion was compounded by the fact that I was raised by a German Catholic governess. Being privileged is a burden; being Jewish is a burden.

It is important for counselors to understand these dynamics, or they may make costly mistakes. Perceiving their White neighbors as more acceptable, a light-skinned Black family forbade the daughter to associate with her ethnic peers, almost all of them darker, who lived in the next block. Years later, when the daughter was in treatment for depression her social worker believed these events to be a myth. She therefore missed the opportunity to help her client explore her sense of isolation from her ethnic group and link it to the rejection and loneliness she had experienced generally.

Disproving the stereotype is yet another strategy for managing membership in a denigrated group. A Puerto Rican teacher described her resentment of the stereotype that Hispanics cannot tolerate pain. This response had compelled her to behave during childbirth "so that it could be seen that Hispanic women are brave and deal very well with pain." Her sensitivity to the reputation of her ethnic group was also reflected in her relentless criticism of Puerto Rican parents whom she felt were out of control and too often loud and impulsive.

The presence of negative identity creates certain imperatives for practitioners who need to understand how to help their clients build a strong, positive sense of identity and how to achieve it for themselves. When teachers, clinicians, and other service-providers have failed to experience their own identity as worthwhile, they may fail to value that of their clients. Moreover, failure to change their own negative identity can mean they avoid dealing with their clients' ethnic issues, because such a focus mobilizes the pain that is associated with their own negative identity. And in this failure, they unintentionally reinforce poor self-esteem and a sense of emotional isolation for clients.

An Afro-American administrator made this statement:

Down South where I lived, we were also taught the importance of religion, obeying our elders, sticking with the

family, and helping each other out. But we also were taught
to feel inferior, value White, and to do what White folks said.

As supervisor of an all-White staff, she now found that these
early experiences (which had left her very angry) had limited her
ability to use her authority appropriately. The importance of
monitoring herself to continually reinforce her belief that she
was competent to do the job and capable of managing the feelings mobilized required the expenditure of large amounts of energy.

But dodging ethnic issues is not the only inappropriate behavior which helpers may engage in when they are poorly equipped
in relation to their own ethnicity. Their response and their own
needs may push them to misunderstand, distort, exaggerate, or
minimize the significance of the client's ethnic identity experiences. Feeling immobilized and unable to handle the complexities, they may swing into action inappropriately.

An Irish-American social worker had been a devout Catholic
throughout childhood and adolescence. She was intensely disappointed when she failed to receive from the Church an annul-
ment of her troubled teenage marriage and, having renounced Catholicism, she became Unitarian. She regarded herself as a world
citizen who had traveled widely and had "many intercultural experiences." When her Irish-Catholic client, pregnant with her
fifth child, was advised by her physician that completion of the
pregnancy would endanger her health, she was angered at her
client's intention to go to term with the pregnancy. Immobilized
by her own feelings, the worker was unable to help her client to
explore any alternative available within her belief system. Her
sense of entrapment in relation to cultural issues with clients became understandable only when she was able to analyze the
meaning for herself of being Irish Catholic. Only then did she
confront the negative feelings she had struggled to control concerning her Irish identity, the Catholic church, and her intensely
ethnocentric Irish father toward whom she had intense ambivalence.

Readier to confront herself was a Puerto Rican social work student who described how her upbringing, which had taught her
denial, left her feeling ethnically isolated and ignorant of her ethnic connection:

I was raised in Puerto Rico, where I went to a private
school. My family was very much into money and success. It

was not until I came to the States and learned about Puerto
Rican culture that I realized how different we were in not
valuing family and personalism more. When I got ready to
come to the States to school, my father cautioned me against
hanging around with anyone who was Spanish-speaking.
When I came here, I didn't understand why people saw me
as Puerto Rican when I felt American. I resented the
Spanish-speaking community and when I went to work there
(the welfare office), I was very hard on clients because I
didn't understand why they behaved the way they did. I
think the ulcer I got was related to how mixed up I was and
still am. I feel I have been robbed of my cultural identity,
and I want it back.

Another Puerto Rican student who recognized the negativism
marking her sense of ethnicity and the intense ambivalence she
felt concerning her Puerto Rican client's fatalistic "acceptance
of pessimism and lack of motivation for change," acknowledged
that her own ethnic confusion had negatively affected her work.
She reacted with irritation to the client's statement that "we
come to this earth to suffer and should accept our sufferings and
punishment from God," and insisted that the client must trust
her doctor. Reflecting on the influence of her behavior upon the
client's failure to continue treatment she considered what would
have been a better strategy: to discuss the client's acceptance, to
let her know that the clinician saw that she was trying hard to
be faithful to her religious beliefs, and to suggest in passing that
God also guided her doctor who had a different opinion about
the outcome. This same student was able to see that although she
had several negative experiences with persons of Irish descent,
the intense fear with which she approached her Irish client and
her expectation of rejection stemmed partly from her own negative feelings about her Puerto Rican identity. Thus, she was surprised that when—with great trepidation—she asked her Irish client how she felt about having a Puerto Rican social worker, the
client responded with warmth and empathy that she "too had
been an immigrant and told stories of her victimization both in
the U.S. and in Europe."

Where there is comfort and clarity about their own ethnic connectedness, and some knowledge about the client's, clinicians
can look with less distortion at the cross-cultural interface, being

clear on how their own "internal program" of ethnic meaning can affect their thinking and behavior in the helping encounter.

Values as Important in Ethnic Meaning

Ethnic meaning can be crystallized when one is able to identify the ethnic values one has embraced. Clarity about ethnic values makes explicit the similarities and differences between oneself and others, and between one's present values and those embraced in the past. As the guideposts which people live by, values give an understanding of how people can be alike in a general way but also different in very specific ways. Values are markers of connection to others and of differences *from* others, of the specific ways in which one is not the same as others and therefore unique. Differences between persons who belong to the same group as well as differences between persons belonging to different groups can be highlighted by a focus on values. Differences in ethnic behavioral styles and psychological characteristics which tend to be consistent with values are better understood. For example, Blacks tend to be energetic, confrontational, interactive, animated, and casual (which is consistent with values of strength, persistence, and flexibility) while Anglo-Saxons tend to be cool, quiet, deliberate, noninteractive, and differentiating, i.e., one person speaks, then the other speaks (which is consistent with values of autonomy, mastery, planning, and success). But these behavioral styles are never embraced by all members of those groups, which makes for wide variations that must be understood.

Identifying one's own values makes clear how similar cultural experiences can evoke different responses in people. A female psychiatric trainee, the grandchild of Holocaust victims, reacted in a way totally different from the women in the earlier example. She had responded to her parents' perpetual grieving and ongoing focus on their family and ethnic tragedy with the feeling that "Jewishness was rammed down my throat—I got sick of hearing about it and wanted to get far away." The intensity of her feeling was manifest in her trembling voice. She was reminded by her colleagues that her response indicated intense feelings lying behind her attempts to run away, and that facing these feelings was necessary to transcend them and to acquire a sense of value as an ethnic person.

People who are primarily ethnic in their connection may also embrace American values, becoming "hyphenated Americans." American values closely approximate those considered to be Anglo-Saxon or WASP and are the essence of the melting pot. Clinicians need to understand the way in which they themselves and their clients emphasize not only ethnic values but also the prevailing norms in our society. Clarity about these norms is essential since they constitute the context for everyone's sense of meaning irrespective of ethnic connections. Here is a list of American values compiled by students in a cross-cultural class:

Hard work	Organization	Mastery/Problem
Materialism	Profit: Money	solving
Affluence	before People	The future
Friendliness	Mobility	Individualism
Honesty	Status/	Self-reliance/
Justice	Superiority	Independence,
Freedom	Planning	Autonomy
Egalitarianism	Spaced/Distance	Technology
Achievement	in Relationships	Innovation
Power	Space in Living	Imperialism
Youth	Efficiency	Racism

In examining this list, one is impressed with the degree of contradiction that exists in this group's view of American values alone; for example, the juxtaposition of justice and egalitarianism alongside ownership, possession, power, status, money, affluence. Inconsistency such as this can create tension and value conflicts that affect people's functioning.

No other cultural group emphasizes autonomy and independence as much as Americans do. This is so despite the fact that individualism is a Western concept that is not exclusively American. This unusual association of individualism and Western culture is dramatically illustrated in the fact that the English language is the only language that capitalizes the pronoun "I" (Marsella and Pedersen 1981). The experiences of nonimmigrants and immigrants alike validate this strong American emphasis. This statement by a Vietnamese teacher dramatizes the difference:

We don't live a personal life, but we belong to the family and the culture and its traditions. Sometime we might want to do something that is not good for them like the marriage. We have to depend on the family so we don't do it.

The independence that Americans value can inspire a special sense of isolation among immigrants:

I am a West Indian from Trinidad; I have also found it difficult being in this country. When I first came, I found people unfriendly and cold. The support of family and friends is so important. You even live with your family after you have become an adult until you marry. I felt a lot of loneliness when I came here. Now I am more comfortable because I've become more conservative, and I enjoy our West Indian community where we can have our festivals and enjoy each other.

The differences that exist between American values and personal ethnic values often become a source of conflict for immigrants. This conflict is often reflected in generational struggles between family members, especially parents and children or teenagers. An Iranian immigrant describes her fear that her son will reject Iranian values:

I am a Moslem physician from Iran. In our culture feelings are easily expressed, people are open, share readily, and argue a lot. When we were preparing to come here, my husband was warned that we would be seen as impulsive and unsophisticated. It has been a difficult adjustment, made more difficult by my six and one-half year old son who insists on doing everything the American way: eat at McDonald's, go to a Christian church. I'm afraid he's rejecting his Iranian heritage which I want him to have. I'm afraid of the freedom children have here in America and the rebelliousness of teenagers. It is really hard because by our Iranian values children stay close and even live at home until age 40 with their parents' support. I feel so much conflict about how much to let him be American.

One's own values and personal ethnic meaning are better understood when there is clarity about American values as the context.

There are other benefits to obtaining clarity about one's own values. It helps guard against use of that well-known defense, expectation of sameness. This makes people comfortable but reinforces a helper's need to see clients as like themselves and thus to ignore differences that may mean ignoring a client's uniqueness and strengths. Practitioners must recognize how their own values constitute a lens through which they see their clients and realize the handicap that can be. A devout Polish Catholic student felt powerless about how to help her Jewish client, who "did not believe in a resurrection or hereafter," with the loss involved in her impending death: "How could I help her work through her depression if I could not relay that sense of hope so important to me?" This student's struggle to see that her own cultural value that one should solve one's own problem ("Heaven forbid if I cannot find a solution to a problem myself.") had prevented her from seeing that her Jewish client's expectation of searching for help, of turning to experts, and readily relying on them did not mean the client was not capable of handling the situation. It also becomes possible to speculate about how clients' values may affect their perceptions of their helpers. An Anglo-Saxon clinician, understanding her own values of autonomy and emotional control, wondered if her Italian client might see her as cold and uninvolved.

How one responds to the values of others that are different is critical self-knowledge for helpers. A German-American social worker felt engulfed by the Jewish family of her hospitalized client who was terminal. Her own background of emotional control left her unprepared for the family's ready expression of feelings: "What I found the most difficult was the father crying." Helpers are readier to appreciate the adaptive nature of their clients' behavior and life-style when they are clear about their own values and the general significance of values in determining people's functioning.

An Irish student resolved to be more patient and try harder with her poor Black client to gain his trust. The knowledge that her client's values of toughness, struggle, and "running a game" had been adaptive in his battle for survival moved her to resolve that "I won't get turned off by his resistance or get angry when I see him looking for a fight or trying to manipulate me. I realize I have to get beyond those behaviors if my client is going to trust me and that means more work for me." Clarity about values also points up the energy that must be expended by the helper to transcend value difference. A social worker of Irish descent struggled to understand her Italian client's argumentative style. Her insight about the differences that existed between herself and her client in the management of feelings facilitated a more appropri-ate response from her. She reflected on the way in which Italians ventilate their anger as opposed to "we Irish suppress anger and let it build up which may lead to withdrawal and emotional cutoff." Recognizing the cultural basis for the anxiety that her client's intense feelings mobilized helped her to remain involved. It also helped her to see that "this mode of fighting does not in-validate the tenderness this husband and wife show for each other." Her own Irish style of "not questioning the doctor, of suf-fering in silence, and offering it up to God" required making an effort to understand this client's dramatic expression of pain and her relentless demands to see the doctor and get his opinion.

Awareness of one's own values provides clarity about the way in which one is ambivalent or in conflict about them, under-standing that can determine the helper's effectiveness with cli-ents. An Anglo-Saxon social worker who described herself as struggling to become less individualistic and more expressive and "laid back" checked her automatic tendency to push her West Indian client, who was ambitious, driving, and upwardly mobile, to see American values in a more negative light.

> As a WASP, I was taught to feel proud to be emotionally controlled. It really upset me when I found out that people can share feelings openly and that it could be a good thing. I've spent a lot of energy trying to overcome this, and now what I have to do is watch not pushing others to do the same.

An Irish social worker found her efforts to work with a French-Canadian female client compromised by her own conflict. The client came from a working-class family and had come to treat-ment because of guilt and shame following a brief marital affair. She had been abused as a child by her strict disciplinarian father and now felt trapped and helpless in her marriage to an abusive, alcoholic spouse. The social worker described her own frustra-tion that the client did not want to use treatment to raise her self-esteem and free herself from her situation. Instead, she viewed treatment as a confessional from which she sought an easing of her guilt rather than change, support rather than an opportunity to understand her situation and to work through her problems and grow. The worker's own conflict had complicated her efforts to help the client. She explained:

I struggle to figure out how much of her ambivalence that is so frustrating to me and makes me angry is related to her cultural belief that being trapped and a martyr in an alcoholic and abusive marriage is her fate and how much is based on her psychological need for punishment because she believes she is a bad person. It is hard to do this thinking since my own conflict about moral judgment and the Church means I am unclear for myself. I experience anxiety about rejecting the morality of the Church and a sense of being smothered when I try to accept it. I waiver back and forth in my judgment about the client's guilt and how it ought to be managed!

One's own conflicts, therefore, which may be multidetermined, can complicate the work because they provide a barrier to the careful thinking that is necessary. In this particular instance the social worker also noted the extra energy it required for her to stay invested and empathic with her client's lack of interest in getting a graduate equivalency degree and becoming upwardly mobile.

A French-Canadian social worker who had considered himself as "some species of WASP" now discovered that a major factor in his driven sense of industry stemmed from "the family's tyrannical French-Canadian roots." In acknowledging his identity he noted "the powerful role of the male who must maintain dominance and the emotional ambivalence in which closeness was demanded but emotionality avoided." He was clear about the conflict these values constituted for him and expressed his desire to arrive at his own unique values and "extricate" himself from the ethnic values he saw as unhealthy for himself and his relationship with others. This realization had been driven home to him when he recognized that he had labeled his Anglo-Saxon male client as "too weak and ineffectual because he could not manage his wife and child." He had done this without attempting to understand how his client's experiences with parenting expectations might be different from his. He also was aware that his own conflict about hard work had spawned negative feelings toward his client's "dogged pursuit of money and security."

Ethnic-value conflict on the part of clinicians can constitute special jeopardy in work with intermarried couples. For here, the clinician is confronted with value conflict between two clients as well as conflict between his or her own values and those of the clients. This situation is especially loaded when one member of the couple has a similar background to that of the helper:

> I am working with this couple; the wife is Irish, the husband is Italian. The husband's loyalty to his father, now widowed, and his insistence on visiting him every day, which is expectable behavior for Italians, is not understood by his wife. Since I'm Italian too, I find myself getting annoyed at her and have to watch my tendency to support the husband. It has helped to understand that Irish families tend to be more nuclear and less extended and to know that I have to look at my own issues.

Practitioners need to understand how the complexities involved in ethnic dynamics can affect the helping encounter. A general understanding is not enough. They must be able to see the specific way in which information applies or does not apply to a particular client and also to themselves. They need to understand the pervasive significance of ethnic meaning—the importance for a given individual that ethnic meaning be clear, positive, and integrated; the consequences of ambivalent, confused, fragmented, and/or negative identity for how people behave; and how societal status assignment and individual experiences can shape this sense of ethnic meaning, determining its quality. This understanding must be applied to the helping relationship. When helpers can be clear and mainly positive about their self-definition and its meaning about their group definition and connectedness, they can appreciate the similarities and differences between themselves and members of other ethnic groups, as well as between themselves and members of their own ethnic group. An understanding of their own sense of ethnic meaning can facilitate an awareness of their vulnerability to ethnic value conflict and identity confusion as a result of a cultural process, and the costs and consequences involved. This will enhance their potential for effectiveness, because anxieties, ambivalence, and negative feelings about their own cultural background will not immobilize them or prevent constructive engagement with clients.

5

Understanding Race

Entrapment for Everyone

Race constitutes a different level of cultural meaning than ethnicity. Originally carrying a meaning that referred to biological origin and physical appearance, the concept of race was always more inclusive, embracing a number of ethnic groups within a given racial category. Over time, race has acquired a social meaning in which these biological differences, via the mechanism of stereotyping, have become markers for status assignment within the social system. The status assignment based on skin color identity has evolved into complex social structures that promote a power differential between Whites and various people-of-color. These power-assigning social structures in the form of institutional racism affect the life opportunities, life-styles, and quality of life for both Whites and people-of-color. In so doing they compound, exaggerate, and distort biological and behavioral differences and reinforce misconceptions, myths, and distortions on the part of both groups about one another and themselves. "Although many forms of exclusion and discrimination exist in this country, none is so deeply rooted, persistent, and intractable as that based on color" (Hopps 1982, p. 3). This intractability was evident in the celebrated 1988 television documentary concerning race issues on college campuses. On that occasion, a White student from the University of Michigan made this comment, which he said was hard to admit:

71

When a Black person makes an intelligent remark, I always
think, "This is not what I should be getting from them."
(*Racism 101*, WGBH, Channel 2, May 10, 1988)

And a Black student confessed that he had reached the point
where he could no longer stand being around White people and
had curtailed any opportunity for interaction as much as possible
by staying in his room.

Human service deliverers, trapped in these biases and structures like everyone else, are often unable to be empathic and,
hence, to succeed in cross-racial work. For, helping efforts must
often be directed to situations that exist, at least in part, as a
consequence of racism. Even persons with some sensitivity to
the societal dynamics that sustain racism feel immobilized when
it becomes an issue in the helping encounter. For example a social worker cited her problem with a Black client who complained about put-downs by darker skinned Blacks in her office.
The social worker felt that the isolation of this client had intrapsychic origins but "was afraid to confront her." Said she, "Had
she been White I would immediately have confronted her." In
another example, a supervisor reported reluctance to ask the
Black psychologist he was supervising to identify the race of his
patient although he suspected that race was an important contextual factor in the client's problem. He feared that the supervisee
would become annoyed and think he "was reading race into the
situation when it wasn't there." An Afro-American social worker
described her confusion about how to handle the anger she felt
in relation to a demeaning remark made by her White client. The
client was attempting to express her gratitude for the worker's
help: "None of these other [White] people here have been able to
help me. Just think it had to be a colored girl who could do it."
Freedom from this entrapment is critical to successful treatment
outcome. To achieve such freedom, practitioners need to (1) understand their responses to racism and the consequences of
them, (2) understand how they may threaten the cross-racial encounter, and (3) learn to manage them effectively.

Reviewing experiences related to race and identifying the associated feelings, attitudes, perceptions, and behaviors provide opportunity to acquire such understanding and control. It is important to examine experiences and responses affected by race
separate from ethnic distinctions. When ethnicity is the exclu-

sive unit of attention, the salience of race can be ignored and White people can maintain their ignorance about the meaning of race, both personally and systemically. "Ask a White person his or her race and you may get the response 'Italian,' 'Jewish,' 'Irish,' 'English,' and so on. White people do not see themselves as White" (Katz 1978, p. 13). Other experts agree:

> While Blacks, Puerto Ricans, and other racial and ethnic minorities are forced by racial oppression to be aware of themselves as members of racial groups, Whites are generally not aware of their whiteness. (Adams and Schlesinger 1988, p. 225)

In order to understand what race and racial identity mean to us, we need to examine early experiences that have centered on race, early images of race or color, how we were taught to cope with racial issues, and feelings about being White or a person-of-color, as well as current perceptions of the other racial group. In this search for understanding, the inconsistencies, complexities and confusion that people identify in relation to ethnicity are compounded, and the strong feelings people seemed to harbor regarding ethnicity pale in comparison to those regarding race. Moreover, there is none of the levity and pleasure that character-ize the search for ethnic understanding. Instead, the mood is one of discomfort, struggle, and pain. For Whites, the work re-quires breaking through the denial, projection, rationalization, and other defenses that have maintained the stereotypes and then enduring the anxiety and psychological pain they have served to ward off. For people-of-color it also means enduring the pain and anger which an exploration of racial dynamics in-evitably mobilizes.

Most people experience apprehension in undertaking such a task. For the ideas, attitudes, feelings, and perceptions that must be confronted are held tenaciously. Many of them have remained hidden or obscure despite the fact that they heavily determine people's behavior in cross-racial situations.

> Even acknowledgment of the real status differences and that they have been imperceptively incorporated into the ego can be disquieting. This is especially true of members of majority groups. Such acknowledgment is unwittingly perceived as

negation of past struggles to surmount such unworthy stances. (Adams and Schlesinger 1988, p. 205)

The anxiety that exists for Whites concerning the subject of race should not be underestimated. It is high even for those who believe they have mastered their biases and especially for those who have made the commitment to self-confrontation. For although many would like to believe they are free of racial prejudice and want to view it as operative only in instances of blatant bigotry, there is tension about checking this out. This anxiety has been expressed in terms of fear of discovering bad things about oneself, uneasiness about unexamined values, awareness of the pervasiveness of racism, of one's helplessness to cope, and of a sense of entrapment:

> To be White means to feel safe but sad—and I'm not sure I want to open up that sadness.

The anxiety about discovery of bias can be particularly troublesome since it violates ideals of justice and equality, cardinal American values. This threatens people's image of themselves as just and fair, mobilizing guilt and fear of disapproval from others. Such anxiety prevents comfortable interaction between Whites and people-of-color and thus unless properly managed can affect cross-racial work. Management of this anxiety in the interest of confronting bias and achieving greater comfort and confidence in cross-racial interactions should be seen as an act of courage.

But usually Whites do not feel courageous. They tend instead to plead ignorance and to protest that they have never had to think about the meaning of being White. These psychiatric residents are an example:

> I know I am a Jew and I think about it all the time, but I don't think of myself as White although I know I am. It simply has not been an issue and has no meaning to me.

> And yet we use race in every history we write on patients. A typical first line reads: "This patient is a 20-year-old White male," and we think nothing of it.

On the other hand, people-of-color are often preoccupied with the issue as this psychologist suggests:

> I can never forget that I am Black. I dare not.

The apparent ignorance of Whites and the ever-vigilant, constant awareness of most people-of-color provide startling con-
trasts. Whites manifest ignorance about people-of-color in statements about not knowing them and feeling strange in relating to
them. Further examination reveals that behind this ignorance
and lack of awareness are definite fantasies, images, and attitudes. A psychologist described the following experience:

> I grew up in Wisconsin and never knew any Blacks as a
> child, but I loved Aunt Jemima on the pancake box because
> she seemed so cheerful and caring.

With certain persons such as those who have had little contact
with people-of-color, it is easier to see that their perceptions are
based on stereotypical images and that these images can satisfy
a personal need. In the example above, for instance, the stereotype of the Black woman as mammy and nurturer (Aunt Jemima)
represented a compensatory wish, according to the speaker, for
a maternal figure who was different from his own mother whom
he had perceived as cold and distant. Such fantasies and images
illustrate how social process prompts the use of minorities as a
stabilizing and tension-relieving force for persons who belong to
dominant groups.[1]

> It is not farfetched to say that having scapegoats has been
> protective of the adaptation of the White American
> throughout our country's history. (Bradshaw 1978, p. 1521)

When such fantasies and images drive cross-cultural work they
can push clinicians to behave in ways that benefit the clinician
rather than the client in the helping encounter. A psychiatric
trainee confessed to a fantasy that she could take her Black patient home with her, noting that it did not mean that she would
take care of the patient but that the patient would take care of
her. Practitioners need to understand not only their images and
fantasies but the real experiences that created them and shaped
their feelings.

Whites often express confusion and bewilderment at the behavior of people-of-color:

> On my first job, I encountered lots of hostility, anger, and
> suspicion from Blacks. I didn't understand it. I think they
> were testing me out, but why would I be working in that
> kind of agency, doing that hard outreach work? I would

never go near them if I hated all Blacks. It's been very
painful.

While some will resist the issue by a determined focus on ethnicity or by pleading ignorance, others may describe their experiences of mistreatment by people-of-color. Examples abound of
hostile interactions, especially childhood battles, in which
people-of-color appear as provocative, inconsiderate, rude,
frightening, and dangerous. Sometimes these perceptions appear
to be offered as justification of the bias they have so vehemently
denied and are struggling to understand:

I didn't dislike Blacks till I went into the army. The Blacks
there taught me to hate. Don't they know this separation
stuff only antagonizes people?

Others tell stories of good deeds, helpful acts, and rescuing behaviors in which they have been involved. These examples appear to be offered as proof of their freedom from prejudice. And,
indeed, some are offered by persons who have had an ongoing
commitment to control their bias and fight racism. Others will
offer descriptions of mistreatment of people-of color by others,
especially parents.

There are illustrations of lessons in negative stereotyping,
which demonstrate how parents' management of issues related
to difference teaches children fear, anxiety, and hostility. One individual remembered being taught to see Blacks as dangerous,
especially Black men who "will hurt you for no reason." A common experience involves servants or persons in their parents'
employ. These and other experiences confirm the confusion with
which young children struggle as they learn about the dynamics
of race. They also illustrate the exquisite sensitivity that children
often develop when contradictions exist. A nurse described her
confusion when her family, usually "very moral and ethical except with Blacks," used the servants as dumping grounds for angry feelings. A psychiatrist reported that his earliest memory of
people-of-color was the Black maid who took care of him and the
fact that he and the rest of the family were never allowed to eat
out of the dishes she used. Suggesting that his mother was pro-
foundly disturbed emotionally during the early years of his development and that the stability provided by this Black mother substitute had been fortunate, he linked these events to his
tireless commitment to work with people-of-color. Even subtle

contradictions are picked up by young children as seen in this statement by a psychiatric resident:

In our family we were taught that it was wrong to be prejudiced. But I knew my folks were anyway when my older brother gave his new watch to his Black friend. I had never seen my father so angry and I just knew it was because his friend was Black.

The comment below vividly illustrates how the experiences of a social worker seemed to support her father's instruction in prejudice, and the cost to her in terms of ambivalence and a sense of entrapment:

My father was an architect who worked with housing projects in Chicago. He was very prejudiced, talked about Blacks as out to destroy everything no matter how nice it was. He thought it was of no use to provide them with decent housing. They wanted to be undereducated, didn't want to work, didn't care, and would destroy everything. At Christmas, we would ride into the city to see the lights, and on the elevated we could look right into people's apartments that were beside the track. And the windows were dirty; there were no curtains and the rooms were a mess. When I would see Black kids on the street, I'd thank God I wasn't born Black.

Then in church I learned we should love everyone, that we are all God's children, and I knew what I saw and felt about Blacks wasn't right. My aunt and uncle stayed in their neighborhood after Blacks began to move in. We always visited them there and it was awful how it went down. So I have this tape in my head that Black people ruin things for White people. This was drilled in my brain and I don't want to think that but I still do. (This person seemed close to tears.)

In a few instances parental teaching attempted to instill unbiased, egalitarian attitudes. Usually these experiences are remembered as costly in terms of rejection by other Whites. And when the lesson of nonbias was based on "all people are alike," upon current examination, this experience was deemed unrealistic, naive, and distorting. In our groups, there was never a report of parental teaching of nonbias that promoted the idea that differences are real, not to be judged but acknowledged and respected.

When attention is directed to the meaning of racial identity in the present, the examination moves from parents, teachers, other adults, and peers to the self. Exploring childhood memories or parental attitudes and teaching or the behavior of others is always easier to tackle than the issue of personal bias in the present (Adams and Schlesinger 1988, p. 210). If the exploration occurs in a group, attempts may be made to move the focus to the feelings and behavior of people-of-color and their attitudes about Whites, a strategy often not recognized as avoidance (Katz 1978). People even have objected to being identified as White:

> I have a reaction to being identified as White. It makes me feel guilty. I'd rather be called "majority"—somehow that makes me feel less guilty. Maybe it's because "majority" legitimizes the power and sounds less oppressive.

In the helping encounter denial of White racial identity can have varying effects. Such discounting has a high potential to be destructive, for it constitutes an invitation to clients who are people-of-color to deny who they are, what they see, and what they experience. This in turn reinforces confusion for them and undermines the sound reality testing and judgment needed to cope with their harsh realities.

Fear is another frequently acknowledged response on the part of Whites. A tall, well-built psychiatric resident appeared close to tears as he described his fear of the Blacks he encounters as he walks between buildings of the inner city medical center where he worked.

Anger, too, is acknowledged not only in terms of past mistreatment. People report feeling angry at the process of self-confrontation, of having to face the associated discomfort and pain. There is also anger at the effort that has to be exerted to understand: "It's an overload." People feel overwhelmed. They also feel frightened at the notion of empathizing with people with whom so much pain is connected, about whom so much contradiction exists, and about things they feel helpless to manage. A variety of other issues may be at the root of this intensity. For example, a psychiatric resident was angered when challenged concerning her belief that her identity as a homosexual had prepared her to understand the oppression of people-of-color in a way that other Whites cannot. She passionately defended this conviction. The intensity of her feeling later proved to be related to her guilt about her belief that Whites are innately superior to people-of-color and her guilt about such ideas.

Positive responses about being White are sometimes even harder to acknowledge than negative ones. For many, being White means being safe, accepted, lucky, comfortable, secure, like others, not having to spend energy on struggles to extract necessary supports from the environment. But admission of relief and gratitude about White identity are also associated with guilt. For cross-cultural work, guilt can interfere with the comfort needed to build a trusting relationship and thus with effective intervention.

Whites' perceptions of people-of-color also reflect ambivalence and contradiction. People-of-color have been seen as basically incompetent but supercompetent if they achieve; acceptable as nurturers and caring figures but not as equals; as angry when they appear arrogant (whereas Whites are not); as frightening when they appear competent, act assertively, or demonstrate ability to cope with racism without being demoralized. This list of conflicting reactions to people-of-color further identifies the ambivalence one group expressed:

- Revulsion vs. adoration
- Distaste vs. want to get help from them
- Fear because they are destructive and dangerous versus pain over their despair

Only a diligent effort to identify and clarify these attitudes, feelings, and perceptions can bring order to the confusion and a readiness to move beyond the defenses people use to seek comfort, which immobilize them. These feelings and perceptions run deep. Ordway (1973) describes his psychoanalysis of a White social worker who had been working intensively with Blacks to help them organize self-help programs. Increasingly fatigued because "he felt too keenly the tragedy of Black–White hostilities between friends in both groups and because both Black and White militants constantly play(ed) on his loyalties, sympathies, guilt, and anxieties" (p. 125), he found himself viewed by some Whites as a traitor and by some Blacks as suspicious and dangerous. Analysis of symptoms and dreams revealed murderous wishes to "string 'em up" for the anger, fatigue, and exhaustion Blacks stirred in him as a result of their struggle, negativism, criticisms, hostility, combativeness, and suspicions. Seeing himself as a kind and unprejudiced individual, he was astonished to learn that the pleasant agreeableness in his Black friends, which he had interpreted as shallowness, in reality represented a holding back of their anger, since they saw him as an unsafe person. He was also surprised to learn that his opinion of them as less intelligent and scholastically competent was a denial of his experience in school. When he did acknowledge competence in some, these persons were seen as exceptions and turned into White. He also learned that his perception of Blacks as dangerous was a projection of his fear of retaliation for his own aggressive wishes toward them, for the personal offenses against them carried out at a largely unconscious level. Unacknowledged and uncontrolled, such feelings and perceptions can constitute major roadblocks to effectiveness in clinical work.

In contrast to Whites who, as a group, remain largely ignorant about issues of race and its significance for them, people-of-color demonstrate great familiarity. Their perceptions of Whites focus on Whites' easier access to resources and the absence of barriers for them. "Life is a piece of cake," "If they can't achieve, what's wrong with them?" are typical comments. Whites are seen as protected from true competition with people-of-color since "their headstart through the unequal distribution of resources means they always get a handicap." There is awareness (and often resentment) that Whites may see them as incompetent and frightening. People-of-color are, for the most part, knowledgeable about the ongoing inconsistency, contradiction, and paradox which race creates and the negative consequences of this predicament.

But there is wide variation among people-of-color—depending on such factors as region, degree of destructiveness in the larger social system, and the kind and nature of supports—in the realities and the extensiveness of the coping mechanisms devised. For example, the experiences of Blacks who have grown up in the South range from life within a rigid caste system where there was daily humiliation such as moving to the side of sidewalk or street to let Whites pass and the ongoing threats of the Ku Klux Klan, to life in protected pockets of segregation. Here, a tight network of school, church, and extended family facilitated safety and security, and experiences where Blacks and Whites had cordial relations, acknowledged blood relationships, and even held family reunions.

Despite the fact that many of these experiences occurred during childhood, the feelings can be very much alive to the extent that the recall of them has on a number of occasions provoked tears and some of the original outrage or fear:

> In Mobile, Alabama, I remember walking down the street when I was eight years old and a red-headed White boy yelled, "Hey, nigger, give me some pussy." I was very scared because I'd been warned about the danger of White men. To this day I have an automatic reaction of revulsion to red-headed White males.

Such feelings naturally shape interaction not only with Whites but with other people-of-color and affect the helping encounter. An Afro-American nurse described her decision not to work with a White psychotic patient whose ongoing racial epithets and insults she found intolerable. Although she recognized the pathology that drove such behavior, she felt that the societal context of racism made those insults more loaded than other insults which she could view as less personal. Issues such as this have thrown inpatient hospital staff groups into turmoil in the effort to find the best way of managing such a patient—one that is in the interest of patient recovery and staff comfort and respect.

There is the problem of immigrants who find racism an enigma with which they are rarely prepared to cope. Who is White and who is not and the meaning of that definition have often been perceived differently in their country-of-origin than in the United States. In Puerto Rico, for instance, one individual reported that White is defined not by skin color but by hair texture. Dark-skinned persons with straight hair were considered White; whereas blue-eyed, fair-skinned persons with kinky hair were not. Another workshop member explained her confusion about the meaning of White and Black in the United States, where she herself is not considered White, in contrast to Puerto Rico, where she is. Said she:

> Here any trace of Black blood makes you Black no matter how White you look. There only dark people are called Black. It does become confusing: when do you start calling people Black?

Another described her experience:

Being Puerto Rican has been a struggle. We are mixed
racially and so weren't ready for the racism in this country.
We didn't understand it or know what to do. Since our
family has identified more with the Spanish rather than
African background, we felt very confused. Back in Puerto
Rico I never experienced such a difference because I was
darker than my family. We were different shades, but we
were all basically the same. Here it was a real eye-opener.
I've even been taken for my daughter's maid.

A Cape Verdean protested that her family views itself as neither
Black nor White. But while they explain their unfamiliarity with
labeling themselves according to race, some do, however, admit
that a higher value is often placed on fair skin than dark skin
within their former land of residence. Immigrants-of-color thus
are unprepared to cope with the more polarized meaning of
White and non-White in the attitude of Americans. The stress
that this may cause is reflected in the fact that in one psychiatric
clinic every Puerto Rican patient was found to be the darkest
member in his family.

While negative self-image is often the assumed outcome of societal denigration, many of the responses of people-of-color indicate that they do not necessarily internalize a negative meaning
but can instead develop a positive one through personal struggle
and determination:

It means pain and transcendence—the pain of having less
opportunity and less access. It means being determined and
persevering, finding a way to deal with it so you don't deny
what's happening, but you don't get bogged down so you
can't transcend. And transcending does not, will not come
from Whites, only from ourselves.

In fact, the coping patterns devised by people-of-color vary tre-
mendously. For example, in some cases southern Blacks protected their children from the humiliating racist caste system,
avoiding public encounters with Whites such as riding public
transportation or patronizing stores that humiliated Black cus-
tomers. They never gave first names, and refused to teach their
children, as others did, "Do as White folks said," "Go around to
the back door," "Always address Whites as Mr." A constant

theme is the fear of and the dangerousness of Whites. This image existed even for those who had little contact. For example, a social worker reported learning to read by studying headlines about lynchings of Blacks.

The absence of networks and mutual aid systems to buffer the effects of racism and neutralize or lessen its impact has been felt keenly. A psychologist described how losing the support of nurturing teachers and the encouragement provided by her local community school in "the disaster of desegregation" had created upheaval for her. Said she:

> I thought I won't make it. I was expelled from school when a White teacher tried to make me take home economics instead of physics and I told her, "I'm not going to clean any damn houses." Since then I spend a lot of energy proving to myself that I can make it.

In the experiences of many who have coped successfully, there have not only been supports and mutual aid but clear instructions about the reality of racism and how to manage it. It has been a key responsibility of parents to teach the child how to cope. A male social worker who had grown up in the South explained his training:

> I was given very clear directions about how to deal with racism. The old adage "sticks and stones" was the watchword. I was always told what to do. If you're out late at night and a carload of White males stops you—even for directions—don't wait to find out what they want—take off. I was taught to always say, "Yessir, nosir," because if you didn't someone could make an issue—people who talk back, who smart off, are found dead.

Another social worker described her family's instructions:

> My father taught us how to deal with racism. He said don't let them get you upset. If you do, they have won. He taught us to manage our emotions, to be responsible, to work hard, and be strong. He said always keep your goals in mind, always figure out how you feel, then decide how you want to behave.

Coping mechanisms have involved teaching about the "unreasonableness, craziness, and immorality" of Whites along with a rejection of the notion of Black inferiority. One social worker said, "We didn't feel inferior, but we knew Whites felt superior." Another was taught that Whites were jealous because they didn't have a nice suntan as she did. Said she, "That made me feel better" (a power solution using "better than" as a defense against discomfort).

People-of-color are well aware that being able to assess the significance of race in a given situation, to see the possibilities clearly, and to develop the ability to manage the feelings mobilized are critical survival skills. For example, a social worker described her son's experience trying to determine whether he was being unduly suspicious when a White laboratory technician administered a blood test that was unusually difficult and painful. In trying to manage his perception that race was a factor, he thought of all the other possible explanations: It might have been a bad needle; the technician may have been incompetent or just having a bad day. In the end, he didn't know which one it was but thinking of all the possibilities made him less ready to act on impulse. The presence of many possibilities, however, also meant that he would never know the answer and must be able to live with the ambiguity that "while race may often be the issue, you can't prove it." Processing the possible explanations and managing the consequent ambiguity requires energy and effort, which under the pressure of constant demand can lead to exhaustion. Pierce (1970) identifies the "microaggressions," small acts, often subtle and out of the awareness of both people-of-color and Whites, that exploit, degrade, put down, and express aggression against people-of-color. These acts require them to monitor their helplessness and rage constantly—a necessity that takes a toll in terms of stress and health problems. People-of-color are convinced that being prepared for rejection, humiliation, and mistreatment is adaptive in that it prevents them from being "off balance" and prepares them for taking appropriate action to protect themselves, their self-esteem, and their ability to behave in accordance with goals. So what they see as sound vigilance and a correct reality orientation is often seen as hypersensitivity by Whites. And the behavior that Whites typically regard as an indication of appropriate awareness in people-of-color is viewed by the latter as an indication of naivete and vulnerability to danger. Said one Black, "It is not paranoid because it is based on what has happened in the past." On the other hand, an inflexibly guarded stance *can* result in failure to assess a situation correctly and behave accordingly when danger is not present. Failure to exert that necessary energy and effort to sort out the complexity and tolerate the ambiguity can mean that the attempt to protect oneself can result in automatically stereotyping Whites and seeing them all in a societal role of exploiter and abuser. In the words of one psychologist:

> If you expect it and think it's there when it isn't or if you don't expect it and then are confronted with it, either way you're in trouble.

Only a well-functioning ego can cope with these complexities and contradictions. Sound reality testing is required to assess the confusing and distorted messages delivered, to check out myths and sort out what is real from what is in one's own mind, distinguishing between persons who are trustworthy and dependable and those who are dangerous and exploiting. These mental functions require patience and flexibility in thinking to cope with the uncertainty and ambiguity. Energy and strong but flexible defenses are required to cope with the anger, fear, sadness, and sense of entrapment that are constantly being mobilized.

In addition to clarity about the dynamics of racism and strong ego functioning marked by sound reality testing, good judgment, and effective management of feelings, people-of-color need high self-esteem, a clear and positive sense of racial identity, and strong support networks and mutual aid systems (which require healthy relationships). The development of these attributes must become major goals in intervention with people-of-color. Practitioners, whether they are White or people-of-color, who are uncomfortable about racial meaning and identity, who are unwilling to face their feelings, and unready to confront their own collusion in the perpetuation of racism are poor candidates for helping people-of-color to reach these goals.

When Whites and people-of-color attempt to communicate about racial identity and meaning, the differences in their experiences and in their responses to these experiences impose major impediments. Frustration is high, and efforts to share perceptions, to be heard, and understood will often generate "more heat than light." A teacher describes her sense of entrapment, perceiving the issue of race as tyrannical:

It's like blackmail. If you try to be honest about what you think is going on, you'll be accused of racism. And Black people won't be honest either. There is no place for honesty anymore.

Anger is a common response for everyone. The anger some Whites experience may be a general reaction to confronting feelings that have been hidden and protected. People-of-color become angry, too, since the process stirs up discomfort and anger connected with their experiences as victims. Expectations of people-of-color that they must be vigilant and wary of Whites are perceived by Whites as prejudice; they resent being lumped with all Whites as part of the racist system and not seen as individuals who are in pain, in conflict, and confused, or who have tried to fight racism and help people-of-color. Said one psychiatric resident:

I have been angry because this discussion puts me in the category with all other Whites as racist toward people-of-color. I don't belong there. I worked in the civil rights movement and I resent not being seen as an individual with attitudes that are unique to me.

The pain expressed by people-of-color is also hard for Whites to hear:

I can't help people-of-color except as individuals. I can't do anything about their plight. And although their anger is understandable, it turns me off—I just can't take it.

In cross-cultural work this pain can cause withdrawal (Stempler 1975).

Understanding and empathy fade when Whites turn off or get angry about the guilt and sadness they experience. When such behavior is transferred to the treatment encounter, it can clearly be destructive. For example, consider the effect of feelings expressed by a White psychologist and a Black social work student if transferred to the treatment encounter.

I get a feeling of distance from the Blacks in the group. It's like they are experts telling us how hard it is and making us feel bad.

The student answered:

If I say how it is and that makes you feel bad, should I shut
up and say something to make you feel better that's not true?

The Whites in the group expressed a sense of irritation that the
realities being described by the Blacks in the group not only
made them feel guilty but also threatened and inadequate at the
competence Blacks displayed in understanding and coping. In
another situation, a Black social worker responding to the pleas
of Whites to be seen as individuals offered her scheme for differentiating among different kinds of Whites:

I have figured out a classification of Whites that is based on
their responses to me, and I think it helps me to
individualize them and to see what I'm dealing with. First,
there are those that relate to me as me, accepting me as
Black but seeing me as an individual. Second are those
liberal Whites who try hard to see me as an individual but
are secretly racist, being superkind, super-helpful, etc. Third
are the racists who avoid me; fourth is the racist who will
harm me.

Surprisingly, to her and other people-of-color in the group this
attempt at logic was greeted with anger, and she was accused of
sounding superior and arrogant.

Not only may such feelings affect work with clients who are
people-of-color negatively, they also upset and immobilize practitioners when they attempt to communicate with one another
about their work. A White psychiatric resident asked the Black
administrator of a neighborhood health center to explain his
comment that events at his agency led him to think that Whites
should not treat people-of-color. He responded:

Many of the problems at my center are a result of Whites
who think they know best how to work with people-of-color,
and they don't. They don't want input regarding issues about
child abuse, refuse to understand that forcing an 18-year-old
to return to school where he's in a class with 14-year-olds
with teachers who don't care is destructive. We have a
mechanism for input to professional staff about the needs of
clients. It happens that this mechanism consists of White
professionals, people-of-color (Black, Latino) nonprofessionals
and representatives of the client group. The professionals,

and especially the physicians, will not listen to the opinion of others about what clients need. They think their training has prepared them and there's no need to translate it into ethnic issues. For example, a patient needs a dietary change. There's no way you can make them stop eating rice and beans—you need to examine what in the diet is nutritious and supplement rather than demand they stop. The patient doesn't come back because the professionals don't respect the culture.

His response was greeted with defensiveness:

I feel I try hard and do a good job. If the patient doesn't return it may not only be due to lack of respect. The patient could be resistant to working with Whites, period.

I can see how in the beginning of the work such a question might be asked, but if a clinician is a good person and caring, he can do the work. If there's a problem, it may be the patient.

What does he think we take the Hippocratic Oath for? Physicians give equal treatment to everyone. We work hard to learn to help people; we are ready to help everyone.

While Whites resented the perception that they are all necessarily insensitive or incompetent in dealing with people-of-color and while they experienced this statement as offensive and inaccurate, there was, underneath their defensiveness, the sense that the magnitude of the differences between them and people-of-color seemed to nullify their role as experts. One clinician commented with obvious sadness:

I am thinking that if I can't use my experience to understand another's pain, how can I help?

The inference that their performance was marked by incompetence was so threatening to their professional image that these Whites could not listen to the perceptions of another that differed with theirs. At that moment they could not understand that their determination to give equal treatment could be at the root of the problems being cited since what these clients needed was not treatment equal to that given to Whites but treatment based on their own unique needs. Nor could these White practitioners understand that, despite how hard they worked, their efforts might not be effective and, in fact, were responses based on their own needs rather than those of their clients.

Defining Race and Racism

Because of the confusion and misunderstanding it creates among people, race is a concept that must be understood intellectually as well as emotionally. Defining race and racism can bring contextual clarity to people's confused perceptions, painful feelings, and problem behaviors. Race is a biological term classifying people who have the same physical characteristics. Its meaning is ambiguous although in people's minds it is understood as a measure of difference referring to culture. Within a given racial group there are great cultural differences depending on factors such as region, history, and the realities people have to adapt to. Race in this country has come to take on a meaning that refers to differences between people based on color.

Racism is often equated with prejudice, which is the act of prejudging and expecting certain behavior from specific individuals. But the distinction between prejudice and racism is an important one. Racism raises to the level of social structure the tendency to use superiority as a solution to discomfort about difference. Belief in superiority of Whites and the inferiority of people-of-color based on racial difference is legitimized by societal arrangements that exclude the latter from resources and power and then blame them for their failures, which are due to lack of access. Although these arrangements may exclude some persons who are White, people-of-color are affected in far greater proportions. A single policy or institution[2] cannot be identified as the cause. It is rather the ways in which the total social system in which policies and institutions interlock and reinforce one another in their capacity to deprive and cripple many people-of-color while offering preparation, support, and opportunity to Whites (Knowles and Prewitt 1969). Thus, while both Whites and people-of-color may harbor prejudice or bias, the bias of people-of-color can usually not be used to reinforce advantage since they usually lack such power.

Resistance is high against comprehending the institutional aspect of racism and the fact that this not only ensures that Whites benefit but also exonerates them from responsibility while at the same time blaming people-of-color (Knowles and Prewitt 1969). It is against realization of this social arrangement that Whites are usually the most defended. Acceptance of this fact thus can constitute a peculiarly painful moment in the struggle to understand. A psychiatric resident protested:

> If that's true then there is a real inequality in this group. You (people-of-color) can point a finger and say "racist" and we can't, and that's not fair!

In another situation, a White psychologist asserted:

> It's like I, as a White, have a bias, but you as a person-of-color don't.

This awareness carries particular pain for Whites who have seen themselves as different from Whites whom they view as racists. Often such persons have been involved in antiracism activities, which they see as exonerating them from participation in its effects. One individual struggling valiantly to understand pondered:

> I didn't realize until we defined racism what I've been struggling with. I feel powerless because by that definition no matter what I say or do I can be labeled a racist if the Blacks here don't agree. I feel I've spent all my life trying to fight racism; I've been close to a lot of Blacks.

Acknowledging that he felt he was not getting credit for his efforts, he commented, looking very sad:

> It's so hard.

This young psychiatrist-in-training, whose earlier description of his activities in civil rights was offered as proof that he was "not like those other Whites" and who on another occasion was angered when a Black questioned whether behavior he believed to be helpful and protective was in fact patronizing and controlling, seemed devastated at the implication that he, along with other Whites, could be a beneficiary of racism. The sense of injury that Whites feel stems not only from recognition of themselves as trapped in the systemic process of racism, which benefits them and exploits people-of-color, but from the realization that while for many people-of-color this reality has been obvious, for them it has been hertofore obscure. In addition, the pain of this realization is intense since it calls into question many of the assumptions upon which they have operated. It is both frightening and unsettling, perhaps all the more if it occurs in the presence of people-of-color.

The possible consequences of racism for Whites include:

- It creates a state of "psychological stress" in that Whites' beliefs (in justice, etc.) are in profound contradiction to what they practice.
- It forces people to behave destructively, to act out, deny reality, use projection, transfer blame, dissociate, and justify.
- It creates confusion about the meaning of being White since White people do not see themselves as White.
- It creates a delusion of superiority in that White people are unable to experience themselves and their culture *as it is*, often not being aware of the arrogance it embodies and the disdain for all that is non-White.
- It threatens the sense of positive self-worth.
- It prevents Whites from experiencing and accepting humanity because it forces them to reject empathy for and vulnerability with people of color in favor of a stance that justifies exploitation, degradation, and dehumanization. Thus it limits their intellectual and emotional growth and development of self.
- It creates a dehumanizing stance.

(Katz 1978; Kovel 1970; Knowles and Prewitt 1969; Ordway 1973; C. Pinderhughes 1973; Pierce 1973; Spurlock 1973.)

Racism thus is a costly societal process that can leave Whites seriously handicapped for the task of effective helping. Few Whites are able to say honestly that being White is an identity that brings them a sense of pride. Although some may feel that being White means being powerful, lucky, comfortable, and secure, it also can mean confusion, entrapment, and threatened self-esteem, hardly attributes that would promote helpfulness to people-of-color, who may be dealing with such consequences themselves. A practitioner whose sense of self is distorted and who needs another to project on cannot help that other to feel good about himself, to develop sound judgment, strong reality testing, goal-oriented behavior, the will to struggle against racism, and the skill to work toward change in his oppressed condition. Changing the meaning of White to a more positive one thus becomes an important step in preparation for effectiveness. It involves taking back one's projections and owning up to them, facing the feelings that they defend against, so that one does not need such projections for self-esteem.

Defining race and racism also brings clarity to a number of issues concerning people-of-color. Some of the less obvious mechanisms that people-of-color use to cope with racism and the realities they face as a consequence of their societal status assignment become clear. Some are not as effective as intended. They may even be destructive and contribute to the perpetuation of racism. Protecting Whites and engaging in behaviors that make Whites more comfortable is one such strategy. A tall dark-skinned Black male confessed that, mindful of the fears his appearance stirs up in Whites, he always approaches them smiling. Behaviors like these anger some people-of-color who see them as an affirmation of the stereotype of the grinning, shuffling Black. Such behaviors can subtly encourage exploitation by Whites. In practice, protection can also be unconsciously promoted by White professionals who indirectly communicate anxiety and fear, or deny that differences exist between themselves and their clients. Such behaviors encourage clients to ignore race as an issue to be confronted and to ignore or invalidate their own experiences and realities. People-of-color protect Whites when they do not confront racist behaviors or when they blame themselves for situations that are clearly consequences of racism. This behavior is common in situations where people-of-color are subordinate to Whites in authority. For example, a Latina psychology intern, ordinarily very competent and consistently performing at a high level, accepted a low performance evaluation by her White supervisor. Whereas other colleagues-of-color had recognized that the evaluation was not accurate in terms of her performance and was based on bias in her supervisor, she could not see this and instead blamed herself. One might question whether her acceptance of this evaluation was based on some lack of assertiveness, even fear or discomfort, about challenging the assessment of her performance by a person whose authority derived from being both supervisor and White. While this may indeed have been true, her tendency to protect him was manifest in her refusal to consider the possibility that he might be in error.

Taking Responsibility for Collusion

Often unaware that such behavior colludes in the perpetuation of their painful circumstances, some people-of-color view it as protective of themselves. Because they see no possibility of change in their oppressive circumstances, they prefer to focus their energy where they believe change is possible—in themselves. In so believing, they are able to avoid seeing themselves as powerless and without a choice. Protecting Whites by blaming oneself and embracing stereotypes does not reinforce the positive, clear sense of racial identity that is needed to form a healthy self-concept. Neither does rejecting or denying one's racial identity.

A social worker described her own mother's collusion in the system; she blamed her child instead of racist policies for the family's humiliation:

> Some parents try to protect their children and don't teach them about how dangerous the White world can be and how to deal with it. My mother was like that. When I was nine years old we were travelling south on the train. And when we were not allowed to eat in the dining car and had to bring our food with us, my mother said it was because my brother, then four years old, would act up and embarrass us. So when my brother grew up, he didn't know how to deal with being Black.[3]

Denying one's racial identity in order to cope with the reality of racism and to ward off the pain connected with it can be costly. For it leaves an individual or family isolated and disconnected from other people of their own racial group. Without the supports that can help to neutralize the impact of racism, they are left even more vulnerable to its vagaries. This teacher's experiences and her family's orientation as simply "human," which was based on denial, set her up to be a misfit:

> I am a Black American. My father grew up poor and became well educated. My mother was a White upper middle-class artist. We lived in Haiti and Mexico. I remember we had a Japanese house servant, and there were often people of different backgrounds who were my parents' friends. When I was twelve, my mother died and we were sent to live with

my father's relatives. The prejudice in this country was unbelievable to us. I had not learned to think in terms of Black or White—my identity was human. I couldn't deal with White people hating me because I was Black. But then I didn't fit in with Black people either.

Denigrating those within one's racial group who have been unable to achieve and prosper while idealizing those who have is another approach that can cause problems for individuals and the group. For it can reinforce splitting one's connections within the group and seeing some of its members as "all good" and others as "all bad." Parents have frequently sought to instill motivation in their children by using such an "all good" versus "all bad" or "better than" approach. A social worker who attended Dunbar High School in Washington, D.C., a school historically and nationally known for high achievement, reported "being challenged to perform with the admonition, 'You are the cream of the crop.'" A teacher considered how her parents had used such a strategy with her and her siblings.

They told us "Don't be like those no-good Blacks. Be like Ralph Bunche."

She saw her painful struggle with Black peer group pressures at a White university as a natural consequence of such a strategy. She had felt terrorized by Blacks whom she saw as not committed to excellence but who demanded from her a total commitment to Blackness.

The outlook, however, that most demonstrates collusion on the part of people-of-color and that is approached with the greatest reluctance is the one based on skin color, the idealization of light skin and the devaluing of dark coloring. The power of skin color prejudice has been a clearly recognized trap among Blacks but one that nonetheless has been difficult and painful to acknowledge: It has been "hard to admit to the wider world that some Blacks felt that way about one another even if the socialization in America was such that it was hard not to feel that way" (Gilliam 1982). While this collusive behavior has been more identified with Blacks, other people-of-color readily engage in it too:

Color is a big issue among Filipinos too. When babies are born the first thing they want to know is how light they are. Everybody prays they won't be dark.

In the Caribbean color distinctions are openly acknowledged, and higher valuation is placed on light skin. "The lighter you are, the closer you are to the European end of the continuum and the higher your status in Caribbean society" (Brice 1983, p. 126). West Indian Americans, thus, are very likely to reflect such societal attitudes. These are also attitudes that Whites hold about persons within their own group as these social workers' comments illustrate:

> In my family the blondes are more admired than the dark ones, so I felt less attractive.

> I was ashamed of my kinky hair as a child; it was too close to Blacks' hair. I idolized my blonde friend and I used to dream that I would return in the next life with long, blonde, straight hair.

When people-of-color attempt to examine this issue, they find it is easier to focus on experiences that explain how they were taught such attitudes or how they have been victims of such attitudes than to take responsibility for embracing them:

> Being Black meant you had to be strong, especially if you are dark-skinned. I was not surprised when some White teachers were prejudiced toward me but it was real hard when a Black teacher acted that way too.

A psychologist described the taboo in her family against discussing skin color. In this family her mother's nearly White appearance and her father's dark complexion had created problems in identification for her who resembled neither. Her problems in identification were magnified by the fact that her mother's fair complexion was more highly valued than her own much darker coloring. In addition, it had been forbidden to talk about skin color:

> We had to pretend that these differences did not exist and everyone was the same. It was crazy.

When its existence as an issue is unacknowledged and the matter of responsibility avoided, there is little opportunity for resolution. In a meeting of over 200 professionals gathered to consider issues concerning Black mental health,[4] stories abounded of the way in which the issue of skin color has caused confusion, anger, and pain, constituting one of the most destructive consequences of racism for people-of-color. Dark-skinned persons told of rejection or ostracism by members of the family who were lighter skinned. Lighter-skinned persons told of putdowns, distrust of and rejection by darker-skinned relations. Many complained of others' assumptions that they embraced these biases when, in fact, they did not. The potential for this issue to create misunderstanding and conflict within families and in other relationships is great. But confronting the self, acknowledging not only that one is a victim but also a perpetrator by holding such attitudes and taking responsibility for this collusion in the perpetuation of racism is difficult. However, people can confront themselves and take such responsibility:

> I learned about the pain dark-skinned people used to suffer from my aunt, who was herself very dark-skinned. She disapproved of my dating a dark-skinned boy, whom my mother, who was fair-skinned, liked very much. She told me, "Ain't no need to keep a-darkening up the family." I was shocked and I asked her, "How can you say that—look at you." I'll never forget what she said, "Yes, look at me." Her sense of herself as ugly was so painful that I went into the next room and cried. But I stopped dating dark-skinned men and the tape is still there. I even tried to pass it on to my children. I have carried this burden with me for a long time.

A Puerto Rican social worker, who earlier had acknowledged that in Puerto Rico "dark means inferior," admitted that he harbors such attitudes and cited the expression "Marry lighter, whiter to improve the race." A Jamaican teacher recalled her experiences of being light-skinned in a mostly dark-skinned family. Within the family and at school she was favored because of her color, receiving help and approval that others did not get. She added:

> At home where I lived with my grandmother, aunt, and cousin, I longed to be with my own mother as my cousin was. (My mother had left for the States.) I consoled myself and dealt with my envy of her by thinking about the fact that I was much lighter than she. And I really used that to make myself feel better.

Just as Whites must take responsibility for the projections they use, people-of-color must take responsibility for their racist internalizations.

Understanding racism and taking responsibility for one's collusion *can* improve people's ability to be comfortable with themselves and to deal with people of all races. One can become able to acknowledge the use of stereotypes and projections onto others as a means of enhancing oneself and one's group and of acquiring a sense of comfort. One can acknowledge how responses and the consequences of responses based on stereotyping can block appropriate functioning with people who are racially different. When one does face the pain one has tried to avoid one no longer has the need to run away. An occupational therapist confronted the way in which stereotypes of Blacks had been used in her family to enhance Jewish ethnic pride:

> My family decided to move from the area when Blacks came. They were constantly complaining of how smelly and dirty Blacks are. I can see now that they used all the Jewish lingo to express this distaste. It seemed as though Jewish pride was increased with these epithets about Blacks. My cousin and I used to fight with the family when they talked that way. But then I'd get on the subway and feel revulsion when a Black person was close.

A social worker could see how his inability to resolve his guilt about racism had exacerbated his problems with a Black student he was supervising. He had been unable to exercise his authority as supervisor and responsibility for enforcing standards of competence:

> When I was a social work student, I had a management internship in a factory where I struggled with some of these issues. There was this Black guy that everyone agreed was not pulling his weight. I kept wanting to give the guy a break because I was so guilty about the injustices Blacks have to cope with, but then I had to do my job which was to make him shape up or fire him. I kept going back and forth and was very inconsistent with him. I was scared of this guy's rage, which I felt was justified, and my behavior was making him angrier. I kept vacillating back and forth between making up to Blacks for what's happened in the past and

then treating everyone equally. I stay in conflict because I do feel as though I inherited the debt of racism and I have to help pay this debt.

A teacher reflected on her confusion about the difference between her stance and that of Black teachers and about her paralysis in the face of disrespect from a Black student that had been destructive for both of them:

For several years I taught English and reading in a junior high school that was 99 percent minority—60 percent Black and 35 percent Chicano. I remember the confusion around expectations for these children. The school administration emphasized discipline and holding action rather than active process for them. I was part of a large group of teachers who considered self-esteem and self-expression as first and foremost. Now I wonder if a part of it stemmed from a discomfort with determining what could be expected from kids when they were taught with care, high standards, and an expectation of success rather than failure. I can look back now and better understand why the Black teachers so often had higher standards and requirements for their students than many of the White teachers. I also understand why I was immobilized one day when one youngster called me "honkie-tonk White bitch." I was confused whether to respond to this child as an individual testing limits or a "cultural carrier."

People can learn to assess their everyday experiences and moment-to-moment interactions and cope with the contradiction and sense of entrapment. A physical therapist described her increasing ability to observe herself and question what heretofore had been automatic reactions:

I watched myself last week and found out that when I'm upset and anxious I'm more likely to have prejudiced thoughts. My car's been in the shop all week and in this below zero weather I've been hassling the "T." On the subway platform one day as I stood there freezing and exhausted, there was a group of Black children who made me angry because of their loud, raucous behavior. I caught myself and wondered how I'd feel if they had been White.

People can confront fear and guilt and question their irrational basis, as did the teacher who asked, "Why do the same Black male students whom I have adored and found charming and delightful as little ones, suddenly become frightening to me when they get around sixth grade?" They can learn that while the fears they have may be reality-based, these fears may also be responses to internal needs, i.e., aggressive or sexual drives (C. Pinderhughes 1973) and that these two aspects of the situation must be separated. Fear based on defense against aggressive (and/or sexual) strivings that are projected onto those who are racially different must be acknowledged. The sound reality testing and judgment that is mandatory for practitioners who wish to be effective require that clinicians practice such self-confrontation.

"Therapists [must] have attained sufficient resolution and/or control of their own fears and aggressions that they can mitigate their own racism" (Bradshaw 1978, p. 1523). Working on such resolution, a female psychiatric resident could thus make the following statement:

Why am I afraid? I think it's because of the sexual and aggressive feelings I've been taught are bad and have to be controlled. If I see these bad things in Blacks, I can control them in myself, and I don't have to see them.

Guilt, too, must be confronted, so that it can be divested of its immobilizing effect:

I feel a lot of guilt because people of my race and primarily of my class (and ethnic group, i.e., WASP) have prevented others from having the privileges I've had. I feel awkward and angry that race makes a difference in my favor, and it happens without my doing anything about it.

Guilt can create a sense of powerlessness, demoralization, and poor self-esteem, driving people to atone by seeking punishment—even from those over whom they have had advantage. This is particularly true when guilt over one's collusion in perpetuating racism is compounded by internal guilt (i.e., guilt stemming from anger that is related to early developmental deprivation). These two levels of responses, internal guilt and guilt related to the reality of benefit from racism, can feed one another unless they are sorted out and dealt with separately. For example, a White teacher in great distress protested to a Black psychologist who was exploring his perception of Whites in response to her request:

> You are wrong about me. I don't get off on being White. I feel only pain—about what WASPs have done all over the world (tears). I have tried to change this pain but nothing I do makes me feel better.

Unable to tolerate his perception of Whites as benefiting from racism, which had always pained her deeply, she tearfully proclaimed her powerlessness to do anything about it. In this stance, she provoked him to protect her with this statement:

> Don't let me overwhelm you with my perspective. I'm telling you how I see it. You have to hold on to your perspective— that's how you see it. If I have to guard against encouraging Blacks to act out their anger, you have to guard against encouraging them to trigger your guilt.

When they have not resolved such feelings of guilt and shame, teachers and practitioners can do untold damage by pushing their students and clients to protect them.

The most destructive consequence of guilt and one that is most likely to cause practitioners and teachers to behave inappropriately and defensively is the threat it poses to self-esteem and to everyone's need to feel positive about his identity. White people have as great a need to feel that their racial identity is positive as do people-of-color. The task for them is to find out what they need to do to achieve this.

Openness to themselves and their reactions allows people to acknowledge the impact of race upon many aspects of their lives. For example, race may become a battleground in the struggle for individuation and consolidation of identity:

> When I was in medical school, I had a relationship with a Black female student there. My mother refused to accept it, but my father did not seem to mind. I was determined that my mother was not going to tell me what to do. The situation was complicated by the fact that my mother was dying of cancer. Although I realized the relationship was good for neither of us because of our personal issues, not

race, I couldn't break it off. My girlfriend used to challenge me that I couldn't handle a Black female and, of course, I wasn't ducking a challenge. I was trying to work out handling a woman and at the same time challenging the unjust morality in this country that I had guilt about. But breaking up was so hard to do because I felt so guilty. I just could not get past the thought that I wanted out because she was Black. But I was also angry at myself because I stayed in the relationship. Finally, we did break it off.

This young trainee's review of the pain, guilt, ambivalence, and entrapment that he had experienced in this racial entanglement helped free him from the anger and resentment he had been storing up for many years. Whenever people-of-color lumped him with all Whites, did not individualize him and see him as different, he reacted intensely and cried "reverse racism." When he transferred this stance to his patients and expected them to trust him automatically because he had been a civil rights worker, he was ineffective in dealing with their resistance.

The struggle of a southern female psychologist who had been a civil rights activist to understand her motivations in cross-racial encounters also illustrates how racism can become a battleground for developmental struggles:

My father intensely believed in the inferiority of Blacks and the importance of keeping them in their place. He could even justify it on religious and moral grounds. I spent all my growing-up years trying to make sense of it. I would sit in church and think of the hypocrisy and cringe at the treatment of our washerwoman and other Blacks who worked for us. But I admired, loved, and respected my father.

With intense feeling, she told of battles with her family over their racist beliefs and of her battles through the college newspaper to change racism on the campus of the southern college she attended. Finally she was able to say that although she had worked for change, she later fought against affirmative action because she felt "it went too far." With this statement about her ambivalence over the progress of minorities, her belligerence disappeared and she acknowledged that her battle for equality had been waged more for herself than for Blacks:

I think my stand against racism wasn't based as much on my beliefs in equality as on my need to rebel against my family in my struggle to separate. And what could be a better way to rebel in the South than to be a liberal?

Understanding the institutional nature of racism, while painful, appears to remove blinders for many individuals and often marks the beginning of real empathy. People who had formerly felt confused and rejected are able to put themselves in the position of people-of-color and imagine what it may be like. They can then remember situations in which they were a minority, how that felt, and how the situation may be different for them:

I was once in a situation where I was the only White and it was both painful and scary. But I was able to leave. If I were Black, I would feel furious because I'd be trapped and couldn't leave.

They now can clearly understand what Whites have perceived as the hypersensitivity of people-of-color in their interactions with them:

For the first time I understand why Blacks talk about race all the time. I see that they can't escape it. I want them to stop bringing it up because it's like a barrier, but I see, now, that they have to. It makes me uncomfortable to have it so up front.

I used to feel why are they always harping on it. It pushed me away. I couldn't identify. Now that I see that, I'm not so irritated anymore.

They also become readier to see the behavior of people-of-color in terms of its adaptive aspects and the costs of these adaptations instead of as a confirmation of stereotypes and cause of blame. Behavior that previously appeared enigmatic now seems reasonable. For example, a social worker could suddenly understand that behavior he had judged negatively had in actuality been adaptive in the situation of a poor Black man.

The first Black I ever knew worked at a low position in the warehouse where my father worked. I was struck by the fact that he was always smiling. It seemed somehow silly to me. But now I wonder if he thought he had to do that to be less threatening.

Whites who formerly saw only deficit and pathology can understand the pain and struggle which people-of-color face, the strength and resiliency that can be summoned, and the energy needed to defend against the distortions directed at them.

> It's a no-win situation. If people decide it's better not to fight back, they'll be seen as weak and become vulnerable to further attack. If they decided it's better to fight, they risk retaliation, punishment, and continued escalation of the conflict. Besides if they elect not to fight back, they have to deal with their own anger and its effect on their psychology.

Whites can understand, too, the guardedness and "norm of distrust," as survival mechanisms:

> I had found it distancing and destructive to foster attitudes that people-of-color should be suspicious and distrustful. Now I understand where they are at and where they come from. This is a stance I will be unable to neglect in the future.

And there can be acceptance of the fact that upon first encounter with Whites people-of-color may see race first:

> I now understand what had been so confusing when I was around my Black friends. I have learned how to relate to a Black honestly. I grew a lot in the struggle to understand racism. I see that I have no control over being seen as a racist since I am White and a part of the system. I see how complex it is.

The greater comfort in the presence of racial difference and increased ability to be vulnerable and to confront one's reactions means that one can examine one's responses and perceptions with others. Questions can be asked, responses can be heard. Dialogue becomes possible as in this example where a psychiatric resident exposed his fear:

> I grew up in Detroit, which is a dangerous place. My fears increased after I was robbed by Blacks. I can't get over it (appears close to tears). I must admit that I am scared even walking over to the other hospital buildings.

Turning to the only Black male among his colleagues he acknowledged the problems in their interaction. In expressing this vulnerability he seemed to be asking for help to master his fear.

> I am uncomfortable around you. It's just different than I feel toward the others. Sometimes I feel close to you. At other times you laugh at things I don't understand.

And received this response:

> I can't believe I'm seen that way. What—little me—scary? I don't want to respond defensively. It's hard not to, but I assume your discomfort is that you see me, too, as scary. I can't help you with that. I don't believe your feelings can change until you are ready to get to know Blacks and see them as equals.

When it is safe to be vulnerable, to admit ignorance, and there is expectation that the information needed will be offered helpfully, people can learn from one another. Examples abound of how these new insights can be applied to cross-cultural work: A White social worker described her stereotype of a Black as dependent and unmotivated. The client had talked at length about her desire to get ahead, to get vocational training in something so she could have a life outside of her children. Reflecting on her client's words, "I want to be something, somebody," the worker acknowledged that she found herself surprised at her client's ambition and realized "my surprise was not at her ambitions—it was the fact that she was Black and had them."

A psychiatric resident reflected on his mistake with a female patient:

> I see that I missed the boat with a Black patient I just terminated with. She communicated her anger about the loss by saying, "I'll go out and get me a White boyfriend." I handled her remark in terms of her sexual fantasies about me as a man but not as a White man. Only later did I realize that race had been an issue too.

Now he could question for himself whether his patient had been suggesting that the loss was especially keen because his identity as White had special meaning to her. If so, what had it meant, and had the sexual issue been more difficult for him to handle because the patient was Black? A White male social worker identified his use of projection in his response to a Black female client:

I have been very annoyed at my coworkers for the racist remarks they make about an attractive Black woman who is my client. They said the usual things about Black women as promiscuous and sex-crazed. One day, I accompanied her to a school meeting about her child. I couldn't believe my reactions, me, the unprejudiced, unbiased liberal. I was embarrassed, afraid someone would see me with her. But I also felt "I'm hot stuff. See what I got." I could see what we have been talking about here—I was doing it too—projecting instinctual desires so I could avoid feeling guilty about having them.

A teacher recognized the destructiveness of her tendency to protect Black children:

I see now that my wish to protect the Black child in my class is related to my guilt about White privilege. And I see that it helps no one since the White children complain about what he gets away with and his parents are angry too. They say they don't want their child treated as special.

Expectations that children will function exceptionally well can be as destructive as a conviction of incompetence. A teacher acknowledged that the tendency to see minority children and families as having amazing strength was destructive to the child not only because it created unrealistic expectations but also because it had a selfish motive: it alleviated her own guilt about the privilege associated with being White.

People-of-color will also develop new insights that can affect their work. A Black psychology trainee considered the greater difficulty he had working with Blacks than with White clients. Admitting that he had problems managing anger, both his own and that of his clients, he also acknowledged his tendency to push his Black clients, to be harder and more demanding of them, to be irritated when they were slow in accepting his (expert) help in improving their coping capacities. A Korean psychiatric trainee, recognizing her resentment at being categorized as a person-of-color, could see how this attitude had been responsible for her failure to explore her Black patient's denial and negative sense of racial identity, which were key factors in his problems. A Puerto Rican social worker whose Spanish identification signified her rejection of the racial aspect of her cultural heritage considered this as a possible source of her failure to involve a Black adolescent in treatment.

However, while insight and acknowledgement of responsibility can appear to be liberating, they also involve hazards. The development of self-awareness can appear to add rather than reduce problems. Fears may surface which formerly had been successfully hidden and denied. A White social worker described becoming frightened of going into the Black community when formerly she had not been.

> Last week was a hard week. I'm now feeling afraid to go on home visits in Roxbury and I never used to. I always took a cab with the same driver who was a woman. Yesterday, they sent a new cab driver and I was suspicious of who he was. When he didn't take the same route, I was panic-stricken until I saw the house. Then, another evening, I had to go to a wake for the daughter of my supervisor who lives there. I was terrified to go there at night, but I went. So much fear and so much pain over being scared.

Another social worker observed:

> Take yesterday for instance. I took a White patient to visit a community residence that is located in the Black community. When we came out, there were several young teenagers hanging out nearby and I immediately felt scared. I shouldn't feel this way and I never did before.

But to be cautious in situations where danger may exist does not automatically indicate bias as indicated by this response from a Black colleague:

> I would definitely have noticed those kids, not because they were Black but because they were kids. I notice White kids too. I think it's also a turf thing that gets mixed up with race. When I was a kid our gang taunted any outsider especially Whites. Only a southern accent, which meant you didn't understand the boundaries, could save you.

A sense of fatigue and exhaustion can surface as a result of the struggle to understand the many complexities, to tune in on the sadness, frustration, fear, and anger previously hidden, unarticulated and/or unexpressed; the old denial and ignorance that maintained tranquility and stability have now broken down. Recognition of the tenacity of such feelings can also bring a sense of hopelessness about eliminating them and about the vigilance acquired to monitor them:

> We see how awful "racism" is but everybody keeps on being prejudiced.

> What am I going to do about this prejudice I can't stop feeling?

> It is so much more complicated now. When will it get more manageable?

In one group of psychiatric trainees, a female resident reported this reaction with some embarrassment:

> I was watching my reaction yesterday when I saw a Black woman driving a Mercedes; I realized my assumption was that she got it illegally.

Her colleagues responded to her remark first with levity as they acknowledged their stereotyped images of Blacks who drive Cadillacs and of Latinos and Blacks who drive cars with shoes hanging up and fur pillows inside. But one individual forced the group to confront itself:

> I think we're laughing about this because we feel they shouldn't have these symbols of affluence. We say they should aspire to them, but when they get them, we ridicule them. We don't want them to have them. They're changing our image of the stereotype. It's OK to drive Cadillacs, but not Mercedes. It's too close to what we want.

A mood of depression descended upon the group as they acknowledged their persistence in the use of stereotypes and their reluctance to change their attitudes and to deal with racism. But the sadness appeared related not only to awareness of their entrapment in racism but also to a sense of mourning for the loss of innocence and perceived nonculpability that insight has forced them to give up (Ganter and Yeakel 1980; Katz 1978; Sparks and Phillips 1983). The innocent exploitation of stereotypes, which have protected against unacceptable aspects of self and which have granted an automatic sense of superiority and competence over people-of-color, are not relinquished without pain.

Effective intervention requires that practitioners be able to negotiate this process of mourning, so that they can withstand the stress involved in developing empathic closeness with people-of-color. For closeness to people-of-color means initiation into the systemic entrapment and reveals the necessity to manage their own very real feelings of pain, confusion, fear and helplessness. Energy and stamina are required to withstand this stress. Patience is needed to sort out the complexities. Honesty is necessary to distinguish myth and fantasy from reality. Courage must be summoned to tolerate the intense feelings that have been defended against by the fantasies and myths, and flexibility must be found to tolerate ambiguity and contradiction.

These are capacities that will enable practitioners to persist in their efforts to work effectively with people-of-color and to work toward proving their trustworthiness because they are not paralyzed by perceptions of themselves as not to be trusted, exploitative, and frightening. Like their clients-of-color who need strong ego functioning to cope with the consequences of their entrapment in societal process, practitioners who work with them must have such ego functioning too.

6

Understanding Power

POWER IS AN OFTEN UNSPOKEN but central dynamic in cross-cultural encounters. We have observed its presence in the associations of dominance, superiority, and denigration, with ethnic identity, and group status; in the common perception of difference from others as "better than" or "less than"; and in the dynamics of race (racism), which is itself a power system. In the cross-cultural clinical encounter where power is embodied in both cultural dynamics and clinical role, its existence has been virtually ignored. But the power and lack of power, inherent in the roles of clinician and client and in their cultural group status, can affect clinical process and outcome. Practitioners need to understand how these two dimensions of power can affect their clients, themselves, and their work together. And the self-knowledge that they bring to the cross-cultural clinical interface should include not only awareness of their own cultural identity and meaning but understanding of their power needs and responses as well.

Power Defined

Defining power makes clear its complexities and the various levels upon which it exists: individual, interactive, as well as societal. Power may be defined as the capacity to produce desired effects on others; it can be perceived in terms of mastery over self as well as over nature and other people (Heller 1985, p. 30;

Wrong 1980, p. 2). It involves the capacity to influence, for one's own benefit, the forces that affect one's life. Powerlessness thus is the inability to exert such influence. Power is gratifying: Siu (1978, p. 40) has suggested that "power is the universal solvent of human relations." Basch (1975, p. 513) has stated that "the feeling of controlling one's destiny to some reasonable extent is the essential psychological component of all aspects of life." This means that a sense of power is critical to one's mental health. *Everyone* needs it. Furthermore, powerlessness is painful and people defend against feeling powerless by behavior that brings them a sense of power (McClelland 1975).

People experience the presence or absence of power in many areas of life. For power is a systemic phenomenon, a key factor in functioning, from the individual level where "submission to power is . . . the earliest and most formative experience in human life" (Wrong 1980, p. 3) to the levels of family, group, and social role adaptation (C. Pinderhughes 1983). Internal power is manifest in the individual's sense of mastery or competence. The power relationships between people determine whether their interactions are characterized by dominance-subordination or equality. These styles of interaction are, in turn, affected by the status and roles assigned within the group or the larger society.

Power is also a factor in the clinical relationship. It is inherent in the roles of clinician and client respectively, where the helper is an expert who diagnoses, teaches, and treats, while the client seeks assistance with his need. The power that is inherent in the role of practitioners is such that they are vulnerable to using it to meet their own personal needs. Power may be used by clinicians for aggrandizement, to "satisfy their own needs for power and esteem not met elsewhere" (Heller 1985, p. 161). When so exploited, "power which intends to bolster the image of the therapist is perhaps the most infamous of therapy abuses."

In the cross-cultural helping relationship the compounding of the power differential that exists between helper and client due to their respective cultural identities and group connections can mean that helpers may be doubly vulnerable to invoking the power inherent in this role for their own needs. Helpers may not only encourage clients to aggrandize them in relation to their helping role or personal attributes but also in relation to the presence or absence of aggrandizement granted them by the social system. They may use their helping role to reinforce their own sense of competence by keeping subordinates in a one-down position as patients, incompetents, and persons needing help (Bowen 1978). In so doing, the clinician can reinforce any sense of powerlessness felt by clients due to their need for help and/or their sense of subordination stemming from their cultural role.

A client's sense of powerlessness may be reinforced in the cross-cultural encounter more readily and more frequently than one would suspect. Empowerment requires the use of strategies that enable clients to experience themselves as competent, valuable, and worthwhile both as individuals and as members of their cultural group. They no longer feel trapped in the subordinate cultural group status that prevents them from meeting their goals. The process of empowering requires helpers to use their power appropriately to facilitate this shift. In addition to eschewing the power that derives from using stereotypes, this involves employing strategies that require the ability to be vulnerable, to take a one-down position *when appropriate*, and to let go of the power embodied in the helper role as expert or as a person who is aggrandized as an individual or a member of a cultural group. When practitioners persist in working with cross-cultural clients but fail to engage in such behaviors, they are using the helping encounter largely to benefit themselves.

When they fail to help clients change negative cultural identity; do not help them change self-perceptions of being powerless and victims; do not help them learn to behave in ways that do *not collude* in their own victimization, in the victimization of their group, or in the aggrandizement of helpers and their cultural groups, they reinforce powerlessness in their clients. These behaviors signify that helpers are meeting their own needs for a sense of power by exploiting their clients' failure to have acquired it.

Vigilance is essential to guard against the helper's normal vulnerability to reinforce the culturally different client's sense of powerlessness and subordinance. Vigilance ensures that helpers learn ways of thinking and behaving that enable them to effectively use empowerment strategies with their clients. Understanding one's own experiences, feelings, attitudes, and behaviors related to having or lacking power is an important step in the attainment of such vigilance. It facilitates ability to acknowledge one's own need for a sense of power, to see the ways in which one has experienced power or lack of power and how one has responded, and prepares one to control the seductiveness of the helping role and manage the tendencies to exploit it for one's own purposes. However, many people are embarrassed and even feel guilty when considering their experiences related to having power and what power has meant to them. Power remains a disturbing issue; powerlessness, while more readily approached, is nonetheless also avoided because experiences related to it involve pain and discomfort.

The Multilevel Aspect of Power

In addition to overcoming this reluctance to examine power and powerlessness in cultural roles and in the helping relationship, it is important to place that examination in its broader context—the dynamics of power at all levels of human interaction. Power is a stance that undergirds certain of our societal values: status, perfection, possession, achievement, competition, independence, and so forth. These values, though contrasting sharply with other American values such as justice, equality, and the right of all citizens to pursue happiness, have formed the backdrop for the ethic of the melting pot, which itself embodies the notion of power. In its emphasis on the values and life-styles of persons from a specific class and racial group, i.e., the White middle class, the melting pot has devalued and ignored people-of-color and the poor. The very designation "American" tends to denote White middle class, and hence has also signified power. Here again we note the overlapping nature of ethnicity, race, and power.

The multiple sources and levels on which power or lack of power operate in people's lives are evident. One social worker describes her experience:

Ethnicity and power were big issues for my Irish family. Struggle, surviving, and winning were *always* talked about in my family. My grandparents were immigrants; my father was a self-made man—always adversarial, struggling to get power over his environment. He and his cousins were active in union organizing and he put himself through law school at night. There was much talk in the family about justice and fairness, which was interesting because he was such a forceful personality, and he did not live this in close relationships. I never had a chance to say this to him. My mother who came from a middle class family was powerless to deal with my father in some ways but not others: she used illness and depression to get what she wanted. I, as the eldest child, often felt pulled in different directions by them. I tried hard to negotiate, balance, and distance to avoid being trapped between them. I felt powerless before my father's authoritarianism and only through therapy was I able to move away, to feel enough power myself to select from different options that were available to me, to become integrated and balanced. It's very interesting that in my own treatment it was only when we began to focus on my Irish identity that these issues came together.

In these personal comments, power can be seen as a factor in (1) the adaptation of Irish values, (2) class issues, (3) family interaction, (4) male/female values, (5) the meaning of illness and depression, (6) entrapment in the family drama, and (7) Irish identity (indirectly as a factor), which was only understood after it became a focus in treatment.

Power or powerlessness in one area of people's functioning can obscure its significance in other areas. Another social worker saw how powerlessness with regard to culture and family relationships accounted for her failure to acknowledge that being White would be a privileged status:

As the youngest daughter in a family that had been counting on having a son, I became very sensitive to the sexism in the culture of our western, homesteading family. The White male structure angered me, and I felt powerless in a family and a culture which valued males over female. I did not experience any sense of privilege around being White and was very naive and ignorant about ethnic and racial issues. As a result of my feminism, I tended to identify with other groups in our culture who are granted little power and status such as Indians. Being from a lower middle-class background added to such identification.

Another conceded that the experience of powerlessness as a female and a Jew obscured recognition of the meaning of White as dominant:

I have been aware of powerlessness as Jew from an early age, that I was different and I was hated, that the world hated me and my people. I also felt keenly even when I was very young that privilege and experience were limited because I was female. I felt that it was a cruel act of fate that men had all the fun. As I grew older, I became aware that this powerlessness as a female prevented me from knowing my real self and experiencing all of life. I felt trapped and forced to be something I was not. In high school, I watched a racist system track Whites and Blacks into separate courses. In this one situation, I had power for I was White but I felt none of that because of my Jewishness.

Klein (1980) discusses the consequences of double victimization in her comments about the effectiveness of her treatment model, ethnotherapy, for such persons. She states that the process does not work as well for Jewish women as for men because women's self-rejection is determined by their identification with minority status that stems from sexual as well as ethnic dynamics, thereby causing a double-victim syndrome to operate. It may be inferred, therefore, that this added complexity requires Jewish women to process sex-role issues in addition to ethnic ones in order to achieve the same result that Jewish men do when they process ethnic issues only. Thus, empowerment for persons who occupy powerless roles in more than one area of their lives may require different or expanded strategies than are required for those who do not. These "double victims" may have to work twice as hard to develop coping strategies. On the other hand, it is possible that if one powerless role is linked with other powerless roles, alteration of any one might facilitate alterations in others.

Another important source of self-understanding is the experience of having or lacking power within one's own family. A social worker recalled the sense of powerlessness he connected with his relationship with his father and cited the consequences for his behavior in other situations where he might become powerless:

I avoid situations that risk loss of power. I have painful memories of powerlessness that are especially vivid with my father, and I know this makes me be wary of authority figures. I now believe that to get warm, emotional approval from my father is unrealistic given his cultural orientation [German].

Another reviewed her strong reaction to her perception of her father as passive and powerless. Her recognition of the importance of cultural values in her perception of him was significant in changing their relationship:

> I understand my Irish father better now that I am sorting out what Irishness means. My father identified with old country Irish values of subjugation and victimization. Because of my own conflict between my Irish orientation of subjugation and my American orientation of mastery, I could not tolerate and for a long time did not accept what I saw as his passivity. It has been a relief to depersonalize our conflicts and place them in the context of a battle between values, and not solely between a father and daughter.

A psychologist identified the sense of powerlessness he experienced as a consequence of his parents' conflictual relationship with one another.

> The powerlessness and sense of inferiority I know came from the battles my parents used to have. I thought it was my role to settle their problems, and when I couldn't I felt awful, like I was no good.

This occupational therapist identified her enmeshment in her parents' relationship as a source of her feeling of powerlessness:

> As the only child and grandchild, I received too much attention and often felt powerless about the way I was triangled in with my parents. I felt responsible for their happiness and greatly burdened.

The position of oldest child is frequently a situation that provides a sense of power within the family:

> Being the oldest and having to take care of my younger sibs meant a lot of power for me. I was in charge and telling them what to do—that was heady at times. In some ways, I regret having had that much power because the others are closer to each other than any of them is with me.

> I think my experience within my family helped me a lot to use power appropriately. As the youngest of five, I was pretty powerless in the early days, always being told to shut up and not being listened to. But when my parents took

foster children and I became the eldest, I learned leadership and initiative skills. I learned to lead and to be a part of a group where someone else leads.

The role of family favorite also conveys a sense of power:

I was my father's favorite and he spoiled me. When he died, I fought to become my mother's favorite. I remember a lot of rivalry and conflict, but I was determined to be the special one.

However, the position of family favorite can also become a source of conflict, causing poor relationships among siblings.

A psychologist reviewed how "onliness" with reference to sex identity was both a source of power and nonpower, contributing to her sense of ambivalence about having power:

I was the only girl, third child in a family of five—and that situation presented me with many experiences of feeling powerful and powerless. I was valued as the *only* girl. But I often felt "not as good as" and spent a lot of time proving I was. I felt I had to justify my existence. So the power I felt as an only girl—being special and all that—was a really confusing thing. I didn't want it when I felt I had it and wouldn't acknowledge I had it, but if it seemed I wasn't being acknowledged and special I sought it and felt bad when I didn't have it.

Power or lack of power is often experienced around sex role definition. A common theme for women concerns the pain that models of subordination have created for them. Many emphasize the misery and deep resentment often directed at the mother as role model, as well as at the father:

My significant experience with powerlessness was not about my own but my mother's and how I experienced the relationship between her and my father. I saw her submissiveness to my father, the endless putdowns by him and her perpetual depression as painful. I saw being in the low position as a woman's place and I silently seethed at both her and my father. I secretly vowed never to be in such a powerless position as a female.

One nurse remembered being angry at her mother for not being a better model for dealing with the subordination women had to contend with and for not teaching her to protect herself. She described how, when she became angry, she used the same putdown against her mother that she had heard her father use and then commented:

> And though I loved my father, I knew it was wrong. Only now am I realizing that I was angry because of my own sense of powerlessness, not just about being a woman but about their relationship.

Another described the bitterness she had picked up from her mother about the sacrifices her mother had felt forced to make:

> Women don't have the same choices men do. My mother wanted to be a lawyer. Instead she had to work to educate two brothers: one a lawyer and one a pharmacist. Mother was always angry and when I was a kid, it felt like she was angry at me. It wasn't until recently that I understood differently. I had an awful conflict because of her behavior. I thought I had to stay at home with the kids and some days I hated it, yet I felt it was the most important work there is. When I went to work, I loved it and I felt competent. But my husband is still expecting me to cook and clean. When he does the dishes, he makes a big thing out of it. It's a big deal like he's saying, "See me, see, I'm helping." And most of the time he waits for me to do things he can do for himself.

Yet, it is also important to look at the individual's collusion in the perpetuation of the traditional submissive role from which she is struggling to free herself. This speaker blamed her husband instead of taking responsibility by changing her behavior.

The experiences of men validate the automatic nature of the power that is built into their role. A social worker reflected on this fact:

> We men get power given to us even when we aren't looking for it. I've watched that happen in groups and relationships. I admit it feels good sometimes, and if it's given, I'll take it.

Their experiences, too, show that having power can take a toll. For example, in the words of a male teacher:

> Men pay a price for the power they have because they're afraid of intimacy—of closeness to other men and of real sharing and equality with other men and women.

Uses, Benefits, and Costs of Power

Recognizing the many situations in which power or lack of power may be experienced helps practitioners to clarify the needs, expectations, and tendencies they may bring to the cross-cultural helping encounter. Ambivalence (or fear) about having a position of power can jeopardize the capacity to be comfortable and effective in the role of helper. Early experiences where persons felt dominated by parents, teachers, and other authority figures can result in ambivalence about power especially if they have felt powerless in these relationships (Palmer 1983, p. 121). Failure to confront these feelings and come to terms with them can lead to abdication or inappropriate use of their endowed power in the clinical process.

Important for practitioners to understand are the uses, benefits, and costs of having or lacking power and how these conditions apply to them. They very easily identify the sense of power they get when they develop competence and a sense of mastery in relation to something. They can easily acknowledge the pleasure and self-esteem that such power brings, for it helps them to feel comfortable, competent, confident, happy, and proud. This gratifying sense of power also derives from the ability to be assertive, to have control, and to take responsibility. However, pleasure and gratification as consequences of dominant power, of "power-over" positions, of power from social status or role are less easily acknowledged. Taking responsibility for others is one way of deriving power and thus of securing gratification. When people belong to groups that have high status, they often believe they should assume responsibility for those with less power:

> I identify myself as a White American, which means power, competency, being responsible, and having a sense of social responsibility. We were taught that you can't make piles of money without giving something back.

> I suppose you would put me on the power side of things. What was interesting was how we were taught to deal with it as upper class. It was, you might say, condescending— the notion of the White man's burden—similar to the idea of the Boston Brahmin. It was ingrained in us that we had economic and social power and this meant we had tremendous responsibility for those who did not have those

things. I remember one day a servant's child and I were playing and he took my toy. I screamed but my mother said, "If he wants it, you must let him have it; you must always give it to him because you can get another and he can't. You must never refuse him." And the only time I ever remember being punished by my father was the time I was rude to a servant. My father said, "You must never be rude to someone who is not in a position to be rude back—never." But I always had the idea that they (servants) had an important function and were in some respects better people than we.

But this sense of responsibility may be paternalistic and subject to immediate withdrawal at any sign of a threat to that power:

We were taught we had things on trust and that we should use it for the benefit of all. It was a kind of altruism, but I am certain that had we felt threatened, we would have been the first to react. Looking back, I can see that we could afford to be condescending and magnanimous because we were not threatened—our position was sufficiently secure. It reminded me of the liberals in Boston who rushed down to Selma but, by God, when it started to come in their own backyard, they became as racist as all the others even though it was at an unconscious level.

People who have dominant powerful roles may deny that they have power; they try to avoid becoming aware of it. We have seen this already in reference to ethnic and racial identity and status. A social worker describes his reluctance to acknowledge his double power position as White and male:

I see how much I don't want to admit the advantages I have because I'm a man or how I benefit because I'm White.

A nurse describes her tendency to hide from herself any image that she has power:

I was my father's favorite, but I had the feeling of myself as powerless. I think that was partly because the women in my family had *no* power. So it's a surprise to me that people in this group see me as powerful. I think it's true—I do hide my sense of power from myself: it's a secret.

Practitioners must understand, not deny, the situations in which power exists and has existed for them. They also need to understand how power is used and how they use it. As we have already seen in the examination of difference and race, people sometimes use power to make themselves feel better. This psychologist explained his awareness that he invokes the elite meaning of WASP as a compensation whenever he feels his self-esteem is threatened:

> I can usually control very well the sense of entitlement that goes with being a WASP. However, I notice it gets triggered and I act out (get arrogant) whenever I feel threatened or under stress. I've never seen this so clearly until now.

A social worker reflects on her father's need to use his perceived higher status in order to compensate for his defective self-esteem:

> My father was a Northern Irish Protestant and we were a minority in our town. We were told that we were better than the Irish Catholics who lived around us. Now I wonder if my father didn't use that superiority thing to bolster himself since he was not faring as well as some of his brothers.

Again we see, as in the exploration of ethnicity, difference and race, the use of the stance "better than" to manage anxiety. A psychiatric trainee acknowledged how he uses the stance of "better than" to cope with any feelings of worthlessness:

> I can feel like shit, powerless, and not important, but I can still feel powerful if I know there's somebody I feel better than. Society helps me to believe this about myself and Blacks. It's like I need my prejudice to make me feel better and that makes me feel awful.

The costs of dominant power, especially as related to ethnic, racial, and gender identity are also important to understand. Privilege and special position may be experienced as burdensome, as described by this Black social worker:

> For me, the power that went with oldest child meant being special, and I liked that, but it was also a burden. I also got pushed into being the token Black, taking leadership that I didn't want. It was a demand which I grew to accept but always felt uncomfortable about.

Some of the reactions associated with having power are troublesome and can cause problems. One such response is guilt.

A social worker examined how guilt in relation to her privileged background had complicated her struggle for a sense of competence and meaning:

> I think of myself as being Anglo-Saxon, as having been privileged in a lot of ways. In terms of family ethnic background, race, and class, my world epitomized power. I didn't question any of it until college when I began to feel that life had been too easy—things had been handed to me and I hadn't had to struggle very much. I think I had an awesome sense of the importance of chance in all I had—that I didn't do anything to deserve it and that I had to prove myself. I always had to take on the biggest challenges, and I ended up in the Peace Corps in Africa.

When guilt is a part of the baggage that people bring to the cross-cultural interface, it must be carefully managed. In clinical work, guilt can push clinicians to overfunction and to take responsibility in ways that trap the client into functioning with less competence and autonomy. And there are other costs. A sense of oneself as powerful can create vulnerability to distortion and ignorance of self and of one's reality (Lichtenberg, Reinert, and Levine 1983; Ordway 1973). A teacher observed that this tendency exists for Whites because their position of power, which is reinforced by racism, allows them to "teach White children unreality, superiority, and entitlement. I learned to value ignorance and avoid the truth." A psychiatric trainee discusses this tendency toward lack of self-understanding, particularly on the part of men:

> Having power as a White male has been a double-edged sword. It has meant being responsible, having to take care of someone, but it has also meant more freedom. And the power men have is achieved at a great price. I may be seen as a decision-maker and powerful yet we depend heavily on women to get what we need. But many of us don't even know what we need.

Another says:

> It's the values of the male culture that isolate men. Being strong means being independent, not depending on others. But then to deal with loneliness, we get others to depend on us.

Needing another to see oneself as strong and to take a dependent role means that the powerful one is as dependent as the subordinate one (Lichtenberg, Reinert, and Levine 1983, p. 5). Dominance can impede self-knowledge if one is pushed into a situation where the sole factor in self-definition is as a caretaker for others. Dominance may also be associated with limited ability to be vulnerable to others, which interferes with the capacity for intimacy. The entrapment of people in dominant-subordinate relationships can signify a low level of psychological functioning and self-differentiation (Bowen 1978). Such persons will be highly vulnerable to fused relationships because their sense of themselves depends on the existence of a subordinate other. Without someone who functions in a subordinate position, they experience intense anxiety and instability.

Privilege can distance one from others. A Black teacher considered her family's privileged status as one source of their failure to attain a cohesive sense of identity and to feel connected to other Blacks:

> My background was very unusual. My grandparents were college graduates in the 1890s, which was very unusual for Black people. I think you could say our family were intellectual snobs. We really considered ourselves upper class. . . . Despite the fact that we mostly socialized with Blacks and we had many books about Blacks, we never really came to grips with being Black and what that meant.

> Feeling you have more power than someone else can distance you and make you feel alone. I feel this way about being a White male and an administrator.

The sense of entitlement which power can create ill prepares one to cope with adversity or situations in which one lacks power. An occupational therapist described the consequences of her position within her family as the entitled one:

> That sense of entitlement was very destructive. I always look for it, get angry if I don't have it: I think "how dare they?" and feel doubly powerless when I can't have it. It was unrealistic and didn't prepare me for the real world.

Paradoxically then, power can create greater vulnerability to powerlessness. When one is used to having power, any infringement of it may be perceived as severe. A teacher described how her family's situation—"Mayflower lineage but no big bucks"—had set her up "to feel especially deprived among my wealthy relatives and the private school types who had homes in the Vineyard." A psychiatric resident described his experience as a cherished first child in an Anglo-Saxon family with a lineage of professional achievement. Comparing himself to his Black and female colleagues who recalled experiences where they were blocked in some of their aspirations, he could remember no situation in which "I couldn't be what I wanted to be." This fact, he believed, was partly responsible for his inability to cope with the panic he felt when he realized that he might not be accepted into graduate school because he was gay: "I went to pieces."

The sense of responsibility that is embodied in power roles can become distorted, prompting people to develop a compulsive need for perfection and to have superhuman expectations of themselves. When this occurs, any slight mistake or imperfection can appear major and provoke a sense of failure. Having developed few coping strategies to deal with these experiences of powerlessness, the consequences can be serious. This social worker explains how perfectionism interfered with her ability to work sympathetically and productively with clients:

> Being special as the professor's child and being under great
> pressure to achieve academically has contributed to my need
> for perfection. I have a tendency to have unrealistic
> expectations with clients and to drive them as I have driven
> myself.

Those in positions of power can also develop a tendency to deny their own personal pain and ignore their experiences of powerlessness. This stance can be costly in terms of its potential for distorting reality and for denying and devaluing one's own feelings. This is a commonly accepted consequence associated with the role of men (Miller 1982). Denying one's own pain is also a consequence of power in relation to cultural group status assignment. A psychologist explained how being Anglo-Saxon can prompt him to seal off psychological pain and downplay physical pain:

> One of the things I see coming out of my Anglo-Saxon
> background is never wanting to admit that we suffer, too, at

times. We get to thinking "all those other folks have suffered so much more" and this gets translated into never wanting to admit to the pain one has, feeling one has no right to say it hurts.

Whites have considered how the denial of pain may have pushed them to misperceive the cost of racism to them. Practitioners have examined how in the clinical encounter the power of their helping role may assist them in denying their own pain and enable them to concentrate instead on that of others. In placing an emphasis on the powerlessness of their patients and clients they make themselves more comfortable. Such a stance can push them to avoid a focus on the strengths, competence, and successes of the people they work with, and to give attention instead to their weaknesses and pathology.

Even those in positions of power who do not deny their own pain and experiences of powerlessness, must contend with others disqualifying their pain and failing to empathize. As one social worker protests:

> It bothers me. It sounds like we're saying that people who are White, middle class, or male always have power. That's not true. They can feel and be extremely powerless. I know because I'm WASP.

Any of the behaviors that are responses to having dominant power may become part of the baggage a practitioner brings to the helping situation and undermine efforts to empower clients appropriately.

Responses to Powerlessness

How people handle experiences with powerlessness also has relevance for cross-cultural interaction and work. Many of the feelings and behaviors have already been identified in the examination of ethnicity, difference, and race. Since powerlessness is painful, people tend to respond in ways that will neutralize their pain *with strategies that enable them to turn that powerlessness into a sense of power.* One response that is commonly cited as a strategy for turning powerlessness into power is that of personal mastery and achievement.

Anyone can see I lack power from the color of my skin. I therefore have defined my source of power as becoming well-educated, getting a professional identity where I know I'm successful.

Sometimes I think learning to deal with powerlessness related to ethnic identity takes a lot of maturity. That was true for being Native American anyway. When my children went to school, I watched carefully what went on, especially in their history classes. I sent notes to the teachers about their background along with artifacts we had that I let them know I'd be glad to share. I figured that forewarned was forearmed. What that did was get me invited to speak at school where the kids were clearly identified as Indian in a positive way. So it was not only educational, it was protection. Sometimes the teachers would ask me for suggestions before beginning to use the content.

When people feel powerless, they may attempt to make themselves feel better by developing perceptions that they are better than others. We have also seen in the examination of difference that the defense of superiority may be connected with group and individual psychological processes related to perceiving the self as different. A group may use belief in its own superiority over other groups to create unity and a sense of pride among its members. Individuals may perceive themselves as "better than" others as a defense against the anxiety about difference that originated in early developmental trauma. The cyclical nature of power is demonstrated when individuals who feel powerless and oppressed cope with it by assuming a power stance over others. "There is compelling empirical support for the notion that powerlessness results in the attempt to secure the power of others" (Heller 1985, p. 157). One social worker's early experience is an illustration:

I just remembered the first time I ever felt powerful. I could always be reduced to nothingness by names my older sister called me—she always knew what to call me to make me upset. One day a younger cousin came to visit and I talked him into eating soap. I used what I had learned from my sister. It was a wonderful feeling finding someone I could convince to do something. And it was a White male too [laughter].

An Irish social worker who had grown up in a small Pennsylvania town where she attended Catholic schools described being taught that "we Irish were better than the Italian and Polish kids." Said she, "We even felt superior to our Jewish landlord." A French Canadian who grew up in the Northeast reported that in her community where French Canadians were the majority, her ethnic group "escaped the prejudice so often directed at us, but we looked down on the Italians and the Poles." A Polish social work student recalled that she grew up feeling badly about being poor and that "the only people poorer than us were Blacks and I was glad I was not Black too." Reflecting on the meaning of this behavior, she said, "I guess it made me feel a little better that they were in worse shape. . . . But," she added, "the people whom the community excluded the most were Jews." Ridicule and put-downs, strategies that use "power-over" to defend against powerlessness bring a sense of power to the victim by making a victim of the other.

Put-downs related to lower status may also be directed toward family members. In the following example class status constituted the source of experiencing lesser value:

My family was very low on the economic ladder, but I went to school with kids who were middle-class Anglo-Saxon. I felt keenly that sense of being "not as good as." And my parents felt this too—my mother saw us that way—she mostly blamed my father who was a jerk. And both of them put down Blacks making it clear that we were certainly better than them.

Inspiring fear is another way of turning powerlessness into power. A Black psychologist made this point to a White colleague:

My powerlessness as a Black male in the American system often leaves me with one sure way to get a sense of power— to scare you.

Manipulation, another strategy for turning powerlessness into power, is usually recognized more easily by practitioners in patients and clients than in themselves. A psychiatric trainee noted:

My anorexic patient feels powerless about her body and many other things. She gets tremendous power and feels quite powerful by refusing to eat. In so doing, she reduces the whole staff to powerlessness.

However, one social worker made a personal application:

I needed to see that I wanted to be powerless; it was easier to be powerless. Then you can manipulate other systems sometimes. You have power in a negative sense, but it's power. I need to see it's not healthy, that I need to be powerful in a positive way.

The reader will recall that this strategy was examined as an adaptive mechanism used by people-of-color in the examination of race. Its usefulness was questioned in the light of the cost it exacted. Although manipulation empowers the actor while making the object of the manipulation feel powerless, its use as a defense against powerlessness is not usually acknowledged. A psychiatric trainee shared his hypothesis about the connection between manipulation and powerlessness:.

People who feel powerless often engage in self-destructive behavior not just to get attention but to get others to take responsibility for them, set limits for them, nurture them. I always try to remember that this behavior is an indication of how powerless an individual really feels. The more powerless I feel as a result of such manipulation, the more powerless I think the patient feels. Suicide is the ultimate example.

Poor people frequently use manipulation. A social worker describes the lessons in manipulation she learned from her client:

My client educated me on survival mechanisms in poor neighborhoods. "You get a buck any way you can," she told me. I had found myself worrying about the games she played with people because I could see the trouble she could get into. I was also getting overwhelmed by her manipulation with me: she would tell me horrendous stories of seemingly unsolvable problems, and I stayed overwhelmed.

Managing clients' efforts to manipulate helpers must always be based on appropriate goals and strategies for empowerment.

Conflict about their power role and problems with being vulnerable can prompt practitioners to behave ineffectively either by becoming defensive and moving to a "power-over" stance in order to ease their own discomfort, or failing to set limits when they are needed.

When discomfort is extreme and anger related to powerlessness is perceived as dangerous, people may respond with withdrawal and evasiveness. Women, for example, frequently display evasive behavior in response to their sense of entrapment and anger at their powerless role (Miller 1982). A Black social worker explains its usefulness as a strategy for dealing with racial powerlessness:

> Not fighting back may be your only option when you're
> feeling powerless and don't want to alienate those in power.
> I learned to be diplomatic, indirect, and evasive so I won't
> be seen as a hostile Black . . . But I have to have somewhere
> to vent my anger. It's dangerous for a Black to be alone or
> unsupported in this position.

Paradoxically, accepting the reality of one's powerless position can under certain circumstances bring a sense of power. In such a situation, when the individual has taken the initiative and made the choice to assume a stance of powerlessness, this can become a way of turning the powerlessness that is being experienced into power. Even accommodation and dependency may be seen as strategies for turning powerlessness into power, or of getting close to the source of power (McClelland 1975).

A Black psychologist reflects on how this has applied to him:

> Sometimes I can find comfort in accepting powerlessness by
> not fighting it and therefore not losing. Accepting can be
> active for it is taking initiative.

There are other ways that powerlessness can be turned into power; these strategies also illustrate the systemic nature of power:

- Turning things around so that the negative is seen as positive, for example "bad" means "good"
- Exaggerating the projections of the power group so that one takes the initiative in assuming behavior labeled by the power group as negative, for example being a super stud,

super macho, super dumb, super dependent (E. Pinderhughes 1983).

When people perceive their own condition as marked by a high
degree of powerlessness, they may develop exquisite intolerance
to power behavior in others. They find intolerable any behavior
that conveys a sense of specialness on the part of others, or any
behavior that is characterized by put-downs. Thus a social
worker described her poor Black client's extreme intolerance:

> It was a shock to hear my client say "Easter's comin' and
> when the kids get all dressed up, they get uppity and always
> have to get a beating."

Often such persons scrupulously avoid behavior on their own
part that could be viewed by others as power-determined. They
stress instead friendliness, humility, being "regular" and not
"uppity." Or they may do the opposite and become controlling,
dominating, flaunting symbols of power and status and using
"power-over" behavior as a strategy for achieving a sense of comfort. This defense of identifying with the aggressor protects
against anxiety aroused when one perceives the powerful person, on whom one is dependent, as an attacker. The anxiety is
managed through incorporating characteristics of the person
seen as powerful. Though it brings a sense of power, this strategy
also exacts a high price. Consequences can include self-hatred,
problems with relationships, and problems in the development
of coping skills (E. Pinderhughes 1983).

As noted in the examination of race, many of the responses to
powerlessness which people use to get a sense of power are usually identified as pathological behaviors. In addition to manipulation these include using passive-aggression, being negativistic,
and behaving in ways that reverse one's original behavioral intent.
A psychiatric trainee reflects on his patient's use of oppositional
behavior:

> Not talking can be a way of getting power. My patient
> enraged me yesterday. He read the newspaper forward and
> backward and never said a word. I was furious.

Some of these behaviors can take on a cultural meaning when
they are used extensively by large numbers of persons, becoming
practices that are shared by the group. For example, suspicious-

ness and distrust, oppositional, passive–aggressive, and manipulative behavior are responses to powerlessness used by Afro-Americans, the Irish, and also by the poor, women, and other oppressed groups (McGoldrick 1984; E. Pinderhughes 1983).

The responses which people identify as strategies for dealing with powerlessness illustrate a number of principles about power dynamics. Many of these behaviors, which usually have been viewed as pathological, can now be seen as defensive, adaptive maneuvers for turning powerlessness into power. For example, as noted earlier, people will use behaviors such as opposition, passive aggression, manipulation, accommodation, a dependency, and identification with the aggressor because they feel powerless and believe they have no other choice. While these behaviors are adaptive, they can also be exceedingly costly. When one is reacting, one cannot initiate or be proactive; so when one uses these behaviors, one may gain a sense of power on the one hand but may be handicapped on the other. In reacting, one does not have an opportunity to be self-assertive, to decide on one's goals, to assume leadership, or to know oneself, since one is focused on reacting to another rather than on one's own well-conceived goals, beliefs, and values (E. Pinderhughes 1983).

Intervention based on a full understanding of the dynamics of power (summarized in Table 1) will focus on strengths, reinforcing coping mechanisms that enable constructive self-assertion, goal achievement, exercise of choice, and taking the initiative, all behaviors that emphasize proactive rather than reactive stances. (See Chapter 8.)

TABLE 1 Frequently Described Feelings and Behaviors Related to Differences in Power

More Powerful	Less Powerful
Feelings	
More comfort, more gratification	Less comfort, less gratification
Lucky, safe, and secure	Insecure, anxious, frustrated, vulnerable
More pleasure, less pain	Less pleasure, more pain
Less tendency to depression	Strong tendency to depression

TABLE 1 (Cont.)

More Powerful	Less Powerful
Feelings	
Superior, masterful, entitled	Inferior, incompetent, deprived
Hopeful	Exhausted, trapped, hopeless, helpless, with few choices
High esteem	Low self-esteem
Anger at noncompliance in the less powerful	Anger at inconsiderate control by the powerful
Anger at feelings of powerlessness	
Fear of loss of power by the powerful	Fear of abandonment
Fear of the anger of less powerful	Loneliness
	Fear of the anger of the powerful
Fear of retaliation by the less powerful	Fear of own anger at the powerful
Guilt over injustices that may result from power	
Fear of losing identity as a powerful person	
Sense of burden of responsibility	
Fear of abusing power	
Behavior	
Use opportunity to impact the external system or self	Lack opportunity to impact the external system for self
Use ability to create opportunity	Lack ability to create opportunity
Use ability to take responsibility, exert leadership	Lack ability to take responsibility, exert leadership
Project on the less powerful unacceptable attributes, such as being lazy, dirty, evil, sexual, and irresponsible as justification for maintaining power and control	Project onto the power group acceptable attributes, such as being smart, competent, and attractive
Blame the less powerful for assuming the projections	
Devalue one's own pain and suffering	

(Cont.)

TABLE 1 (*Cont.*)

More Powerful	Less Powerful
Behavior	
Distrustful, guarded, and rigid due to vigilance needed to maintain power and control	Distrustful, guarded, and sensitive to discrimination, often seeming paranoid to the power group
Deny the powerful position and its favorable effects on benefactors and unfavorable effects on victims	Deny the less powerful position and its effects
Display paranoia resulting in delusions of superiority, grandiosity, unrealistic sense of entitlement, arrogant behavior, and tendency to distort reality; consequent unreal assessment of the self and the less powerful	Display paranoia resulting in the acceptance of a dependent position, passivity, and the assumption of stereotypes, such as a physical or stud image, dumbness, delinquency, and addiction; consequent unreal assessment of oneself and the more powerful
Isolate, avoid, and distance from the less powerful; take comfort in sameness; unable to tolerate differences in people; lack enriching cross-cultural experiences	Isolating, avoiding and distancing from the more powerful
Display entitled, controlling, dominating behavior	Utilize autonomous, oppositional, manipulative, and passive–aggressive behavior as a defense against powerlessness
Display rigidity in behavior; have to keep the power	Display rigidity in behavior; to control sense of powerlessness
Have need for a victim, someone to scapegoat and control	Strike out, becoming verbally or physically aggressive to ward off powerlessness
Justify aggression and exercise of power or violence; dehumanizing behavior, and pleasure at human suffering	Identify with the aggressor, leading to self-hatred, self-devaluation, aggressiveness, violence, dehumanizing behavior, and pleasure at human suffering
Identify with the less powerful, leading to a wish to repudiate power	Use deceptions, secrets, half-truths, lies

TABLE 1 (*Cont.*)

More Powerful	Less Powerful
Behavior	
Project aggression outside the group onto the less powerful to enhance group cohesiveness and unity. (This behavior is reinforced by a sense of entitlement.)	Project aggression outside the group onto the more powerful to enhance group cohesiveness and unity. (This behavior is reinforced by a sense of justice.)
	Direct aggression within the ethnic group, resulting in conflictual relationships destructive to group cohesiveness
Experience conflict and confusion resulting from (1) sense of injustice versus need to hold on to the power and (2) wish to share the power versus the fear of rejection by one's own ethnic group	

Power in the Cross-Cultural Encounter: A Dilemma

Examining one's own behavior in the cross-cultural encounter and monitoring the way one manages the feelings, perceptions, and attitudes mobilized as a result of one's clinical and cultural group status role are key to one's ability to practice effectively. Whether the clinician happens to be male, White middle (or upper) class, and/or a member of an ethnic group that enjoys dominant status; whether the clinician is female, a person-of-color, or belongs to an ethnic group of subordinate status, he or she can benefit from the effort to address the following questions about him- or herself and the power dynamics that occur in the clinical process.

1. If the societal projection process provides a sense of competence, stability, and lack of confusion for benefactors--beneficiaries while reinforcing anxiety and greater confusion for victims, and I, as the helper, am a member of the benefactor—beneficiary (or victim group), what does this mean for me in my work with clients who are also victims of this

process? What does this mean if I, as the clinician, am also a member of a victim group?

2. Do I receive gratification in this possibly double power role?
3. Is this gratification a liability in the helping process?
4. In my relationship with clients (victims), do I allow the goals pursued and the strategies used to be influenced by my own need for power and gratification embodied in my professional role?

Many of the dilemmas that characterize the boundary nature of the helping professions (Myers 1982) becomes crystallized in the task of developing this understanding. Addressing these questions also further clarifies the paradoxes that exist in the way power operates. Protests have been offered that it is unrealistic to address a client's powerlessness at all the levels on which it may exist—especially within the context of the clinical encounter. A social worker says:

We can't change a client's powerlessness on all these levels working with them one time a week. Many other things are influential in their lives besides what's going on with us.

If we focus on clients' powerlessness based on social structure, we know that's where the work should be done, but then we'd have to quit the profession or work only with larger systems because that's the focus that's needed.

The contradiction that becomes apparent in the definition of the goal for cross-cultural work mirrors the eternal debate on whether the focus should be on external environmental systems or on internal psychological ones. People also have strong opinions about whether the change needed is in the client's realities or in their view of themselves as capable of dealing with these realities. Not sharing knowledge with clients about how they can cope with external systems and with victimizing structures can be a way of perpetuating their dependency and trapped position, of reinforcing the need for someone to intervene. In the examination of race, the reader will recall, emphasis was placed on intervention that would enable people-of-color to bring about change in the systemic processes that maintain their oppression (Jenkins 1985; Lefley 1986; Sue 1980). But some contend that a focus on change carries vulnerability for helper entrapment, especially for those who are people-of-color. For example, there is a vulnerability due to the commonality of painful circumstance for Black trainees to opt for supportive and activist approaches "because of unconscious fears of and/or identification with intrapsychic aspects of their patients' problems" (Evans 1985, p. 458). In addition, advocacy and a focus on external systems carry vulnerability for client entrapment in that clients may fail to learn how to do for themselves if the practitioner becomes overresponsible, cannot let go, or fails to support clients' efforts to do it themselves. Thus, whichever strategy—a focus on the external or the focus on the internal—practitioners use, they must beware of the opportunities to reinforce their power roles.

The conviction that clients may need help to change their external realities as well as themselves introduces yet another paradox connected with power, namely, that it can be healthy and appropriate to accept unchangeable realities. The critical issue here is who defines that unchangeability. When the person who is the more powerful is also the definer, as is often the situation in the helping encounter, his perspective of what is changeable can be influenced by the very factors that created his dominant position in the first place. The helper's definition, therefore, may not favor changes in the client's subordinate role status. For example, the teacher who prepares the minority child for lowly expectations so he won't be disappointed, the clinician whose treatment goal focuses on acceptance rather than changing the reality, are defining that reality as unchangeable. On the other hand, to hold up expectations that can never be met because of client or system limitations that are realistically unlikely to change can also reinforce a sense of failure and powerlessness. But what remains the critical issue is that unchangeability should never be defined to meet the needs of clinicians (to protect themselves or bolster their self-esteem, sense of competence, and power).

There have also been debates about the level of power that is really embodied in the clinician's role. Some will dismiss the issue of practitioner vulnerability to power abuse with the response that "clients are consumers and they come because we have something to offer" and thus they have the power to come or not come, to work or not work for change. However, the usefulness of power in this respect appears questionable. If the power to stay away is exercised because the client has experienced put-downs or feels that the powerlessness he came to change is instead reinforced (i.e., he is not understood, is misdiagnosed), then his basic sense of powerlessness has not changed. Under such circumstances the client's leaving may be seen as his choice. "But then," as a social worker commented, "I *am* colluding in his staying powerless because I didn't help him change that. And worst of all, I'm blaming him for it." One social worker commented:

> Practitioners do have the greater power because we define reality for the people we work with. That's my definition of power. Men have done this for women—parents for children. In any hierarchical situation, systems of any kind, the people in power define reality. We do diagnoses on people and 51A investigations, and while there are good reasons why we do it that way, unless there is full and equal participation by the people we're working with, we *do* have the upper hand and we have to face that.

Another social worker trainee articulated her guideline for preventing such abuse of power:

> I think the solution is to always help them make choices, to work on moving to a higher level, to be able to make better decisions, no matter where they are.

Empowering behaviors and nonexploitative stances are more likely to characterize their work when practitioners can explore their reactions and look honestly at themselves and the vulnerabilities they must learn to control. In this exploration they can question whether power was a motivation for their choice of profession. This psychologist considered the gratification he derived in both helper and cultural roles:

> As a male who is also White middle class, I have been aware of my power and the powerlessness of others and I have felt sorry for them. I sometimes wonder if I became a clinician to maintain power and control.

They can also consider how a personal need for power can constitute a threat to successful work. For example, clinicians may want the client to make the clinician look good:

> And I wanted to say to him, "Hey, man, you're ruining my reputation as a good clinician if you don't show up."

Or clinicians can refuse to acknowledge their ineffectiveness:

This is where there are traps for me and some seduction. Intellectually, I can accept I'm not the best match for everybody and I may not be the person to do it, but I can get caught in wanting to help, wanting to have an impact, and in wanting so much to help them when I see there is no change in their circumstances and they continue to feel hopeless, I *am* perpetuating their helplessness and I'm keeping them there for me.

Clinicians can refuse to accept responsibility for their ineffectiveness:

We have a certain way of saying we help clients, but the client may not necessarily feel this. So it's an assumption that we have the answer and we don't. If they say you can't help, we feel helpless, but since we're in the power position, we can say it's their choice whether to come or not.

Clinicians can fail to help the client alter his powerless position:

I can help someone do something and feel good about myself as a therapist, feel good and powerful, but if I look at the larger society and see that person's position hasn't changed, I have to know that I'm feeling good about helping him fit into the system better. Furthermore, my position hasn't changed and I haven't given up anything.

Clinicians can make themselves more comfortable by trying to control their clients:

I suddenly could see the interaction between my client and me as a fight for control. I was getting angry. Though I had power through my ethnicity (WASP) and position, I was insecure due to being a student. Here I was working to gain confidence in my skills and this child was challenging me. It was not only that she was Black that contributed to my anger but her age too! And then I was upset with myself that I let this child test my endurance and patience.

Clinicians may refuse to acknowledge the threat that the client's attempt to get a sense of power can pose to the clinician's personal need for power:

I was working with a Black prisoner who was very manipulative and controlling. He tested me constantly, asking where I lived, did I have kids, what am I thinking and constantly bringing up the fact that I am White and he is Black. I focused on his toughness and his fear of dependency as narcissistic, but I wasn't looking at my part. I was battling with him over control. I was angry and upset at his assertive behavior, challenging my authority, but also not staying in his place—inferior and powerless. How dare he!

The issue of the gratification inherent in the power of the clinical role, what it means to the clinician in terms of his own power needs and responses, and how these are managed in the clinical process is key to the process of client empowerment. This is true because in that process the therapeutic relationship actually becomes a "forum for the unfolding of power dynamics" (Heller 1985, p. 169). And a change in therapist power is fundamental to the client change that marks effective treatment.

This necessary shift in power that must occur in successful intervention means that there is a change in clients' perceptions of themselves as victims and without power. They no longer feel powerless nor do they collude in their own victimization or the denigration of their cultural group by aggrandizing the helper and/or the helper's cultural group. Successful intervention means that clients can now see themselves as persons of power who belong to a group that has value and can behave in ways that aim to change their powerless status, including acquiring the resources necessary to cope with this reality. In having made these changes clients have shifted the relationship between themselves and the helper toward a more equal one. For practitioners, this means their powerful role as experts, teachers, therapists has changed as has the meaning attached to their dominant cultural group status as White, high status ethnic, upper or middle class, or male in the eyes of their clients. For them as well as their clients therefore there is a shift in power. In the situation of the helper this shift may involve letting go of a significant source of gratification. Clinicians must understand their reactions to such change and whether or not these reactions to that potential power shift do, in fact, provide a barrier to facilitating the changes necessary for the empowerment of clients. Accordingly, the practitioner must be ready to ask himself these questions:

If a successful outcome would mean a change in the client's collusion in his own subordinate status and thus a change in his perception of me as dominant because of my helper role or my ethnic, racial, sex (or other) identity, how do I react to this change?

Under what circumstances might this be a problem for me?

The systemic nature of power is such that a shift in its balance can automatically stir up a counterreaction. This is first demonstrated in the resistance people have to examining this issue, whether the arena is family sex role or racial status assignment:

> I was powerful as the oldest child who was favored. It's hard for me to say that and I certainly would never have admitted it had someone asked. Not only that, but if my sister tried to push me out of that position, I fought hard to keep it. When my parents tried to be fair, I wanted none of it.

There will often be ambivalence and negative feelings despite an intellectual belief in the rightness of the change. Several male psychiatric residents describe this reluctance in their responses to the changing role of men. Some feel confused and threatened. Some resent it.

> Now when I see a woman getting what I want, while intellectually I see it as OK, my gut reaction is negative. Giving up power is hard to do even when you know it's right.

> I want women to have equal chances, but I still have trouble when they have authority over me.

> Well, as a White male, I feel the rightness of their cause but when they're very strong and come after me, I feel threatened even though it may not be true. There is dissonance for me in terms of being committed to feminism, recognizing the injustices that have been perpetrated against women on the one hand, and what that plays out to be in my own life. It's a struggle for me.

Some who initially favor change will undermine the process when it is underway:

> I'm ambivalent. I want my executive wife not to be as successful as I am. I also want her to be nurturing and care for me while I'm in training.

I try to adapt to these new demands my wife is making
about helping her more and all that but I must admit, I often
purposely don't see the dirt (laughter).

Whether that which is relinquished happens to be stereotypes and
learned judgments or role advantage, dominance, and the superiority embodied in the role or in the social structure, a shift of power
constitutes a psychological loss. The loss that is experienced involves giving up a sense of entitlement, space, automatic attributions to oneself as superior, or "better than." In giving up these
benefits there can also be loss of the associated sense of stability
and tranquility:

Isn't that the root of all prejudice, feeling superior? Equality
takes away that superior position and the entitlement that
goes with it.

Loss of the sense of stability and tranquility that characterizes a
dominant role is clear in these comments related to men's roles:

Sharing power isn't easy. Now that women are changing
society, men are becoming dysfunctional. Right now it's a
painful place for us because we don't have the choices
women have.

We (men) are taught to be tough and independent. So we
have learned to look for support not from our peers (other
men), but from women whom we have been taught to
dominate. Now that women are changing that, we are caught
with no supports.

This loss is also identified in relation to cultural roles, in this
instance, race:

Accepting Blacks as equals *would* mean giving up my
privileged position of being the credible, knowledgeable one,
seeing myself as less competent, becoming less useful in
some tasks because the experience of others would be more
appropriate.

Especially when a power role has served to make the experience of powerlessness in other areas less painful, the loss of that
aggrandizing, gratifying role may be perceived as harmful or
threatening. Again, the experience of men illustrates this:

Yes, that has been one place where we men could expect to feel powerful. And anyway I think a lot of our power is a cover for the dependency we feel.

I'm reluctant to let this power go because very often in my life I have felt powerless. I'm just in the process of discovering my power as a person and as a man and feeling great about that.

This loss can set in motion a process whereby those who have been dominant can begin to feel themselves like victims:

I became a racist in college when Blacks and other minorities banded together against Whites. They were hostile and bigoted, too. It was a horrible experience for me. Intellectually, I understood it, but personally I felt hurt and rejected.

The conflict I have is not about relating on an individual, one-to-one basis. I feel more powerful year by year in the sense that I'm not so vulnerable that the individual is taking my power. But on the level of social policy and with the conditions of abuse and racism, I begin to lose trust that things will ever be equal—someone will always have the edge over the other. As a member of the White race I don't trust them—they may do to me what has been done to them. So on an individual level, that's one thing, but on a policy level race to race is another.

Although I considered myself an eastern liberal, within a few weeks after joining the army, the words "fucking nigger" had found their way into my vocabulary. While most of the officers and high-ranking non-coms were White, the company training cadre in my basic training unit was entirely Black. These men, whose job it was to prepare us for the inevitable combat roles we would assume in a matter of weeks, were brutal and nasty and insensitive. Race hatred was everywhere.

When people in power are threatened enough and feel like victims, they respond to their sense of powerlessness in all the ways we have identified to keep their sense of power. This is a critical issue in all relationships including the clinical encounter when clinicians can feel the power embodied in their role threatened. Clients challenge practitioner power all the time. This is endemic to the clinical process, and managing these threats in a way that forwards the goal of client empowerment is a part of the clinician's role. But when clinicians maintain a personal need for the power embodied in this role, either as the expert or as one whose cultural group status must be aggrandized, and when empowering the client means a shift in that power differential, practitioners may be unable or unwilling to implement the goal of client empowerment. Instead they may engage in behaviors that will undermine this goal or drive the client away.

When they become aware of dynamics related to power in the clinical process, and understand their own power needs and responses, practitioners discover a fundamental fact. If they have a personal need to maintain the power inherent in their clinical or aggrandized cultural role, the necessary shift that must take place in this power differential between themselves and the clients, which facilitates effective outcome, *will constitute a danger for them*. And therein exists a serious dilemma. They are threatened, on the one hand, with the loss of self-esteem as professionals because of failure to faithfully execute the treatment imperative, and, on the other, with loss of the power embedded in their clinical and/or aggrandized cultural role and vulnerable to the pain that such a loss would bring. But this dilemma can remain carefully hidden, maintained by ignorance—ignorance of cultural identity and meaning and how it applies to their personal circumstances, and ignorance of how power operates in the clinical encounter, including the cross-cultural one. While the problem remains latent, there are nevertheless clues to its existence in the behavior of the clinician: anxiety, a sense of immobilization, avoidance, or other unhelpful behaviors.

The Solution to the Dilemma

Power sharing can be a solution to this dilemma. It becomes a gain, not a loss, because it brings a different sense of power. Power, then, will be experienced not as a consequence of dominance, but as freedom from it. There is freedom from the entrapment embedded in the dominant position, from the sense of conflict, the fear, and the stress, the rigidity, and need for sameness.

There is also freedom from fearing the loss of power, from the pressure to hold on, from the distortion in thinking, from the inability to grow, and from the intolerance for difference. This freedom can manifest itself in several ways: There can be a sense of pride in self and one's identity:

> I see how important pride in identity is not only in terms of ethnicity but also race. I see the importance of knowing and understanding. My grandparents come from southern Italy, which in Italy is second class. I've recognized my mother's feelings of inferiority and my own and their connection with my negative reaction to her. And I understand how these issues could set me up to need the superiority racism offers. I know now that when Whites feel good enough about who they are as unique individuals they can allow people-of-color to have power too. In coming to grips with the power I sought through racism, I have never felt so Italian, so Catholic, so human.

There can be new understanding of clients' reluctance to change:

> I have some idea now of how clients feel when we ask them to evaluate their assumptions and test out their ideas. I've learned from this process how hard that can be. As a White person, I see, too, how hard it is to stop blaming others for my racism, just as it is hard for my clients to take responsibility for their lives and stop being stuck with blaming their parents and society. I will remember this and be more empathic with clients.

There can be better understanding of how clients use defensive behavior to get a sense of power:

> I was no longer worried about the games my client played with people and the trouble she might get into because I was able to validate her behavior of manipulation as adaptive to the powerlessness she experienced and at the same time to show her the price it cost her.

> I could see that the pervasive powerlessness of my client meant that with few choices externally and an internal sense of being powerless, the one choice she had was to say "no" to me. And thus I could wait patiently while sending messages that she could return whenever she was ready.

The increased comfort with difference facilitates the ability to take an appropriate nonpower stance:

> I had approached the relationship with D very naively, denying that race makes a difference and putting more energy in emphasizing our similarities than our differences. It was when I began driving to D's workplace (another site in the industrial setting where we usually met), *equalizing our relationship and discussing our differences,* that our relationship began to grow. Her continual distrust of me made me angry but this anger was really at a system that would make help difficult for D to accept and make me unacceptable. I had to remind myself that my anger was not at D but at both of our experiences. When we were able to share our feelings of powerlessness, the racial situation in general, and what was going on inside the corporation, she opened up and shared a great deal.

A female psychiatric trainee describes her plan to change her behavior, which she now recognizes as related to poor tolerance for difference:

> The confrontation about my ideas as a woman was significant. I learned that other people don't feel and think the same as I do, and because of this I had stopped engaging with those who think differently. I want to make a commitment to change that, to become more active. I want to be able to engage with those who think differently. I will stop tolerating ethnic and racist jokes.

There is greater readiness to manage client resistance that has a cultural basis:

> The issue of race and power is always there—I see that now. We may reinforce the client's powerlessness in subtle ways when we don't realize they are bringing it up. My client insisted there was no problem with my being White. But the issue of White and the power of Whites were all over the interview when I studied them. After I raised this a number of times, she shared her reluctance.

There is greater readiness to consider treatment alternatives that focus on the use of external systems as supports for clients:

I acted on the suggestion that I help my patient to take action by joining a women's group. My supervisor (male) disagreed with me, insisting that such action would avoid helping her see how she sets herself up. I felt we had looked at that enough. When she joined the group, there was a definite shift in her depression.

I had a Hispanic client who was manic-depressive and is now recovering. She became very hopeful when we planned for her to work with a community action group to deal with racism and the lack of services.

There is greater readiness to acknowledge power struggles with clients and the part one's own needs play. One trainee described her battle with a poor Black client. She described her client's adaptation to poverty, the stressful family situation, and her contradictory behavior; she refused to use available preventive services (which included support, medication follow-up, socialization, and skills training) but persisted in using hospitalization and her family in a kind of revolving door solution. The client would arrive in crisis at the hospital when she had to get away from the stress of the family and, after a brief stay, would then demand to get out because she now felt the family needed her. The worker said:

I entered the treatment arena with her, armed with my problem-solving strategies, my individualistic values and need for success, and she retaliated by "yessing" me to death, undermining any constructive plans we made, being as withholding as possible and intensely determined not to let me help. What I didn't see was that by this behavior she was enabling herself to feel as empowered as she knew how to be. I couldn't see that. Caught as we were in this paradox, neither of us found any satisfaction in our relationship. My goal was to help her stay healthy and hers was to maintain her cyclical pattern. I could not understand why she kept up such destructive patterns; it made perfect sense to me that she'd want to stay out of the hospital. Evidently, my goal was just that—my goal, not hers. She had absolutely no desire to change her pattern of living and I honestly believe she gained quite a sense of satisfaction from the fact that I was running around, beating my head against the wall, and getting nowhere. She even *told* me that she had no intention of changing, but I didn't believe her. I needed to believe that I could step in and change her life to the way it 'should' be. No wonder we got nowhere.

There is greater readiness to take action on other levels, which enhances one's clinical role and removes the sense of immobilization that may exist:

I need to see where I can make a difference. There *are* things I lobby for that can help people stop being victims: getting more Black kids into treatment, seeing that certain populations get serviced. This means operating outside of the clinical encounter.

I've started doing some research on violence in inpatient services, and I'm collecting data on the connection with ineffective treatment. I'm finding a lot of violence between people-of-color.

Operating outside of the clinical encounter by speaking out and working to change people's oppressive realities (in relation to policies and inadequate funding) can also give helpers a sense of power because they no longer feel powerless about changing the conditions that had made their clients powerless. Said one social worker:

I won't be stuck anymore.

7

Assessment

ENHANCEMENT OF SOCIAL FUNCTIONING, facilitating people's ability to cope with their realities and to improve the quality of their lives are recognized goals of effective work with all clients. In the pursuit of these goals, practitioners must pay attention to culture as a factor in problem formation, problem resolution, and in the clinical process itself, which includes assessment, relationship development, intervention, and outcome. The perspectives, capacities, competencies, and abilities that enable practitioners to focus successfully on culture in their work have been identified in earlier chapters. Among them are the following:

1. The ability to be comfortable with difference in others (and thus not be trapped in anxiety about difference or in defensive behavior to ward it off

2. The ability to control, and even change false beliefs, assumptions, and stereotypes, which eliminates the need to use defensive behavior to protect oneself

3. The ability to respect and appreciate the values, beliefs, and practices of persons who are culturally different and to perceive such persons through their own cultural lenses instead of the practitioner's

4. The ability to think flexibly and to recognize that one's own way of thinking and behaving is not the only way, and

5. The ability to behave flexibly. This is demonstrated by the readiness to engage in the extra steps required to sort

147

through general knowledge about a cultural group and to
see the specific way in which knowledge applies, or does
not apply, to a given client

The importance of these steps, which take extra time, effort, and
energy, is illustrated in the following remarks:

Yesterday a new client came in, sat down, and the first three
words she said were, "I'm Irish Catholic." I didn't know
what that meant to her, but I remember thinking is she
struggling with conflict about her Irish identity, is she having
conflict with her husband (her last name sounded Italian), is
she questioning what I am, and does this mean she wonders
if I can help her? Well, I later found out she was concerned
with being accepted by me and in some way thought I'd see
Irish as negative. I understood this when she said, "We don't
drink or fool around and we're very quiet and moral."

Purpose and Steps in Assessment

Assessment, the initial step in the process of intervention, is
completed with more accuracy when practitioners have developed these capacities. The work of assessment includes (1) gathering data on the client and his problem; (2) analyzing the data,
identifying the most critical factors, and defining the interrela-
tionships, i.e., inferring meaning; (3) developing an effective
intervention plan. In order to develop an effective plan of intervention, the clinician should be able to determine what is the nature of the client's need or problem; what are the factors contributing to its maintenance; what are the client's perceptions,
capacities, and strengths; what needs to be supported, modified,
or changed.

In determining the nature of the problem and the factors maintaining it, the practitioner must elicit the client's view of the
problem and his response to the referral. She must understand
how the client experiences the problem, the degree of distress
being experienced by him and by persons with whom he interacts, what he has done to deal with the problem, and his response
to the referral. The inferences she draws in the process of analyzing the data as she identifies critical factors and defines interrela-
tionships depend on several factors. First, these inferences de-

pend on the theoretical base being used by the clinician, which, in turn, determines the kind of behavior and the areas of functioning to be focused on as factors which perpetuate the problem (Northern 1987). For example, if the theoretical base is psychosocial and the problem is school phobia, the child's early relationship with the mother and the separation process may be inferred as the cause. If the theoretical base is cognitive, behaviors that reinforce his wish to stay home and not attend school will be inferred as the cause.

Second, these inferences will depend on established norms or expected behaviors that define what is adequate or not adequate in the behaviors or areas of human functioning being examined, and because norms vary in different cultures, assessment of culturally different clients using traditional White middle-class norms, or norms based on the clinician's culture, may result in erroneous inferences. For example, to assess a Latino child as school phobic would have to take into account the fact that Latino families do not push the child to separate as early as Americans do.

To ensure that their own cultural lens is not the basis of assessment, practitioners should determine the nature of the problem, and the factors maintaining it, by asking the following questions (Jacobsen 1988; Lum 1986; Ho 1987).

1. To what extent is the problem related to issues of transition such as migration and immigration?

2. To what extent is the client's understanding of the problem based on a cultural explanation, for example, "evil curse," "mal ojo," and so forth?

3. Is the behavior that is a problem considered normal within the culture or is it considered dysfunctional?

4. To what extent is the problem a manifestation of environmental lack or insufficiency, or lack of access to resources and supports?

5. To what extent is the problem related to cultural conflict in identity, values, or relationships?

6. To what extent is the behavior a consequence of psychological conflict or characterological problems?

7. What are the cultural strengths and assets available to the client such as cultural values and practices, social networks, and support systems?

Competencies Needed for Assessment

Practitioners are not only asked to work with a range of cultural groups, but within these groups, they must assist persons from a range of social classes, levels of education, and acculturation. These are contextual factors that must be considered in understanding the client's problem. Practitioners, thus, must be sensitive to a continuum of cultural beliefs and socioeconomic issues. They must use flexible thinking to sort out a variety of dimensions and be cautious in generalizing about a specific individual or family based on cultural knowledge of that group, since what may be characteristic of the group may not be relevant to that individual. Clients may be struggling with the issues of migration and the stressors of adapting to a new environment, where loss of family, neighborhood, or homeland, along with a change in culture and language, can be powerful stressors (Bernal and Gutierrez 1988).

In assessing these clients, practitioners must avoid "confusing a client's appropriate cultural response (to stress) with neurotic transference" (Brislin and Pedersen 1976) or confusing a response that represents culture shock with a response that indicates serious pathology. In one case a 15-year-old Puerto Rican male was erroneously diagnosed as schizophrenic by an Anglo clinician because he talked of seeing the devil who tried to get him to do bad things. Investigation by a Puerto Rican clinician revealed that this youngster, who had recently arrived in the United States, was experiencing culture shock, material deprivation due to reduced financial circumstances, trauma over separating from his father, and humiliation over his life situation. The diagnosis of stress reaction (adjustment disorder with mixed emotional features) saved him from being treated for schizophrenia, which would have required powerful tranquilizers and hospitalization in a long-term treatment facility, "possibly resulting in the development of more chronic emotional problems" (Ramos-McKay, Comas-Diaz, and Rivera 1988, p. 217). In such instances the presence or absence of a precipitating stressful situation preceding the onset of symptoms and the existence of symptoms that are labile would contradict the diagnosis of psychosis. When such behavior represents culture shock, it will abate quickly. In another case, an alert and empathic Anglo practitioner was flexible enough to change his idea that his Mexican-

American female client's punctuated speech and emotional intensity indicated a borderline personality rather than a culturally endorsed way of handling stress (Martinez 1988).

Behavior that is reactive to chronic stress as well as the acute stress of transition must also be assessed correctly. Behavior under these circumstances can also be erroneously diagnosed as psychotic. For example, a young man was assessed by the admitting physician as a "crazy Indian" who was impulsive and potentially violent. Strapped to the bed after being brought in by police, he was anxious and agitated. Upon learning that the evaluating psychiatrist was Indian, he relaxed and told his story. His four-year-old son was taken from him and placed in a White foster home by a judge's ruling, because they had been found sleeping beside a building after he had consumed a bottle of wine. They had camped for the night since they had become sleepy and, by nightfall, were still far from home. Totally without reserves and in a strange city, in his outrage over being separated from his son, the patient had threatened the judge, asserting that he was ready to die to teach the judge a lesson. The evaluating psychiatrist who saw this as a reactive condition was sure the patient would have been diagnosed as psychotic and/or alcoholic, deemed dangerous, and placed in a psychiatric ward by persons unfamiliar with the Native American experience (Thompson, Blueye, Smith, & Walker 1983).

Whether or not the behavior that appears dysfunctional or pathological to the practitioner represents dysfunction within the client's culture is a significant issue to be determined in the assessment process. Practitioners must be on the lookout for signs that indicate the meaning of the behavior being observed or described, since ordinary yardsticks cannot be used.

It is important, therefore, that practitioners evaluate carefully. The client's behavior in the interview is one source of data for the appraisal. For example, an Italian client who speaks rapidly and shows a great deal of emotionality must be assessed as to whether her behavior should be considered culturally adaptive or unstable, hyperactive, hysterical, or controlling. A client's gift to her practitioner will not automatically be seen as a power move or as an expression of unworthiness (a traditional psychodynamic interpretation) but will question whether such a gesture represents a culturally endorsed expression of generosity and friendliness (Lum 1986; McGoldrick 1983). The self-care and responsibility that some Black parents demand of their children will be viewed as a possible adaptation to their harsh environment and not necessarily pathological. The knowledge that Puerto Ricans are highly spiritual and fatalistic helps the social worker think twice about whether her client who has a conviction that she will die is really suicidal. The behavior of the Irish client who came to the office to cancel her appointment with the psychiatrist will not be seen automatically as stemming from dependency needs but also will be considered in the context of the Irish values of obedience and conformity. If a clinician understands that Latinos value interdependence and that once they trust the helper, they expect support, he will *not* assume automatically that this expectation is an indication of a high dependency need or oral longing. Rigid machismo behavior in a Latino male will be examined further to determine whether it is a consequence of sex-role expectation, a result of social stress (for example, lack of work), or an aspect of developmental process. The Black mother's slow pace in planning her son's discharge from the hospital will become less frustrating to her social worker when she considers that while it may be an indication of ambivalence or rejection, it may instead be consistent with the adaptive values embraced by people who contend with social and political powerlessness by living in the present and not planning for the future. The nodding of a Japanese client will be recognized as communicating the message, "I'm listening"; it does not necessarily mean that the client agrees with the clinician's assessment or with the treatment plan under discussion (Lum 1986).

The practitioner who can think broadly and behave flexibly will remember that what constitutes pathological behavior can vary greatly among different ethnic groups. Thus, when the client is an Asian or Latino (groups that value affiliation), isolation or distanced relationships among family members may be a sign of greater stress and greater dysfunction than they would among Anglo-Saxons (who value independence). When stress reinforces rigidity and exaggerates the use of normal cultural practices, care must be taken to determine the degree of dysfunction that may exist. For example, when the affiliativeness valued by Latinos becomes exaggerated under stress, they may display intrusive behavior and overinvolvement that is not necessarily based on psychological dependency. When the individualism of American and Anglo-Saxon culture becomes exaggerated due to stress or isolation, the alienation, anomie, and denial that people manifest may not be related to deficits stemming from developmental trauma. The severe punishment used by Black parents that can easily slip into abuse may not be a consequence of developmental deprivation.

Even the severity of alcoholism must be viewed in the context of cultural practices, its determination being a matter of an "internal comparison within that culture" (Thompson et al. 1983). At the same time, heavy drinking among Indians is associated with a variety of factors: dependency conflict, genetic predisposition, anxiety, feelings of alienation, helplessness, deprivation, frustration, and powerlessness related to change from an Indian economy of hunting and gathering with a low degree of social complexities and consequent entrapment in a culturally disadvantaged position.

Rigid, exaggerated behavior is an expectable response to stress. For example, among women, especially minority women, the role of supporter and nurturer can become characterized by exaggerated submissiveness to the male, overprotection of children, and sacrifice of self. Under stress, the culturally based tendency toward self-negation of Chicano mothers can become extreme (Falicov 1983). Afro-American mothers under such conditions often become intensely involved with their children (Hale 1980). Interference with the culturally prescribed role of provider causes minority males to experience stress, conflict, and poor self-esteem. For example, Asian males may perceive themselves as a source of shame to self and family lineage (Shon and Ja 1983). Under such stress they and others may exaggerate their dominant role, intensify demands for female accommodation, become less supportive, more unavailable, and even abusive (Pinderhughes 1986).

The degree to which culturally based behavior can be maladaptive is also important to assess. For example, maintaining a connection to their cultural groups is critical for minority group individuals, because it helps to buffer the effects of racism and oppression. But this need can also reinforce cultural prescriptions that prevent escape. In Asian families, for instance, separation and divorce are not viable options for Asian women who are ostracized and relegated to outcast status as a consequence (Shon and Ja 1983). Many, although intensely dissatisfied and frustrated, feel powerless to change either the behavior of those with whom they interact or the oppressive circumstances that fuel it. Instead, when unable to change the situation, they blame themselves, often feeling that they are failures.

Clinicians must also be alert to the fact that behavior observed in the interview may be a critically based maneuver to cope with stress. Avoidance and detachment may then be evaluated as possible indications of mistrust of the interviewer which the client entertains based on his societal experience (Lum 1986, p. 156). The clinician, then, will be less likely to assume that behavior manifested in the interview is the essence of the client's behavioral style rather than a sign of this mistrust. Since silence can be a culturally valid way of responding for Asians and since taboos exist against freely discussing physical and emotional problems, a client's reluctance to answer questions, his guarded affect, and flatness must not be considered routinely a sign of depression or mental illness. And even when the client's perceptions and responses are determined to be a sign of dysfunction, the practitioner must monitor his own responses to make sure there is no distortion or projection that is fed by his own need. (Greenson discusses his struggle to recognize that the experiences described by his analytic patient were real, not fantasies or a sign of paranoia which he himself had wanted to believe [Greenson et al. 1982]).

Clinicians who are self-aware and who understand their own cultural baggage, including their power needs and responses, will have no problem in considering environmental support or insufficiency as a factor in the etiology of the problem to be addressed. The stresses related to deprived minority group status are frequently related to socioeconomic factors, not cultural ones (Leighton 1982). In the case of minorities and the poor, clinicians will refuse to ignore the effects of the societal projection process upon both their minority clients and themselves. Knowledge of these realities will not threaten and immobilize them. Relationships to the wider society will be assessed to determine the degree of exposure to negative valuation (and thus to the hazard of developing feelings of low self-esteem and powerlessness) that can occur as a consequence of cultural group membership (Solomon 1982, p. 166). Despite the fact that practitioners may have been beneficiaries in the societal process that victimizes their clients, they must be able to look honestly at those effects upon the client.

In one child psychiatry clinic, information needed to complete an assessment required that the clinician make a home visit. The trainee assigned to the case refused to make such a visit, first claiming that the family was "too resistant," then that the visit would cause him to miss his scheduled patients and seminars, and finally admitting that he was "too afraid," even when offered a guide. Since home visits were made at the discretion of the clinician and the department in which he was a trainee, his resistance was not seen as a "problem," and the home visit was not made in spite of efforts by the Afro-American team member to the contrary (Wyatt 1982, p. 142).

Despite responses on their part of guilt, shame, or fear concerning the advantages their position has granted them, clinicians must strive to assess clients' situations accurately. Unless clinicians can manage their responses to their own societal position, they may not evaluate correctly the contradictory nature of a minority client's social role, which, as we have seen, may have sustained stability and tranquility for the practitioner while reinforcing tension, conflict, and contradiction for the client. For example, in work with minorities clinicians will not shrink from evaluating the affronts and assaults that are associated with the client's societal role (Solomon 1982, p. 176). Nor will they fail to assess the way in which experiences with institutional racism can influence how clients see the world and how they handle life cycle events. They will recognize the enormously contradictory demands with which clients as victims of the societal projection process are confronted. Despite being faced with ongoing conflict, confusion, and contradiction, minority clients are called upon to function competently and with organization, sustaining family solidarity and cohesion. And despite being surrounded by a hostile, nonsupportive environment, they must find ways to maintain intimate, caring relationships, to raise children to be loving, competent, and strong, and to secure a sense of esteem for self and group.

Significance of Strengths and Adaptive Behavior

Assessment of culturally different clients is never complete unless it includes an evaluation of the strengths that enable people to cope with such conditions. Clinicians must be free to focus on these strengths. When they have been beneficiaries in the social system and are unaware of its significance for them, they may find this hard to do. Their role in societal processes can seduce them to view the behavior of their clients, who are members of victim groups, in stereotypical ways. They will thus tend to see behavior in terms of weakness or pathology. They may also remain unaware that the beliefs they hold can be stereotypes representing unacceptable impulses existing within themselves that their position in society permits them to project onto persons from victim groups, and that their clients may be such persons (Ferguson 1982, p. 217). As we have repeatedly illustrated in the examination of the experiential data, stereotypical thinking allows the thinker to stabilize and tranquilize himself, because he can disavow rejected aspects of himself and see them as existing in the other. In so doing the thinker can ward off anxiety about these impulses in himself and anxiety about the situation of difference between himself and another. The use of stereotypes to understand the client-victim may make practitioners more comfortable, reinforcing for them a sense of tranquility and stability. Thus, they may be unaware that they engage in such thinking about a client or that the purpose of such thinking is to make themselves feel more comfortable. This explains some practitioners' readiness to interpret cultural differences as deficiency (Lum 1986, p. 164). It also explains the tendency for practitioners to formulate diagnostic and dynamic questions in such a way as to validate their own false beliefs and to elicit information that will support these beliefs (Ferguson 1982, p. 217).

One social worker, accustomed to the dependent and helpless posture some Blacks have used to gain access to societal resources, evaluated a "short, solidly built man with a strong, deep voice, a forthright posture, a very self-assured and stern personality" as aggressive (Weaver 1982, p. 112). Another social worker admitted a greater readiness to "focus upon pain and suffering" than on coping skills and strengths. Another admitted being so "devastated" by the struggles and deprivations faced by her client that she saw her client as having no strengths or coping abilities, as having no choices available. Greenson has suggested that the contempt of some Whites whereby they see Blacks as lazy, stupid, etc. can hide an envy of their strengths—in his work with a Black analysand he identified such feelings in himself in relation to the issue of sexual prowess (Greenson et al. 1982). Finding weakness and pathology in others is consistent with the role of expert and competent one and it reinforces such a self-image.

Among the strengths that clinicians must be able to identify in clients are coping abilities, natural support systems, problem-solving abilities, and tolerance of stress (Lum 1986). Identification of support systems is a major issue in assessment. People from groups that have been victimized by societal projection are especially vulnerable if they are isolated. Among Mexican-American psychiatric patients, for example, the most disturbed were disconnected from their religious life (Martinez 1988, p. 191). Isolation from extended families and the community supports that can help neutralize the consequences of their societal position and enable them to fulfill family, work, and other roles can also have destructive effects. Strong group connections can nourish self-esteem and the ego strength needed to cope effectively and to achieve personal and social goals (Solomon 1982, p. 171). Careful attention to the strengths and nutritive quality of these supports means that the practitioner must be able to see the positives in many seemingly negative situations.

When practitioners are able to focus on strengths they can understand even problematic behavior as the client's adaptive attempt to survive the paradoxical imperatives of his systemic role. Passive aggression and dependency have been cultural adaptations used by Puerto Ricans to cope with the powerlessness they have experienced in relation to the impact of colonialism and their denigrated societal status (Ramos-McKay, Comas-Diaz, and Rivera 1988, p. 213). Even dependency can be seen as a strategy for coping with powerlessness since it represents a way of being close to a source of power (McClelland 1975).

Many of these behavioral strategies for survival have given rise to stereotypes. Examples include the passive and stoic behavior of the Asian, obedient and carefree behavior in Blacks, the quiet, smiling presentation of the Asian-American, the sleepy demeanor of the Mexican, the stoic behavior of the Native American, all of which are behaviors "covering despair over social, economic and political oppression" (Lum 1986, p. 74). These are not cultural adaptations in the sense that they are a part of the ethnic fabric that facilitates group cohesiveness and individual integration in a people; rather they are a consequence of socioeconomic conditions (Leighton 1982). These should be recognized as people's attempts to cope with powerlessness and achieve some degree of comfort. Paradoxically, the need for comfort and a sense of power may be such that people's attempts to gain it can even include assuming negative attributions and stereotypes in the extreme.

Practitioners must be able to identify these and other strategies that people use to cope with the powerlessness associated with low cultural group status and to gain a sense of comfort in surviving their harsh conditions and paradoxical realities. Such strategies include the practice of assuming negative attributions and stereotypes, the extreme use of aggressive accommodation, and aggressive passivity (Chestang 1972), turning around the meaning of negative attributions (Draper 1979), using paradox, humor, subtlety, deception, and various forms of manipulation, emphasizing struggle and power in relationships. It is important to identify these maneuvers and to assess the degree to which these behaviors are rigidly adhered to because, for the most part, they represent a reactive, defensive response to the initiative of others (individuals, groups, or the larger social system). When these behaviors constitute the total repertoire of an individual, he will be unable to behave with initiative, self-assertion, and leadership. His only choice is to provoke others so that he can then engage in the reactive behaviors with which he is familiar. He thus has no possibility of being able to pursue his own goals or develop a sense of mastery and competence, because all his energy is consumed in reacting to the initiatives of others. It is the rigidity with which these behaviors are used that makes them so destructive. If people employ the behaviors at one time but at other times are able to make choices, assume leadership, to set their own goals and pursue them (even with assistance), then such behavior should not be considered dysfunctional. That individual is able to demonstrate healthy flexibility.

When a practitioner is himself a beneficiary of the very process that induces these rigidified responsive behavioral manifestations in his clients, he may find it hard to assess the behaviors objectively as survival mechanisms, which may be effective at some times but costly at others. But to assess correctly, to plan effectively, and empower his client, he must manage the feelings mobilized by this recognition of his own beneficiary status and eschew the vulnerability to behave rigidly himself, summarily viewing these behaviors as pathology or failing to check out the client's capacity for flexibility.

While balancing all these factors in the equation of clients' problems, the flexible thinker will not overlook internal factors. To do this would be as inappropriate as ignoring the external. Jacobsen (1988, p. 145) discusses a case where a focus on the client's cultural adjustment during a two-year treatment period ignored a "biological diagnosis" of "mania and depression." This is a distinct risk for clinicians when they become knowledgeable about cultural dynamics. They "overculturize" (Leighton 1982) when they automatically view behavior as culturally based and fail to consider other factors such as internal functioning and trauma due to developmental process. When psychological and characterological problems appear to exist alongside issues of transition and cultural conflict, more sorting out is needed. The role of psychological conflict and the degree to which it is reinforced by elements of culture (and vice versa) *must* be assessed.

There are hazards too in working with persons from one's own cultural background. For example, there is the danger of overidentification, which can cloud the thinking of competent clinicians so that they misperceive the severity and extent of the problem. We have already encountered many examples of this in our examination of the experiential data. A Jewish psychiatrist who treated a Jewish female patient failed to diagnose her thought disorder and to treat her appropriately. The client, a 25-year-old daughter of Nazi concentration camp survivors who were the lone survivors of their families, became depressed at age 17. In an interview, she manifested symptoms of severe dysfunction, loose associations, blocking, bizarre affect, auditory hallucinations, and poor concentration. At age 21 the patient was treated by a psychiatrist because of persistent school difficulty and problems in maintaining relationships and holding a job. Her parents now reported that earlier she had been given medication and there was no further contact. Now that her symptoms had returned, her parents were seeking evaluation from another psychiatrist. A phone call to her original psychiatrist revealed that he had been reluctant to diagnose the patient as having a thought disorder, had treated her for a milder condition, and never pushed for a follow-up because he strongly identified with her father's concentration camp experiences and felt sorry for his plight (Jacobsen 1988, p. 142).

How does one go about ensuring that these inbuilt vulnerabilities in clinicians due to their cultural group identity and experiences do not interfere with the assessment? Strategies do exist to help decide whether behavior represents a cultural response to stress, indicates serious pathology, or symbolizes mistrust within the therapeutic relationship. As already noted, practitioners must faithfully check out their own responses and be open to recognizing when they are using stereotypes. They must keep an open mind, examining possibilities other than the ones that first have come to mind. In interviewing, they will use "techniques which encourage the patient to tell his own story in his own way, ensuring that the client explains what otherwise might be taken for granted" (Leighton 1982, p. 12). Being careful to tune in on feedback (to really listen!) and to modify their initial hypothesis, they faithfully monitor the client's responses to comments, interpretations, suggestions, and advice and recognize that "each party may have to process messages twice before real communication takes place" (Ferguson 1982, p. 218). They will explore the cultural dimension in assessment or get assistance with what may be culturally related treatment difficulties from a colleague or consultant of the client's ethnic background (Jacobsen 1988, p. 145; Lum 1986, p. 156).

A critical issue in the assessment of clients is the significance and meaning of cultural identity and the degree to which it is positive and not marked by fragmentation or conflict. Practitioners must be aware of and empathic with the paralyzing effect of identity conflict, which can cause clients to experience confusion, a sense of fragmentation, isolation, and alienation. Value, role, and identity conflicts are risks for many Americans who have roots in pre-American cultures. Persons-of-color are particularly vulnerable to such conflicts for two reasons: First, their exclusion from total participation in the American mainstream prevents total connection and identification with it. Second, the difference between the values and behavioral practices of their own culture and those of American culture are great. There is "American individuality, freedom of choice, and self-determinism on the one hand, and collective decision making, family obligation, and self-restraint on the other" (Lum 1986, p. 149). Affiliativeness, collaterality in relationships, and interdependence are values that are emphasized by all these groups. Such values support extended family and cultural group cohesiveness and contrast sharply with American values of autonomy and independence. For example, Native Americans may see the individualism of American culture as requiring competitiveness that allows only one or a few to succeed, often at the expense of others (Attneave 1983). The Chinese may equate American values with selfishness (Ryan 1985). The necessity of having to relate to more than one culture is a primary cause of cultural identity conflict. There are few possible adaptational responses to this cultural imperative. Among them are: (1) striving to melt or assimilate into the mainstream; (2) striving to remain separate from the mainstream while embracing one's culture of origin in a positive way ("preserving or revitalizing"); (3) striving to integrate the culture of origin with the mainstream; (4) remaining marginal to both (Spiegel 1984). The third option usually offers the best chance for reduction of value conflict. Marginality involves alienation, isolation from both cultures, fragmentation, and confusion. The other two options also involve conflict, since they require renunciation of one of the two cultures at the same time that contact in some form is practically compulsory. Integration, which is the most desirable option, is not available to people-of-color because of their excluded position in American society. They thus must exist in a state of biculturalism, relating to two worlds but being unable to totally integrate them. This means that people-of-color must remain permanently in a state that is only transitory for White ethnics who experience this condition only as immigrants. Their total acceptance into the society means that they later can become free to integrate (take from each) the two cultures. People-of-color, on the other hand, must find ways to live with this duality and to minimize its destructive potential.

Conflict in values and roles can breed disharmony in relationships; promote intergenerational clashes within nuclear and/or extended family members; fuel internal identity conflict, negative identity, and self-esteem; and destroy ethnic cohesiveness. Culture conflict is manifest in cultural and family roles, defensive behaviors, self-hatred, negative identity, and marginality and is a common source of the problems clients bring. The toll that Black children may pay for cultural conflict can be great if they are separated from cultural ties, the extended family, and systems that interpret the meaning of their culture and, at the same time, are unable to replace this with "something of equal psychological value." In such instances the pressure at school for acceptance, which is based on how much they fashion themselves in the image of the melting pot, if succumbed to, will result in education coming to mean giving up of their sense of self to "blindly find new identity" (Powell 1982, pp. 308–309). How much clients have developed the internal skills and knowledge that will facilitate a well-balanced positive cultural identity and how much they have available to them cultural practices and kinship patterns that facilitate survival in their societal role must be assessed (Lum 1986, p. 149).

While biculturalism can certainly take an extensive toll, it must be remembered that under some circumstances it also can foster amazing strength in people. Whether or not it is a strength, whether the ambivalence and conflict can be managed without extensive toll are critical factors to assess. Also to be determined is the degree to which this duality is (1) backed up by the sound use of coping mechanisms such as cognition, intelligence, judgment, reality testing, coherence, flexibility, and high self-concept, and (2) guided by ethnic values and beliefs about living (Lum 1986, p. 73) that enable people to cope with the consequences of their societal position.

The freedom to assess these factors accurately depends on practitioners' clarity and understanding of themselves and their own cultural identity, including the societal position of their own cultural group. To use diagnostic thinking that transcends stereotypes, is flexible, and is marked by appreciation of cultural difference means that in the assessment of their clients practitioners must also assess themselves.

8

Treatment

THE CAPACITIES, PERSPECTIVES AND COMPETENCIES that have been identified as critical for accurate assessment have equal significance for treatment. "Cultural competence" (Green 1982, pp. 52–53) demands that clinicians develop flexibility in thinking and behavior, because they must learn to adapt professional tasks and work styles to the values, expectations, and preferences of specific clients. This means that practitioners must choose from a variety of strategies that are useful for the range of cultural groups and social classes, levels of education, and levels of acculturation that exist among clients.

Engaging clients and building trusting relationships with them in this context requires great flexibility. Because many cultural groups emphasize collateral and affiliative values, many clients who belong to these groups may expect practitioners to be open, friendly, and relaxed, and to function with mutuality and reciprocity. For example, the value of personalismo (the personal aspect in interaction) for Puerto Ricans emphasizes an individual's inner qualities, whether or not he or she is a good person. Mutual generosity, capacity for intimacy, and personal investment in others are valued (Lum 1986, p. 83) and looked for in practitioners. In order to convey this expected mutuality and reciprocity, practitioners must be comfortable with themselves, with who they are, and at ease with their own cultural identity as well as that of their clients. In work with certain cultural groups, a stance of informality is required and clinicians must be willing to organize the setting so that it creates a comfortable, relaxed

163

atmosphere. Some experts even suggest offering light refreshments. These are recommendations for engaging lower-income Afro-American clients (Solomon 1982) and other minorities (Lum 1986).

The success of a service program for at-risk Puerto Rican parents underscores the importance of such strategies. The program emphasized "engaging parents and children in normalizing activities" (visiting, socializing, drop-in, painting furniture). It provided extensive outreach, marked by readiness to pick up immediately on crisis situations, meeting informally with clients in a relaxed atmosphere, and encouraging clients to "have a sense of ownership about the agency and to feel free to recommend changes in planned programs" (McGowan 1988, p. 25).

Working with certain cultural groups requires that practitioners be ready to respect and build on values centering on family, authority, hierarchy, spirituality, and identity (Lum 1986). With Native Americans, for example, intervention should enhance values of family cooperation, reciprocity, extended family, and corporate survival. Thus, one clinician encouraged his Native American clients in the joint use of property such as an automobile, sharing tasks such as hauling water, cutting wood, doing errands, exchanging child care services, and caring for the elderly (Medicine 1981).

Because cultural support groups can be expecially critical in helping people-of-color cope with discriminatory or hostile experiences, clinicians must be ready and able to link people with natural supports such as extended family, church, fraternal and social groups. Some people use religion to help them cope with powerlessness, uncertainty, and depreciation (Mendes 1982, p. 204). In addition to spiritual fulfillment and emotional support, institutionalized religion and the church meet social needs. Thus, practitioners' failure to consider the use of religion and church-based support systems as effective treatment resources (Gary 1978; Solomon 1976) can be particularly unfortunate.

When natural support groups do not exist or are too dysfunctional (as for example in the situation of severely pathological extended families locked into rigidly destructive functioning), helping systems such as social services, support and treatment groups should be used. Well-organized, appropriately funded services that are carefully coordinated with others in the community are necessary to avoid inflicting more powerlessness upon clients as a result of agency turmoil, competition, and inadequacies that leave helpers also caught in systemic conflict and contradiction, demoralized, and, like their clients, powerless.

Clinicians must be flexible and able to use a variety of treatment strategies. This was clearly illustrated in the case of a 29-year-old depressed, psychotic Black Cuban male who was treated with pharmacology and psychotherapy. The latter focused on helping the patient get in touch with his Cuban culture. This included the use of Spanish language in the therapy and discussions about his family in Cuba, his experience of leaving Cuba, and beginning life in the United States. In addition to bilingual–bicultural professional staff, other strategies used included occupational therapy, patient participation in groups with other Spanish-speaking patients, and connection of the client with support groups, school, and work opportunities (Bernal and Gutierrez 1988, pp. 254–256).

The task of engaging clients will meet with greater success when procedures can be used that are consistent with clients' values. For example, observing "certain relationship protocols with clients from Asian and Latino groups involves addressing the client with his or her surname, making formal introductions, acknowledging the elderly or head of household as the authority and conveying respect through other means" (Lum 1986, p. 69; Garcia-Preto 1983). The values that practitioners must respect and the systems upon which they must build may be in direct contradiction to the values they hold or the values that have been the foundation for traditional treatment strategies. For example, a practitioner holding feminist values may be offended by Asian or Latino cultural practices whereby all women are subordinated to all males, and there is the expectation of deference to the father as the family authority. Practitioners' ability to be flexible and to maintain their commitment to a Latino family will be tested in situations where macho values prevent the father from seeking the help he may need. It is necessary to find new ways of reaching him in order to demonstrate his importance (Garcia-Preto 1988). The clinician must "not undercut or negate the importance of the family or of the father as family authority but, instead, must support and strengthen the role of father as a good authority" (Lum 1986, p. 102).

This presents a real dilemma for some practitioners who, having assured themselves that their response is not serving their own needs, honestly believe that certain family and even cultural values may be damaging to individuals, for example, women. While some professionals believe that cultural values and, in this instance, paternal authority, must always be supported, others may look for ways to help clients change those values that appear harmful. The bottom line must be the degree to which the client wishes to change his values, recognizing the cost he may be required to pay.

Since resolving psychological conflict and connecting feelings to behavior are unfamiliar to many Latinos, practitioners will be better off in the beginning not trying to "work through" feelings, or confronting or pushing for exploration of feelings beyond simple expression (Garcia-Preto 1988). Instead they will emphasize their clients' desire to show that they care for and support each other and will find ways to help them do this. Only with the greatest caution would the clinician confront an Asian client for whom saving face takes priority over honesty, openness, and confrontation. And despite the fact that it seems to be reinforcing enmeshment, the practitioner will be ready to help the son in the family of such a client to live up to the cultural expectation that he be supportive of his parents. A practitioner would do otherwise only when convinced that such a stance would interfere with the client's emotional health and to his achievement of personal and social goals.

Instead of beginning immediately to explore the problem, it is advisable that clinicians "practice self-disclosure," which means that they find a point of mutual interest to focus on in order to build the relationship. Not the same as "small talk," self-disclosure is marked by clinicians' sharing something about their background, work, family, or values (Lee 1983; Lum 1986, p. 105). The use of humor and sharing a brief story can also facilitate engagement because, like self-disclosure, they indicate openness and mutuality on the part of the practitioner. Letting the client take the lead in introducing his problem, having the confidence that he will eventually focus on his reason for coming is also important. Following the client's lead is especially important since many subjects may be taboo.

Using openness, mutuality, reciprocity, and self-disclosure are strategies that require practitioners to be patient, flexible, and comfortable with themselves and with culturally different others. These are not behaviors that practitioners can manifest if they are in conflict about themselves. For the denial and avoidance maneuvers they will use to protect themselves against discomfort associated with their cultural identity means that they cannot be open in manner or reciprocal and mutual in stance. Their need for protection will prompt them to be closed, tight, and rigid.

Even if the practitioner does not practice self-disclosure, many minority clients who are often mistrustful of professionals will push clinicians to reveal something about themselves. (Lum 1986; Lee 1983; Shon and Ja 1983; Solomon 1982). They will check out practitioners by asking about their personal life, background, opinion, or values. This behavior is their way of testing to assess the practitioner as a person. Before they can depend on the competency of the practitioner they feel they must assess his or her background. They may remain distant and aloof until the practioner has passed the test. For example, Blacks may be preoccupied with "sizing up" and "checking out" the expert irrespective of race (Gibbs 1980). They are striving to assess her trustworthiness prior to engaging in task-related activities. Practitioners must be able to "participate in this reality testing and respond with genuine caring and empathy" (Lum 1986, p. 83). They must also be aware of these maneuvers as clients' strategies for overcoming resistance. They must respect the fact that evaluating practitioners' inner character and perhaps testing their comfort with closeness is the client's way of managing reservations about them.

To some cultural groups, practioners are safe only when they can be adopted as "relatives." Indo-Chinese clients, for example, have to establish a vicarious family-type relationship with the clinician, even assigning him a kinship position (Lum 1986). Tolerating this closeness, which is so different from the distance and objectivity emphasized in most traditional approaches, requires flexibility and comfort with oneself. For clinicians who need the power embodied in their clinical and societal roles, being tested on interpersonal competence will be intolerable; having to assume a family kinship relationship will be unacceptable. These behaviors require an alteration in the power differential that is inherent in those roles.

Using self-disclosure is also a way of equalizing the relationship, of assuming a nonpower, nonhierarchical stance. Such a stance can be important in work with any client who is distrustful of others and who fears being used or exploited. Fears of exploitation and abuse are common responses that clients bring when they have experienced rejection, denigration, or deprivation. Whether such experiences have been a consequence of family interaction or other experiences, including those connected with cultural identity, practitioners must respond in ways to diminish such fears. Equalizing the relationship and adopting a nonhierarchical, nonpower stance accomplishes such a purpose.

A nonpower, nonhierarchical stance is particularly useful for engaging Afro-American clients who often measure the interpersonal competence of practitioners by their ability to diminish the perceived power differential between themselves and the client (Gibbs 1980, p. 200). Helping the client to perceive the practitioner as a peer and collaborator can be critical to success with persons from this cultural group. Research has documented a connection between such a stance and client improvement. Treatment effectiveness with clients from a low-income, predominately Afro-American neighborhood was related to democratic values or non-authoritarianism on the part of the therapist (Solomon 1982, p. 178).

Research also revealed that despite their acknowledgement of the importance of such a stance, a group of social workers objected strongly to the necessity of adopting it. The researcher concluded that such a stance is not easy for practitioners because they are deprived "of many of their customary protections, myths and sources of individual satisfaction ... they found it difficult to experience the loss of control that is inevitable" (McGowan 1988, p. 25).

Not only must practitioners be able to equalize their relationship with clients when this is indicated, but in some situations they must be able to take a "one-down" position. For example, there are numerous situations where clinicians must have the ability to take a learner, nonexpert role. Practitioners routinely must become learners about the realities of the client's life and the meaning that the client attributes to the culture. Greenson allowed his analysand to educate him about Black life and reality (Greenson, Toney, Lim, and Romero 1982, p. 183). He identified the dangers inherent in this task, the feelings and behaviors he noted in himself. He described, for example, his resistance to hearing information that disputed his beliefs, his sense of disbelief, the constant feelings of shame and guilt that he struggled to manage, and the battle he had to wage with his own prejudice (and also that of his patient).

In order to effectively work with culturally different others, practitioners must be ready to visit the client's community, to become involved in the culture (Leighton 1982), to walk the streets, observing people at work and home, and to meet with community leaders (Green 1982; Lum 1986). When distance from culturally different others is necessary for comfort, when practitioners cannot control their fears or need to hang onto their fantasies, beliefs, or stereotypes, they cannot engage in these tasks.

Accepting the expertise of others with different belief systems is another task that demands the ability to assume a nonpower stance. In dealing with clients when religion and spirituality are intricately connected with culture or with the client's perception of the problem, clinicians must be able to enlist priests, ministers, or other religious specialists as consultants (Mendes 1982). In fact, the use of cultural helpers, persons such as community leaders, neighbors, and others who are familiar with the culture and have knowledge about norms and cultural practices can be key to effectiveness.

Both collaboration and practitioner-as-learner are illustrated in the following episode. Here the practitioner became a learner, not about the client's culture, but in relation to a skill which the client possessed:

After a year of work, Mrs. H., a Black middle-aged client, was judged by her first therapist, a White social work student, as too resistant to engage in treatment. Her second therapist, also a White social work student, engaged her rapidly in discussing her concerns about her grandson. However, it was not until several months later that a real change occurred in the relationship. The worker received a sewing machine for Christmas. She noted that Mrs. H., despite the poverty and other problems with which she struggled, had developed a talent in handwork and asked if Mrs. H. would teach her to sew. After several lessons and shopping for material, Mrs. H. demonstrated a new level of trust and felt safe enough to reveal herself to the worker. What she had guarded carefully was a fear of falling apart, of disappearing, or going crazy. At the end of several months, some modest treatment goals, thought to be impossible by the first worker and her clinical team, were realized. (E. Pinderhughes 1983)

In this example the assumption of a teaching role enabled the client to experience a sense of power in relation to the clinician; this changed not only the helping relationship but the course of intervention and the client's coping strategies.

A clinician's use of self-disclosure and reciprocity also helped a poor, depressed, acting-out adolescent Black male with an extreme sense of inadequacy and incompetence (manifested in inability to read beyond first-grade level) to develop a sense of competence and an expectation of mutual interaction with others. The therapist observed the client's "hidden hunger" for the children's picture books that were located in the treatment room. She also observed his sense of shame about this incompetence and made him comfortable by commenting that she enjoyed them, too (self-disclosure). They began to read some books together, and this became a major strategy in the treatment process. When the client then brought in his comic books, they read these together, too. In return for being "taught to read," the client taught the therapist how to protect herself from muggers, robbers, and rapists (Paster 1985, pp. 413–416).

When clinicians stubbornly persist in working with clients and refuse to employ these strategies which are critical for their empowerment, such clinicians are exploiting their clients and using them to protect themselves. Passing by or failing to pick up a reference to ethnic or racial identity or responding to such a reference by assigning an interpretation different from the one offered by the client are examples of such self-protection. When practitioners are uncomfortable about differences or cultural issues, they are then more likely to engage in maneuvers which protect them from facing the discomfort that would be mobilized by the exploration of such issues. This avoidance gives clients the impression that the subject is unimportant or even dangerous (Lum 1986). It also encourages clients to deny or minimize their own cultural background. Colluding in avoidance of the subject of cultural identity can also be motivated by anxieties which the client has. Although in some instances the client's avoidance of the subject may be based on his wish to identify with the clinician, when the clinician colludes in avoiding the topic of cultural identity, he implicitly reinforces denial of the client's sense of self (Greenson et al. 1982, p. 188). For example, Toney described the treatment of a Black female whose conflict about her cultural identity was left unresolved because of a therapist's collusion. The patient's ambivalence about being Black was ignored as well as her reaction of surprise that in moving from a predominately White neighborhood to a Black one, she had found the Black neighborhood to be "superior." The therapist's discomfort with the subject and his "need to appear in a certain light" to the client had prompted him to ignore the patient's conflict and to assume that her earlier perception that all Black neighborhoods are bad was an accurate assumption because it mirrored his own. His silence reinforced her reluctance to say directly that she would rather live in a Black neighborhood. She feared making such a statement because it might offend the therapist. Not only did this push the client to protect the therapist's erroneous (defensive) belief, but the therapist lost an opportunity to help the client explore her cultural identity and reinforce her sense of it as positive.

We have already noted that a focus on strengths is a basic treatment strategy that practitioners must be willing and able to use. A focus on strengths builds on client assets. Such a strategy is the reverse of traditional approaches focusing on weakness or pathology. Instead of uncovering the dysfunctional aspect of a problem, the clinician should be ready to interpret the problem as symptomatic of a positive striving that has been blocked by an obstacle in the client's life (Lum 1986, p. 71). In one case the client's guilt about unwed pregnancy prompted her to use her religious beliefs to punish herself, which caused her to experience an immobilizing depression. Using the client's religious tenets and focusing on the positives and affirmations that are implicit in these beliefs, the practitioner was able to demonstrate to the client how her focus on the negative—on sin, guilt, and suffering—was a distortion of these tenets. After an exploration of her negative preoccupations, the client was advised to "get in touch with her long-standing guilt about her sexual behavior and to avail herself of her religion's rituals of atonement and receiving of forgiveness." The client recovered from her depression and functioned more effectively (Mendes 1982, p. 208).

Clinicians who use stereotypical thinking cannot focus on strengths because stereotypes usually prompt them to have low expectations for their clients. To expect incompetence or deficiency can be deadly, for it can seduce clients into adopting behavior consistent with such expectations, thus setting in motion the process of the self-fulfilling prophecy. This issue is examined

by Geller (1988, p. 128), who suggests the likelihood that therapists have unwittingly provoked Black clients to engage in behaviors that validate the therapists' hidden attitudes. These dynamics operate in the clinical arena just as they do in education,
where minority children internalize the low-expectancy communications of teachers which reflect societal stereotypes.

As a result, the children perceive themselves as incapable
rather than unknowledgeable or blocked from access (Howard
and Hammond 1985, p. 21). The solution is to change expectations and beliefs about the self as incompetent and incapable and
to develop mastery. Clinicians as well as teachers must recognize
the validity of this solution for the work they do.

Relabeling

A focus on strengths in work with populations whose realities
have forced them to cope with extreme powerlessness credits
their struggle to survive and conveys the message that the solutions they have sought to their problems show how hard they
have struggled to be loyal to their culture. Identifying strengths
or relabeling certain behaviors as illustrations of people's determination to survive and do the best they can credits their efforts
to deal with the contradictions inherent in their societal position.
Relabeling is a very effective strategy for dealing with ambivalence and contradiction. This is a fact well understood by family
therapists. Relabeling survival behaviors such as opposition,
stubbornness, reaction formation, passive aggression, manipulation, domination, striking back, and even dependency and passivity can help clients learn that these maneuvers, which they
have chosen, are based on the natural wish of all people to have a
sense of power and be strong. Thus it offers validation for clients'
struggle to cope with the powerlessness embodied in their societal roles, and for their efforts to manage the systemic confusion
and contradiction in which they are trapped. Credit is given to
the adaptability, creativity, and resilience that the use of these
mechanisms present.

A social worker described a successful intervention with a
Puerto Rican client. Using his insight about cultural adaptations,
he recognized the adaptive aspect of the mother's "overprotec-

tiveness." This behavior was seen as related to cultural values and also to the mother's wish to protect her son from the hostile outside environment. He was able to explain to her the usefulness of her protection in the past but to point out its current cost in hindering her son's desired development. He also helped the child to see that his passive–aggressive behavior which had been useful to help manage his anger in a safe way up to now would not help him compete in sports at school, or to make decisions about his life.

By relabeling, the clinician can help a Black mother who tries to compensate for the failure of "support systems" to do their job and becomes controlling, overly central, and smothering to learn that her heroic efforts to organize the family are exhausting her. A Puerto Rican wife who is tolerating abuse can be told that she is trying too hard to show her love (Garcia-Preto 1983). A Mexican woman who blames herself and feels like a failure when she cannot alter her paradoxical situation can be told she is demonstrating how responsible she feels for everyone's happiness and how much she is trying to be loyal to her cultural role (Falicov 1983). An overfunctioning father who is seen as too authoritative and controlling can learn that his effort to provide for and protect his family in the face of disorganizing, non-supportive, often racist external systems has been heroic. Underfunctioning in such a context becomes a strategy to keep peace, avoid conflict, promote harmony, and/or protect family members. Backing off, an underfunctioning father may be told, may be his way of reducing stress in the family, and while it signifies his caring and a wish to make things better for his family, his family needs him to be more closely involved (C. Pinderhughes 1986).

When there has been a focus on strengths and adaptations clients can learn that in some instances it is not they nor their adaptive mechanisms that are at fault but rather the degree to which these have become exaggerated and the inflexibility that marks their use. For example, hard work, toughness, struggle, strength, persistence, determination, adaptability, creativity and caution may have been critical strategies for managing their oppressive societal position. Under stress, however, adaptability can easily slip into inconsistency, toughness and strength into abuse and power behavior, persistence into stubbornness, caution into immobilization, and hard work into driven dedication (C. Pinderhughes 1986).

Adding New Behaviors

Treatment strategies based on concepts of client empowerment (E. Pinderhughes 1983) will not only moderate exaggerated, rigid behaviors in clients but will help them to add new behaviors to their repertoire of effective responses. When an overinvolved Latina mother is helped to see that she can teach her child responsibility by letting him execute more tasks himself she can back off (Falicov 1983). However adaptive certain of these behaviors have been, and despite the fact they may have conveyed a sense of strength and power, clients can be helped to see that many of them can also be costly, exacting a high price. For example, dominance and striking back can keep power struggles going, reinforcing a power stance where winning is an imperative and one must be in charge and/or put others down. Autonomy facilitates going it alone and can create isolation. None of these behaviors supports the reciprocal, collateral behavior that is needed for harmonious relationships. Moreover, the use of behaviors such as opposition, acting in ways that belie one's underneath feelings, passive aggression, manipulation, and dependency mean that one is *always reacting instead of acting* and therefore cannot make decisions, make choices, take initiative, assume responsibility, or exert leadership (E. Pinderhughes 1983). When one is preoccupied with reacting to the initiative of another, one cannot maintain one's own behavioral intent nor behave according to one's own goals and beliefs. Such behavior does not foster the strong and positive sense of self and the high degree of self-differentiation that people need to cope with their realities. Effective intervention means showing clients that there are *other ways to be strong*. For example, making the decision not to escalate a battle, to take a one-down position and to be vulnerable, are also ways of taking initiative and showing strength. Tolerance for vulnerability can be an important capacity to develop for persons whose survival strategies have pushed them to become rigid and defensively power oriented.

Being assertive in ways that do not reinforce power relationships or put others down is another way of being strong that is not reactive. So is the ability to negotiate and compromise. Such abilities are enhanced by strategies that encourage people as individuals and as members of families to share perspectives and to identify their *personal* goals, values, and beliefs. For example, a clinician working with a dysfunctional family attempted repeatedly through relabeling to block the family members' continuance of escalating battles with one another. Finally, she insisted that each person's comments be limited to observations about his or her own behavior. Whenever anyone began to focus on the behavior of another, even when not in an attacking mode, the speaker was immediately interrupted. Without other family members to focus on, the lack of clarity on the part of individuals about their own wishes, beliefs, goals, and meaning became obvious. Long silences and an atmosphere of depression prevailed before some members were able to begin making statements about individual perceptions and feelings. The more one becomes clear about one's own beliefs, goals, and objectives, the more one is able to accept differences from others and the less one is inclined to get into conflict with others over these differences.

Sharing perspectives, values, beliefs, and sources of meaning in a person's life helps to clarify the ambiguity, contradictions and ambivalence inherent in dual identity and to enhance the readiness to cope with these. As we have already noted, for minority persons of color, resolution of this duality may not be possible because of the dynamics involved in their societal role. Thus identification and clarification of this duality and the vulnerability it can create for interpersonal and individual conflict may be the best that can be expected (Harris and Balgopal 1980). To do this work, practitioners must have a strong sense of self and cultural identity and a capacity for tolerating ambivalence and contradiction.

Practitioners must be willing to take the time and energy to sort out these complexities and to assist in the development of these new behaviors, which may be unfamiliar and foreign to their values. They must be able to manage the impatience and annoyance they may feel and not run away, despite the kinds of fears described by one worker:

> I was really afraid to be important to her. I was afraid to see her pain and experience it with her. I was afraid if I got too close, I'd feel the helplessness of her life and become as immobilized by it as she was.

This worker succeeded in confronting her fears, and was then able to engage her Haitian client.

Some workers find themselves responding to these additional burdens by exaggerating things that make the treatment difficult (Greenson et al. 1982, p. 188). A White social worker described the avoidance she found herself using when her work with minority clients appeared stressful: "At the first sign of resistance, I withdraw. When they talk about flaky Whites, I go blank."

The work is not made easier by the fact that clients who are people-of-color have their prejudices and stereotypes, too, and will invoke defenses and resistances based on them. While their testing behavior may have evolved out of their experiences and represent an expectable approach to strangers who belong to a powerful oppressive group (either in terms of race, ethnicity, or class), it may also be fed by internal demands such as anxiety about difference, or anxiety about aspects of themselves that they project defensively. Perceptions of Whites as angry, dangerous, and "out to get them" may be based on internal need as well as reality. The same may be true of the way they perceive practitioners from their own ethnic group as exploiting or rejecting. Behavior that defends against internal anxiety can prompt clients to distance and resist so that they will be unable to take advantage of the assistance offered by practitioners. Openness and acceptance on the part of clients may be difficult to induce, but a successful outcome requires that clients be helped to suspend and control their prejudices too. Again, by ensuring that clients perceive them as trustworthy and respectful, practitioners can enable clients to lower defenses and face the anxiety that their prejudices and stereotypes have protected them from.

Practitioners who are people-of-color bring their own baggage, too, which must be managed in the interest of the client. A Puerto Rican social worker considered how her tendency to manage racism by avoiding Whites did not prepare her for the White client to whom she had just been assigned. She had justified her avoidance by a conviction that the pain of Whites was minor compared to that of her people. "Why should I waste my time with problems that are molehills instead of mountains. I couldn't see that they have serious pain too."

The baggage that minority practitioners bring can also seriously threaten work with persons from their own group. A Mexican-American psychologist resented intensely any reference to herself as minority or a person-of-color. She was incensed on discovering that her assignment to an inner city mental health center had been predicated on the assumption that she would be empathic and effective with the Black and Mexican clients there. She viewed this assignment as an inferior one and had great difficulty with clients who saw race or ethnicity as a common bond with her. In the cross-cultural seminar that she and all other staff members were required to attend it became clear that she did not perceive herself as a minority person and that this meaning was related to her background; she had grown up in a community that was predominantly Mexican. Her resentfulness in being assigned Mexican and Black clients however appeared to indicate that she had some confusion about others' perception of her as minority, and some ambivalence and sense of negativity in relation to her Mexican-American identity. Similarly, a psychologist who identified herself as Chicana described her struggle to achieve positive identity and reflected on how her previous identity conflict and use of denial had ill-prepared her for work with clients of her own background. Growing up in a White middle-class suburban community, she perceived herself as like her peers. Said she:

> I did not want to be Chicana. When my Anglo boyfriend's parents refused to accept me, I was devastated and tried to deny even more. I refused to join the Chicano group at college, had only Anglo friends, and even married Anglo. When I began to get interested in my Chicana identity, the marriage broke up. My marriage had meant that I had to deny who I was. At that point I was totally incapable of helping my people.

Because she had rejected her cultural heritage, this young psychologist managed, at that point in her development, to avoid assignment to any Mexican-American clients. This was no doubt fortunate, since her sense of negativity about her cultural background would have made her dangerous to these clients. She, however, worked hard to change this negative cultural meaning. Eventually, she was able to acquire a positive sense of value and a strong sense of security about her identity, becoming deeply committed to helping clients from her own background. She also found that her newfound sense of competence and comfort extended to work with clients who were not Mexican Americans. She was even able to handle denigration and put-downs of Latino cultures by these clients who often were unaware of her identity.

Instead of ignoring these cultural micro-aggressions, her strategy was one of helpful exploration in which she would identify herself as Chicana and examine with these clients the sources of their attitudes. Such behavior requires strong, positive cultural identity and sense of self.

But other responses to one's cultural identity can also result in unhelpful interactions with clients. Practitioners may have a cultural blind spot, perceiving those who share their cultural identity as just like themselves. In such situations they may assume that the client's experience has been exactly like their own, failing to recognize the uniqueness of the client or to explore specific meanings for him (Spiegel 1984).

Appropriate Exercise of Power

While practitioners must be ready to use equalizing and one-down procedures when necessary, they must also take care to exercise power appropriately. They must be comfortable with appropriate exercise of their power and able to set limits and make demands of clients in accordance with treatment goals. An Anglo social worker was terrified of her power as a house parent in a children's home. She was immobilized about "making a decision about discharge that could determine the course of my Latino client's life." In professional situations she had usually found ways to avoid such tasks.

Clinicians must be able to handle the manipulative, provocative behavior of clients who, as we have learned, may use such behavior to defend against a pervasive sense of powerlessness. Clients learn to use manipulation because it works. Consider, for example, the case of a frustrated Afro-American mother who found that her teenaged son's condition showed no change after an eight-week inpatient hospitalization except for an increase in his use of "slick," manipulative behavior. Angered at this outcome, the mother responded with manipulation, too. Intimidating the White staff who could not cope with her loud talking nor effectively silence her, she "was literally running the session." In situations like this practitioners too often withdraw or get rid of the client instead of using skills they have to be "directive, confrontive, active and limit-setting when it is in the best interest of the client" (Ferguson 1982).

Clinicians must be aware that their responses to their own position in society may interfere with their readiness to use their
power. We have seen the importance of recognizing these responses and being able to control them so that they do not interfere. When clinicians cannot do this, they will "work out their
own conflict on their clientele" (Ferguson 1982, p. 128). In essence, they will get their clients to protect them.

The capacity of the clinician to exercise power appropriately
is most rigorously tested in work with inner-city adolescents,
whose experiences with powerlessness have been pervasive. Culture and power have influenced the gamut of issues with which
they struggle—"sexuality, aggression, dependence, impulse control, grandiosity, omnipotence, helplessness, poverty, injustice,
racism, unreasonable authority and more" (Paster 1985, p. 413).
The strategies that are effective in work with this population can
be executed successfully only by persons who are comfortable
with themselves and with their own power needs. High self-
esteem, which we have learned is in part dependent on a clear
and positive sense of cultural identity, is needed along with a
strong sense of self-differentiation. Practitioners must have attained a level of functioning wherein their "own life goals are
not too dependent on therapeutic outcome" (Paster 1985, p. 412),
to guarantee that goals and process will be determined in accordance with client, not practitioner, needs.

Only when practitioners have acquired these capacities can
they creatively combine mutuality and reciprocity with setting
limits and making demands, a competency that is critical in work
with this population. Only such attributes and capacities will enable practitioners to control the feelings mobilized by the power
tactics these clients will use, and to behave appropriately with
them. Clients use these tactics to defend against their sense of
terror that treatment will change them against their will. They
are used to defend against their underlying fear that closeness
with the practitioner will cause them to fuse or disappear. These
clients will go to any lengths to dazzle the practitioner with their
"omnipotent grandiosity" and to intimidate and negatively ex-
pose the practitioner's shortcomings. Their efforts to one-up the
therapist will be mixed with evidence that they also want limits
to be set and are struggling mightily with dependency needs
and perceptions of the clinician as omnipotent.

Client behavior that reinforces this perception of omnipotence in the clinician can be seductive, just as behavior that one-ups the clinician can produce serious discomfort. Responding appropriately to both sets of behaviors requires that clinicians be comfortable about themselves, well differentiated, flexible, firmly in charge of their own power needs and responses and of the feelings such clients mobilize. Our discussion of power dynamics in the examination of the experiential data gathered from practitioners' experiences illustrated the struggles they get into when they cannot do this.

In rejecting clients' perceptions of them as omnipotent, clinicians must foster an image of themselves as accepting and non-manipulative, i.e., honest and nonpunitive, as individuals who will not retaliate or escalate a power struggle. This can be done (1) by demonstrating mutuality in setting goals, using humor, telling stories; (2) by offering the client opportunity to exercise choice among options. For example, while empathy is offered concerning the client's ambivalence about making a commitment to treatment, there is explicit recognition that the client may wish to leave. After a brief agreed-upon trial of treatment, he is offered an opportunity to decide if he wishes to continue. The client's perception of the clinician as omnipotent is also rejected by establishing clearly that the client is the authority on his own feelings and the one responsible for his own behavior (and that he therefore is not controlled by the clinician).

But at the same time, clinicians must also foster an image of themselves as able to set limits and make demands appropriately. They can do this by identifying and empathizing with the feelings underlying the client's power-driven behavior, by taking a stand about destructive activities, and by demanding that clients recognize their own best interests and live up to high positive standards of behavior and accomplishment. Expectation is key here, for only if clinicians believe that a client can change can they hold out such expectations. And the expectations can only be held out when practitioners are free of stereotypical perceptions of clients that are based on their own societal roles and on their own need to maintain these.

Practitioners must be ready and able to help their clients cope with cultural conflict. Being caught between two cultures because of transitions such as intermarriage, immigration, or other transitions can lead to conflict on a variety of levels. There can be conflict in values, in identity, and in relationships. Practitioners may work on any or all of these levels to help clients relieve the pain and discomfort that are embodied in cultural conflict. The most common area of focus is identity conflict. Here treatment goals center on helping the client to achieve a sense of integration and consolidation. As noted earlier, full integration of fragmented identity and resolution of conflict is not always possible for persons from certain groups. This is particularly true for denigrated groups who are denied full access to the larger society and for whose members structural societal arrangements will always involve some exclusion. Such persons must be able to achieve a strong, coherent sense of biculturalism and be able to minimize the associated conflict and confusion.

Biculturalism or the ability to live in two worlds to tolerate the associated conflicts in cultural values and cultural practices can be an important asset. Practitioners must be able to help their clients achieve this state and to reduce the destructive conflict and confusion inherent in the bicultural condition. This task is indeed a challenge. Sometimes practitioners will find that being able to help clients achieve this goal involves a change in themselves as well as the client. A group of teachers in a private school learned this as a consequence of a meeting in which they were discussing their distress about a number of problems related to Black, inner-city students. They resented the parents whom they saw as too demanding of their children. They could not empathize with the parents' usually unspoken expectation that a Black child had to be pushed to perform as well as or better than Whites in order to compete with them. They also resented the parents' demand that teachers understand the two worlds in which their children had to live. One teacher put it this way:

> A mother explained when I was questioning her values about allowing him to fight, "I'll take care of his behavior; you take care of his education. Where we live he has to be tough and be able to fight. I'm not going to stop that. You set your standards here and I'll see that he understands he has to abide by them."

In this example, the parent perceived a reality in which her child had to live in two different worlds and seemed ready to help her child manage this. But the teachers, who also needed to understand and support the child's ability to do it, did not. These teachers learned that if they were to be able to support the child's efforts to negotiate this duality, they, as well as the child and his parents, must be able to cope with the conflict in values.

As they struggled with the problems this created for them, the teachers acknowledged their conviction that their own values and those of the school were the more desirable. They judged extremely negatively the parents' attitude toward authority and reflected on the conflict they perceived between the attitude of the school and that of the parents in regard to discipline. They described their experiences with parents who were "rigid and harsh," who stood over their children demanding that they perform. This attitude that discipline required the presence of an adult at all times meant to them that the children had little judgment of their own competence and were completely dependent on the adults' provision of structure. This was repugnant to the teachers, who noted that some of the children were frightened whenever report cards were issued, and some teachers admitted they sometimes distorted the report to protect the child from the parent's wrath. They began to understand that such efforts to help the children could, in fact, be undermining the children's ability to tolerate the inconsistency between home and school. What the children needed was a sense that while the values at school were different, those of their parents were not being undermined. The teachers, thus, needed to be able to convey respect for the cultural values of the families of their students, which were so different from their own. They must be able to function as a bridge, respecting the children's cultural values while simultaneously upholding the values of the school. Time, energy, and effort on their part were needed to negotiate this biculturalism, which was critical to the task of helping these children compete with children who did not have this baggage. Thus, while they expected the parents and children to change, they, the teachers, must change too.

The overall goal of assisting the client to enhance cultural identity means resolving conflicts "within the family, between the family and the community, or in the wider context in which the family is embedded" (McGoldrick 1983, p. 23). Uncertainty on the part of clinicians as to whether or not specific behavior indicates value or identity conflict requires that they observe carefully and explore thoroughly to determine the answer. Discomfort about their own backgrounds can feed clinicians' sense of confusion and a feeling of being intrusive about opening up such a subject. Clarity of thinking and comfort with their own cultural identities are important to facilitate the readiness to pick up the many nuances and variations in relation to cultural identity that bring people pain.

Practitioners who are uncomfortable with difference may be unable to demonstrate the flexibility in behavior that is necessary to cope with the differing perception they encounter in clients. As the leader of a group of parents whose children were hospitalized in an inpatient service, a White social worker was uncertain about how to proceed with a Black mother. The goal of the group was stated as developing ability to become able to communicate feeling through examining past and present experiences in which feelings may have been buried and not recognized. While the social worker evaluated this client, the only Black in the group, as possessing a presence of strength and competence, she was troubled that the client did not respond to invitations from the worker to discuss her background or "look at all sources of her pain." The worker felt that any more direct invitation to discuss her racial experiences in the group would "put her on the spot," and thus left the suggestion vague. In the worker's mind also was a question as to whether the client was already alienated from cultural connection, since she now lived in an all-White neighborhood.

The students of color in the class were certain that there was no real evidence that this client's behavior was rooted in cultural conflict. Rather, they believed that the client may have felt reasonably that the group would not be empathic to her experiences, which were so different from those of the others, and that the group would not extend support to her. They, therefore, felt that the issue should not have been allowed to drop, that the leader should have recognized the reality of the client's difference from the other members of the group, invited her to discuss her reactions to this, and invited the group to give its support. Clearly they did not have the anxiety about confronting the client, nor about inviting the support of the group, that the White class members had. They also questioned why the issue of this mother's being the only Black in the group had not been raised even privately with her before she joined the group. Aware that the client's real feelings might vary from extreme discomfort to almost none at all (especially since being the only one in a group is a common experience for Blacks), their understanding differed greatly from that of Whites, some of whom had never thought about the issue. Others, like the leader, were aware of the issue but uncertain what to do and also fearful that bringing it up would cause the client to feel pushed into discussing something she was not ready to, and thus would become alienated. Since it is possible that the client might not have been ready to discuss her racial experiences in the group, it would have been useful to acknowledge that her racial identity embodied experiences that had special significance to her that might not be understood by others in the group. This would have raised the issue of race in a nonthreatening way and avoided protecting either the Black group member or the others.

When practitioners have a negative sense of cultural identity and are uncomfortable with differences, this must be confronted so that it will not affect their work negatively. A Filipino psychiatric resident who had grown up alienated from her cultural connection had internalized a negative sense of her cultural self. Now in a compulsory cross-cultural seminar that required her to examine her cultural experiences, she remembered a significant episode that occurred at age ten. While trying on a dress she had looked in the mirror and asked herself, "Who is that Chinese girl?" Now, attempting to deal with the feelings that for so many years had caused her to dissociate her Asian identity from her image of herself and to use such denial as a defense, she reacted with headaches, which she experienced regularly on the day of the seminar. She also found herself scheduling her patients into the seminar time slot. Her expression of discomfort with her identity escalated dramatically when she was assigned to work with a fellow countryman who had been hospitalized with a suicidal depression and drug addiction. Her response approached panic:

> There are rumors that he has been assigned to my ward so I can treat him. I am scared of the expectations. I'd have to be super-good to treat him. Everyone is watching. So much has happened around this case. Another countryman whom I'd never met and who is on the staff at the hospital came immediately up, nervously demanding to know what's wrong with him. He then brought in a lot of other countrymen who have been in and out. They have a whole network. But how dare he get sick. Doesn't he know the trouble with us now? We have to be strong!

Fortunately, the compulsory self-examination that was required by the cross-cultural seminar enabled her to confront her anxiety and self-hatred. The success of her efforts was manifest in her work with a Black male patient who was hospitalized with severe depression precipitated by problems at work. Whereas she had previously avoided any focus on the meaning that cultural identity might have for this fair-skinned male who was married interracially and living in a White neighborhood, she became able to explore, empathize with her client's feelings of isolation and abandonment, and help him to link this response to his cultural identity with other responses that mirrored an internal sense of rejection and abandonment.

Resolution of cultural identity conflict constitutes a step in differentiation and requires selecting from one's cultural values, beliefs, and practices those which one wishes to emphasize. It is important that people separate those that have essential meaning from those embraced "for emotional reasons," and doing this involves developing awareness of cultural variability. (McGoldrick 1983, p. 23). Indeed, when cultural conflict becomes reflected in problematic relationships between family members, practitioners must help each to identify his or her own particular values and to understand how, because of different perceptions and experiences, these may differ from another's.

Several experts have discussed the significance of dealing with identity conflict and consolidating fragmented identity. Klein has described her model, ethnotherapy, that seeks resolution from a structured examination of positive, negative, and ambivalent aspects, and of the meaning one connects to one's cultural group. There is also a focus on the sources of that personally internalized meaning, including the key figures with whom one has identified, and the definition of the group by the majority culture. This method, conducted in a group format, mobilizes the powerful fears and stereotypes that have been internalized vis-à-vis the cultural group and "divest[s] them of their magical power" and at the same time uses examination of collective conflicts to facilitate examination of personal, culturally connected issues (Klein 1976, p. 11).

The steps in the model suggested by Comas-Diaz (1988, pp. 342–344) consist of (1) "mirroring the fragmented identity" (i.e., the clinician underscores areas in the client's life where the fragmented identity is manifest); (2) exploring the areas of inconsistency within his own cultural background and then between that background and the second culture; and (3) mediating the conflict by helping the client to "name" the identity conflict, and to connect different aspects of the conflicted identity to the self, which moves the client closer to a more integrated cultural identity. A key element in this strategy is the clinician's use of self to identify areas of commonality in her cultural experience and that of the client. For example, a recently migrated Jamaican woman found that her valued identity as light-skinned and Jamaican was threatened by perception of her in this country as Black. The client was assisted to redefine her identity as a Jamaican woman living in the United States. This was done through an exploration of Jamaican identity, her experiences of culture shock and mourning for lost aspects of her culture, the perceptions of herself as connected with the Jamaican community in her present location, and her perception of the differences between Jamaican women in Jamaica and those living in the United States. She was then able to consolidate her identity perception of herself as a Jamaican in the United States, became more comfortable with herself as she achieved this integration, and was able to cope with cultural inconsistencies such as being labeled "Black" when her Jamaican identity had been "colored."

As mentioned, a critical issue in the success of this intervention was the therapist's use of the areas of commonality in cultural experience that existed between her and the client. These areas, which included Caribbean background, upbringing in Catholic faith, and the experience of cross-cultural transition, were named to enable the client to observe her clinician's comfort with herself and her cultural identity in the United States. Using themselves in this way, especially when pain, discomfort, and negativity have been involved in their cultural self-definition, requires practitioners to have attained clarity and a sense of positive value about their own cultural identity. When clinicians have achieved this and are secure, they can use their cultural experience as a source of empathy rather than a source of anxiety that must be defended against. An Irish social worker explained her success with a West Indian client: After months of work, the client was ready to examine her experience of abuse at the hands of an Irish stepfather after which she was sent away to live with relatives. The worker used her own Irish identity to forward the work. Acknowledging that she herself was Irish, the worker told the client that she found it disheartening to learn that someone who had shared her culture had inflicted so much pain. She also empathized with the client's anger at her stepfather's unfeeling response and abuse, clearing the way for the client to develop strategies to manage its consequences. Such strategies may be controversial since they contradict the prohibition against the clinician's allowing issues from his personal life to intrude upon the clinical process. Such prohibitions exist for very good reasons, one of which is that they protect against a focus on the clinician's needs and thus clinician abuse of the client. These strategies must be carefully used to bridge differences and promote identification with the clinician. They are not needed if resistance is low or when the relationship is already strong, and should be used with caution when clients are preoccupied with curiosity about the clinician.

When clinicians themselves have successfully transcended conflict over cultural values, they can use their experience as a tool. A Canadian social worker used her own experience with conflict over her French and Anglo-Saxon roots, which was compounded by the family's frequent moves, to help her client. She saw these experiences with transition and her struggle to establish her own values of survival as preparation for effective assistance to her Panamanian female client. Viewing herself as a "resource of cultural information[1] with intense sensitivity about negotiating a new culture," she saw her success with the client as the result of being able to translate her experience into one that was useful for her client.

Functioning as a cultural broker, she encouraged the client to compare her life in the U.S. with that in Panama, to examine the sense of loss she had experienced, to identify the goals and values of American and Panamanian culture, determining what she perceived as useful here and what American values she wanted to adopt and have her children learn. In family sessions the worker's support enabled the client to move beyond a conflicted relationship with her mother to a physical separation that before had been culturally incongruent and had seemed frightening (i.e., the American value of individualism had seemed threatening to her Panamanian value of affiliation). Living apart they were able to plan joint endeavors that benefited the client's children as well as the client and her mother. Part of this worker's strategy to help her Panamanian client, who was unprepared to cope with racism and the harassment she encountered here in the U.S., involved education about fair housing laws and assistance in the apartment search with the worker, herself, checking some of the "taken" apartments to see if refusal was racially motivated.

In long-term psychotherapy, identity conflict is a theme throughout the process. It is returned to again and again as exploration links the conflict with various issues involved in the client's functioning. A psychologist, son of an Anglo-Saxon mother and Afro-American father, whose parents never married and who grew up as the only non-White member of his nuclear (including three siblings) and extended family, had had no contact with other Afro-Americans. Although he was readily identifiable as Black, there had been no opportunity to develop a sense of Black as meaning anything other than negative societal stereotypes. He had no sense of affiliation with other Blacks and was devastated when he encountered rejection from Whites because of his racial identity. In response, he had developed a compulsive need for success, which was fueled by a fierce determination to prove that he was different from the stereotype, that he was special and therefore not Black. The effort that this compulsion required had kept him perpetually exhausted and was now creating health problems; at age 28 he already suffered from high blood pressure. Constantly confronted with identification by others as Black, he was continually engaged in determined efforts to prove otherwise. But he found himself entrapped and thoroughly frightened when, as a clinician-in-training, he was sought after as a therapist for Black males, especially for adolescents in the throes of identity crisis. He became unable to function at his usual perfectionistic level and the sense of immobilization and panic that he experienced due to his identity conflict became unbearable when he was assigned a racially mixed 8-year-old male whose Black father had deserted. In treatment, the resolution of this ethnic identity conflict involved an examination of the way his ethnic/racial identity and its meaning had permeated every level of his functioning including his image of himself as an individual, as a male, as a family member, as a friend, a worker, and a professional.

For example, he handled the issue of psychological fusion with his mother by invoking the specter of race and how different they were. He used race as a reason why he could not experience anger at his mother: how could he when she had sacrificed so much to rear a child other mothers would easily have aborted or abandoned? He used race to explain his sense of distance in the family and to avoid acknowledging how this distance defended against his fear of fusion, and so forth. Until he achieved some comfort with his racial identity, none of these issues could be explored. It was necessary to explore his experiences, his perceptions, and his feelings in each of the areas noted above so that they could be integrated into his image of himself as an Afro-American whose sense of himself involved openness and acceptance and whose cultural identity meant pride and value. He was also encouraged to have real experiences that would reinforce this new image: learn Black history, find Black friends.

In another case the conflict immobilizing the client stemmed not so much from identity conflict as conflict in relationships fueled by differences in the definition of the client's cultural identity. A client, who identified herself as Spanish American, grew up in northern New Mexico where her family had lived under conditions of relative sociocultural isolation for generations. With no previous history of difficulty she became extremely conflicted at college upon engagement with Chicano students who were personally assertive, less inhibited in personal decorum, and more liberal politically. Unable to cope with rejection and disdain from these peers because of her "Spanish" identification, she began to question her own culturally learned passivity, conservatism in politics, and in sexual mores in contrast to their different behavioral preferences (Ruiz and Padilla 1977). Her identification as Spanish was probably not, as her peers believed, an attempt to deny her "Mexicanness," since she did identify with Latino culture, although this identity was less strong than theirs. While her problem of personal low self-esteem, loneliness, and mild depression may have been fueled by intrapsychic sources, intervention was directed to her estrangement from her Chicano peers. To reinforce a sense of self-esteem, she was reminded of her strengths (good mind, study habits, perseverance) and encouraged to interact with and confront her Chicano peers. She was prepared for this with the information that to Chicanos, Mexican Americans who identify themselves as Spanish are believed to be denying their heritage and that her peers did not know that her self-definition did not represent a deliberate effort on her part to renounce this identity. This successful intervention did not focus on her ambivalence or depression but on developing self-assertive skills and on expanding the definition of Chicano for both her cultural peers and herself.

Efforts to empower clients must not leave individuals disconnected from their cultural supports, except for very good reasons. Such reasons include the presence of a clear, nonambivalent intention to maintain a cut-off from family and other cultural systems or the existence of an extremely disorganized, dysfunctional family system which prevents a member from reaching goals of self-actualization and which remains unmotivated for change. Empowerment efforts can produce isolation for clients when change is engineered in such a way that the violation of cultural prescriptions compounds the conflicts that clients already have and pushes them to abandon their cultural roots. As we have seen, isolation from the cultural group can cause disastrous consequences. For example, care must be used with strategies that promote egalitarianism since incorrectly used they conflict with well-known customs in some cultures that emphasize hierarchical relationships and respect for authority in the person of experts, high status individuals, older persons, and males. Especially in immigrant and first generation families, many such cultural prescriptions remain strong. This is consistent with the caveat that work with Puerto Rican families must respect the male as the traditional head of the family (Garcia-Preto 1983). This concern is echoed with regard to East Asian families where roles are specifically hierarchical and more formalized by rules and behavior "to a greater extent than in most other cultures" (Shon and Ja 1983, p. 209). Strategies that facilitate independence and self-assertion may run counter to cultural values emphasizing collaterality and affiliation. Clinicians are warned against pushing Mexican or East Asian adolescents to become independent and leave home, which may violate cultural injunctions that young people remain close to parents and create problems for the mother who may depend on her children to negotiate a cultural transition (Falicov 1983; Shon and Ja 1983).

Judgment must be exercised by the practitioner as to the *kind* and *degree* of change in cultural practices or in connection to resources that should be available. Changes that move in the direction of clients' desired goals and at the same time help them to remain involved with important cultural systems may be hard to engineer but critical. Practitioners, thus, must be ready to reinforce supportive connections as well as forge new ones. A psychiatrist was working with a first-generation, middle-aged Italian couple who reported that their stable marriage and gratifying relationship had recently broken down. It appeared that the reason for the deterioration was the husband's severe kidney ailment. But the psychiatrist discovered that, in fact, the real cause was the death of the priest to whom the wife had regularly vented her frustrations over the years. His role as buffer was a cultural tradition that had permitted the marriage to be experienced as relatively gratifying to both partners, and with his death, the wife had nowhere to "unload." The psychiatrist, after careful evaluation of the intense and repetitive complaints of the wife, determined that despite her threats and although greatly stressed, she was intensely invested in her family and did not want to leave. In fact, no one in the family, including the wife herself, was willing to support her ambivalent demands for separation. He then assumed the buffer role which he saw as critical for the recovery of the patient. Open conflict between the partners ceased. However, when he went on vacation, a social worker was assigned to the wife who did not learn of the psychiatrist's strategy. Upon hearing the same complaints that the wife had unloaded on the priest and the psychiatrist, this clinician pursued different goals, focusing on the wife's autonomy, a life of her own, and divorce. Support such as that supplied by the priest and the psychiatrist does not constitute true empowerment, and there are those who would view it as a reinforcement of the female subordinate role. Nevertheless, that support constituted a viable option since it was key in the achievement of comfort for the wife with a difficult relationship that she was unwilling to terminate.

The role of broker or mediator is a key one for practitioners whether they are helping clients deal with value, identity, or relationship conflict. Mediating and resolving conflict in any of these areas can be critical in preserving relationships and preventing relationship breakdown and isolation. The use of mediation means that empowerment efforts are directed toward the relationship rather than toward any one individual. This skill requires that practitioners be able to offer solutions that are satisfactory to all parties. They must be able to help people compromise. For example, in a Polish second-generation family, the parents were distressed at their adult daughter's plan to live independently, which violated cultural expectations. The daughter, on the other hand, was depressed at this cultural limitation to her growth. The clinician helped effect a compromise whereby the parents were involved in choosing and approving of the apartment, and the daughter promised to visit once or twice weekly (Jalali 1988). Negotiation and compromise under these conditions can be seen as an act that encourages growth in both parties. Both are assisted to become bicultural and to have a foot in the culture of the other rather than each remaining connected only to one culture. This is the most challenging task for clinicians. For it means that they must respect both cultural "sides," despite the fact that they may feel more affinity, empathy, or understanding for one than the other. In the examination of ethnicity, we saw this vulnerability of the clinician reflected in the behavior of the Italian social worker who was working with an intermarried couple. She had found herself emotionally supporting the Italian husband in his struggles with his Irish wife.

An Underlying Goal

The achievement of a higher level of self-differentiation and sense of self is an underlying goal of work with many clients. This is particularly true of work with clients from groups where values of affiliation and collaterality often cause them to behave under stress in ways that reinforce poor self-differentiation and an inadequate sense of self (E. Pinderhughes 1982). Work with poor Puerto Rican families, many of whom are labeled unmotivated and unreachable and who are frequently misdiagnosed, has been demonstrated to improve self-differentiation (Ramos-McKay, Comas-Diaz, and Rivera 1988). One approach begins with a didactic process whereby clients are taught to think of themselves as individual human beings who do not have to sacrifice themselves in order to live, who have choices and the capacity to develop, grow, and compete. Innovative adaptations of therapeutic methods that incorporate cultural values and practices have been devised. These techniques place a heavy emphasis on understanding the connections between problems and feelings. Apparently this emphasis has been important because of the cultural prohibition against direct expression of anger, autonomy, or aggression, which can create vulnerability to a variety of dysfunctional behaviors. Strategies have included the use of "future-past techniques" in group treatment with alcoholics. This is a strategy which builds on the value of respect for the elderly using older women to communicate with younger ones in a dialogue that has therapeutic effects. Another technique incorporates the use of espiritistas in a back-and-forth communication with specific individuals in an audience which facilitates catharsis. Other strategies have involved the use of music and drama to identify emotional responses, which is followed by the use of discussion to connect these to personal life situations.

A case example is offered of a poorly educated male from a rural area whose family was disorganized. Recently discharged from hospitalization with a diagnosis of schizophrenia, his participation in such a group eventually enabled him to function at a significantly higher level. At first an observer, he gradually began to risk sharing his own ideas and fears, then moved to discussing his frustrations with other people. As a result, he began to look at himself within his family situation, and began "a long and painful process of transformation." His sense of his own strength helped him to look at his behavior and to recognize what did not work and what needed changing. Eventually divorced, he was able to form a new relationship, and because he proved a responsible, nurturing parent, was granted custody of his children (Ramos-McKay, Comas-Diaz, and Rivera 1988, p. 228).

The necessity of reinforcing cultural connections, identity, and meaning should not mean that cultural adaptations which prove dysfunctional should be reinforced. Any cultural practices that promote difficulties rather than personal growth and change must receive thorough evaluation. The use of folk-healing, for example, which is an attempt by people to get power and control of an unpredictable environment, can reinforce denial of personal responsiblity as a prominent defense. It can be used by helpers as a means of helping individuals adapt to a prevailing social system. This compromises that universal goal of practitioners: "to help clients gain self-trust and control over their lives" (Garcia-Preto 1983, p. 180). When such a goal is kept in mind, clinicians are not confused in their work with clients who proclaim that attempts to help them are destroying their "culture."

In certain cases where cultural adaptations have proved rigid and maladaptive, experts have suggested that exposure to clinicians whose style is based on different values can be helpful. For example, a therapist with a client whose cultural values prompt her to deny feelings might elect "to bring the melting pot into the room" (Jolopinto 1983, p. 49). As in the situation where the natural reserve of an Irish practitioner may provide an excellent balance for Italian impulsiveness (and vice versa), the clinician's style may serve as an antidote (McGoldrick 1983). Such use of one's "cultural self," however, must clearly be based on the goals and needs of the client.

Including the Social Context

Empowerment in work with certain oppressed groups is defined as altering the interaction of the client with the problem environment (Lum 1986, p. 211); changing the paralyzing consequences of negative valuation by the wider society (Solomon 1982, p. 166); assisting the client to develop the ability to cope constructively with the forces that have entrapped him in his systemic role (E. Pinderhughes 1986). Power as well as culture become key dynamics in the structuring of treatment strategies to achieve these goals. Persons from cultural groups whose societal position has created oppressive and stressful realities will benefit from such a focus which directs change efforts toward these larger social systems. Clients must be made aware of the range of effects these systems may have on them. A beginning can be made with a simple educational approach that clarifies the perpetual ambivalence, ambiguity, polarity, and contradiction of the context within which many clients are struggling to function. When clients are informed of their rights and entitlements and are educated as to the effects of the system in which they are entrapped, they become able to sort out what belongs to the system and what belongs to the self. They can understand that the changes which need to occur involve their own responses to the outside systems.

In the following case, treatment for depression focused on changing the client's relationship to the "wider ethnosystem" (Solomon 1982, p. 177). A Black, 50-year-old widower, depressed after his wife's death, became suicidal following treatment that focused on his early development and relationship with caretakers. When treatment focused on his despair over lack of opportunity to develop skills that would have allowed him gratifying employment and growth, he was connected with a self-help group that focused on midlife career changes. As a consequence, he successfully negotiated a franchise as manager of an auto parts store.

Alteration of the social context (Bell, Bland, Houston, and Jones 1983) refers to helping clients change systems that are non-supportive into systems that are. Clients learn that in addition to change in their own responses to outside systems, there must be changes in the responses of outside systems to them.

"Politicization" helps minorities who are people-of-color to identify racism and its part in their problem and learn the skills to cope with it, which include finding ways to direct their anger toward effecting social change (Zuniga-Martinez 1988). A psychoanalyst, addressing the need for such activity in work with female clients queried, "Is it too much to ask of therapists that they attempt to bring such issues to the attention of clients and perhaps a personal example of action as well?" (Siedenberg 1984, p. 4).

Solutions that direct efforts toward societal change are particularly useful when they also promote cultural group cohesion. For example, strategies that enable Indian women to increase competence and self-esteem by helping their people and working for the group can foster the group cohesion needed to effect societal change and can provide an acceptable and needed outlet for aggression (Blanchard 1981).

Central to these goals are strategies that enable clients to exert their own power to secure needed resources. Such strategies include teaching and modeling skills in making alliances, building coalitions, overcoming organizational barriers, and engaging in political action. But whether the needed changes are in themselves, their situations, or the causes of their situations, it is essential that clients learn to perceive themselves as causal agents (Ferguson 1982; Solomon 1982). A social action–based intervention that addresses these goals is used to empower ordinarily unmotivated inner-city youth (Paster 1986). Consistent with the needs and styles of cultural subgroups, it is designed to interrupt these clients' ongoing pervasive experiences with powerlessness by providing meaningful experiences that alter self-conceptions as powerless and worthless and, at the same time, are directed toward system change. Through group action and social advocacy around a community problem, clients learn skills such as planning, delaying, problem-solving, listening to others, and constructive interaction with authority figures. Negative self-concept is altered to one of adequacy, competence, and self-worth. Change occurs as a result of the sense of belonging that results from connection to a group that is successful in influencing powerful others. Participants learn that they can exert some influence over forces in their lives, and that thus they can develop a sense of power individually and collectively. As they learn to value themselves more, the outside authority becomes less idealized, the perceived power differential between them is reduced, and they perceive themselves as critical in the changes that occur. This model requires workers who have attained a sense of self and ability to manage their power needs such that they can "give up the central role of leader and rescuer for one of support and guidance.

Clearly the enormous complexities that mark cultural dynamics and the plethora of approaches that can be used to help people require that practitioners be knowledgeable, flexible, creative, innovative, unafraid of risks, and, at the same time, patient and careful to exercise sound judgment. Most importantly, the soundness of their judgment and the degree of their commitment to their clients will be marked by their ability to use the power embodied in their clinical and social roles in ways that effectively empower their clients.

9

Afterword: Beyond the Cultural Interface

Nonclinical Roles

In the many roles beyond that of therapist-enabler-clinician which practitioners must assume in order to secure services for clients, knowledge of cultural dynamics, of how ethnicity, race, and power influence human functioning, are critical. Helping clients to negotiate the multiple systems that must be involved in their problem-solving efforts requires practitioners to function in a gamut of roles including advocate, teacher, mediator, broker, conferee, liaison, limit-setter, adviser, coach, group leader, consultant, researcher, and organizer. Depending on the structuring of services and the existence or nonexistence of resources, these various roles may be considered as the responsibility of the clinican or they may be performed separately by others. For example, in social agencies such a separate function may be assumed by the case manager, who is responsible for seeing that services are coordinated and that the service delivery system is responsive to the needs of clients.

Case managers, practitioners, and others take on these roles to help clients gain access and learn to use resources in the service delivery network. In these roles they assess, plan, link, monitor, and advocate on behalf of clients in order to remove obstacles to accessibility in relation to eligibility, regulations, and policies. They also maintain relationships with service providers and administrators in other systems who will expedite referrals; ensure responsiveness of services to clients' needs; guard against frag-

197

mentation of services by ensuring continuity of care among institutions, and between phases of illness and recovery; and develop resource systems when none is available (Rubin 1987).

No matter the structure of the agency, effectiveness in executing these roles in ways that validate clients' cultural identity, that enhance clients' ability to function biculturally, and that facilitate mastery and competence hinges on practitioners' understanding of cultural dynamics and on their comfort and security about themselves and their own cultural identity, including their power needs and responses. Without these capacities they will not be prepared to engage clients whose resistance or non-use of services may be related to a variety of issues: ignorance of the existence of the service; expectation that the services will be delivered in a manner so unfamiliar as to create discomfort and confusion; expectation that service will be extended to them with discourtesy and lack of respect; or emphasis on cultural values that do not emphasize seeking help from outsiders.

The assignment of service providers, and the activities in which they engage to assist clients, must be consistent with cultural expectations. For example, approach must respect the significance of privacy and/or anonymity emphasized by Eastern European groups (among whom are Czechoslovakians, Hungarians, Poles, and others), who may not want neighbors and friends to know of their need for help and involvement with helping services (DeVore & Schlesinger 1987). Home visits must take into account the expectation of Italians that in their home the visitor will accept the hospitality that is extended. The persistent, aggressive stance considered so necessary for outreach in resistant cases, must be modified accordingly.

Linking a client successfully with services he or she needs may require the practitioner to accompany the client to appointments, observing how the client interacts with other service deliverers and providing feedback both to them and to the client that will facilitate a better fit between them. These tasks are presumably easier when the services being sought are located in the ethnic community and the practitioners involved thoroughly understand the expectations and practices of the client's cultural group. Even in such agencies, however, some monitoring may be needed to ensure that people do not become the victims of gaps in services and fall between the cracks.

A critical function may be that of interpreting cultural expectations and practices to other practitioners involved with the client so that services can be structured more appropriately. For example, it was important for a day care teacher to learn that her assumption of developmental delay in the 4-year-old Puerto Rican child who waited for her to button his coat might be incorrect, because Latino families do not value independence as do others and mothers may not push children to do this for themselves.

It was equally important that the practitioner explain to the clinic administrator the refusal of an elderly Afro-American woman to keep her appointment with the medical service that was monitoring her diabetic condition. Her "no-show" was due to a sense of outrage at being addressed by her first name. This American practice has been particularly offensive to Afro-Americans as a result of practices during and after slavery where the essence of their powerless societal position was personified in the practice of never addressing them with the usual courtesy of Mr., Mrs., or Miss. The worker sought a guarantee that this information would be the basis for a change of policy within the hospital, so that first names were used only when it was the choice of the patient.

In another instance, a practitioner prepared a teacher for a conference with the anxious parent of a pupil who was performing poorly. The teacher's ability to approach the parent with respect in the face of her apparent indifference about the child's performance was enhanced when she learned that the parent expected to be criticized and blamed as she had been in the past.

And in yet another instance a clinician alerted a protective worker to the fact that Native Americans place a high value on self-reliance in young children, which might mean that evaluation of a parent as negligent and exploitative because she discouraged play while emphasizing work and contributing to the family might be incorrect.

The input from a case manager enabled therapists in the mental health agency to which she referred clients to engage those who were extremely frightened and resistant by telephone first. In one instance it took six months for an Afro-American client to come into the agency. In another case, when a mother who was struggling to stay off welfare by holding two jobs and could not keep appointments at the agency, the therapist held sessions in the client's place of employment on her lunch hour.

It is the task of the service provider to interpret the agency and its policy to the client so that clients will not be confused and overwhelmed by expectations and demands that are different from what was expected. For example, expectation about promptness in appointments is needed information for clients of non-Western cultural groups. When agencies cannot be flexible about this, assisting the client to conform to the policy can be part of a process that ensures a gradual adaptation to the mainstream. This may require special support on the part of the practitioner so that the adaptation process is not experienced as oppressive.

A critical function which practitioners may be called upon to perform is that of removing barriers raised by agencies or other practitioners whose services may be critical but who resist engagement with culturally different clients because of the complexities involved in serving them. Case managers and others who have acquired cultural competence will be ready to advocate for their clients, confronting the resisting system with its failure, articulating how the culturally insensitive behavior must be changed in the interest of a client. They will also be ready to help clients gain access to services which have been denied because of bias. For example, when a White social worker is so prepared she can use her understanding effectively in approaching the colleague who is certain that the Afro-American client being referred for employment counseling does not want to get off welfare and that work with her would be a waste of her time. The practitioner would first investigate reasons for the colleague's opinion and make an effort to help him view her client not as the stereotype being invoked but as a person not only deserving but having the right to such a service. Her ability to help him see the client as a valued person, who can complete training successfully and whose performance may be gratifying, will surely depend on the practitioner's clarity about her own identity as a White person and her ability to imbue this identity with positive meaning. Confusion about her own racial identity and uncertainty about its meaning can prevent the practitioner from behaving appropriately on behalf of her client. As we learned in the examination of the experiential data, it is often very difficult for White people to confront other White people about their racial stereotypes. If the worker does not have clarity and a sense of value about her racial identity and about the behavior she wishes to engage in to reinforce that positive value, she will react with

confusion and inactivity, will be unable to challenge the stereotype and may fail to secure the needed service for her client.

Should the practitioner, instead, be plagued with guilt about her
racial identity, which we have learned can also be a severe handicap in helping people-of-color, she may behave abrasively, an-
tagonizing the counselor, so that if and when her advocacy for
the client should result in the client's gaining access, the negative expectations of the counselor, now compounded by anger over the encounter with the practitioner, could constitute
major roadblocks to the client's success. Clear thinking, a
reasoned approach about her client's right to the service, and a
well-articulated expectation that she can succeed will accomplish more than righteous indignation born of guilt. But such a
stance can only be taken by persons firmly grounded in their
own cultural identity and self-value.

Should a reasoned approach to the employment counselor fail,
then may be the time for the practitioner to engage in confrontation tactics, taking steps to assure that bias will not prevent her
client's access to needed services. There, too, cultural self-understanding will be critical. Our examination of the experiential data
has shown the prevalence of bias in service deliverers as in the
larger populations. Thus, confronting bias when it blocks access
for clients must be part of the advocacy-linking role of the practitioner.

When services are nonexistent, practitioners may find it necessary to develop them. This may involve organizing citizens and
appealing to businesses and foundations for resources and funds.
Appeals are most frequently made to ethnic systems within the
community itself including such systems as churches and church
groups, social groups, lodges, veterans' groups, political clubs,
business and service groups, unions, sports and athletic clubs,
civil rights or social action groups, family associations (Chinese),
tribal councils (Native American), and clan networks (Native
American). A practitioner involved in planning a discharge for
her elderly Haitian client approached the local Catholic church
about the need for a social center for the elderly. Their goal of
locating services may propel practitioners into community organizing, program development, and assistance to citizen's groups
in their attempts to help clients acquire and exercise power on
their own behalf. Asian-American practitioners joined with ac-
tivists to organize poor and powerless clients into grass-roots or-

ganizations that developed a variety of social services and engaged in political activity (Lum 1986, p. 184). The efforts of a practitioner who documented the inability of agencies to assist clients in finding housing under conditions of housing shortage and the imminent dislocation of ethnic residents due to gentrification resulted in a class advocacy suit against the city. This led to the creation of a low-cost housing program within the gentrified area and appropriation of funds to finance the venture.

Planning and Administration

The significance of culture in people's functioning must be recognized by planners and administrators as well as practitioners. Agencies must be created that facilitate the efforts of practitioners to use helping strategies that validate people's culture and enhance their cultural identity. Services should be so organized that attempts to empower clients, to help them reduce their personal feelings of powerlessness, and to counteract denigration of themselves and their cultural groups do not leave practitioners trapped and overwhelmed with powerlessness themselves. Policies should be set that strengthen the health of the ethnic community and reinforce action, self-esteem, pride, self-assertion, and mastery among its members; that promote the ability to cope with the overwhelming problems stemming from their confusing and contradictory roles within the social system; and that facilitate the ability to embrace biculturalism as a strength, whereby they are able to function in the American mainstream and remain connected to the ethnic community if that is desired. The stance of the agency must be to block the destructiveness of societal systems upon its clientele and monitor itself to ensure that it does not join them in their oppressive roles. Failure to take such a stance means the agency is maintaining its clients in their system-balancing, societal roles. For example, policies will not block the support practitioners need to reach out to Chinese clients whose honor and pride may prevent their acknowledgement of problems. The sanction of the agency to engage in outreach means that it is financing this use of the practitioner's time. In addition, policies will not force clients to deny their cultural identity or embrace assimilation and thus cultural annihilation, as have programs offered to Native Americans in need of child welfare services. Nor will policies reinforce the entrapment of Afro-American mothers and others striving to get off welfare by forcing them to take jobs with no hope of growth and development and no chance to get out of poverty. Such conditions reinforce an "alienated commodity identity" (Keefe 1984), a consequence of the value assigned to "producer"–"consumer" roles in an economy that requires some persons to stay trapped in unemployment or denigrated jobs.

Experts suggest that agency ideology supporting commitment to the significance of culture exists along a continuum which includes melting pot ideology, cultural pluralism, and promotion of ethnic identity (Jenkins 1981). The melting pot ideology, which has characterized the perspective of most agencies in the United States, reinforces adaptation to the dominant American culture. The pluralistic agency is structured to reinforce recognition and acceptance of cultural difference. The ethnic agency, which is in the main administered and staffed by persons from the specific ethnic group being served and mediates between the functions of the cultural group and the service delivery system, is viewed as the most efficient way to deliver services that promote ethnic cohesiveness and identity. For obvious reasons it remains the best alternative to empowering the group (Jenkins 1981).

For example, an ethnic agency that was Afro-American in identity articulated its goal of supporting the individual and collective strength of Afro-Americans through programs that developed positive cultural awareness, developed strategies for individuals and groups to combat racism, and taught clients how to understand the dynamics of power, authority, leadership, and responsibility. It set as its goal an agency stance that refused to join other institutions in behaviors maintaining racism or oppressive relationships. Accordingly it monitored its relationships with schools and hospitals accepting referrals only after the referral source was evaluated and judged not to be compounding the client's powerlessness. For example, whether "hyperactive" children were referred for evaluation because of the teacher's or school system's inadequacy or the child's need was a matter to be determined before acceptance of the referral. This necessitated engagement with parents or referral source prior to acceptance, since referrals were accepted only after any parental ambivalence about the referral was resolved and the referring source had cooperated in evaluating its possible input to the problem.

At one time the agency perceived its hard-won consulting program in the schools to be "backfiring" because it appeared as though it was being used to justify labeling children as incompetent instead of addressing school system failure. The agency closed down the program, studied its effects, and only reinstituted it when the policy described above had been clearly hammered out. A large percentage of its clientele were on welfare and there were constant battles waged with the Welfare Department over procedures that requested documentation of service for reimbursement and that necessitated the divulgence of personal information about clients, which was seen as demeaning to their sense of dignity and power. As a result, the agency set about raising funds to reduce its dependency on such external systems. As part of its policy of ethnic commitment, the agency also celebrated holidays commemorating Afro-American heroes and refused to engage in activities reinforcing "victim" identity, such as "charity endeavors" where clients' stories were published in the newspaper to secure money for Christmas. Instead, it channeled its efforts into developing skills, competence, and independence for its clients. A Puerto Rican agency, committing itself to prevention, supported practitioner efforts to join with the community in the establishment of a cultural center devoted to the enhancement of identity and pride and a family life center program with an educational focus that was disseminated through lectures, talks, workshops, radio-TV programs, newspaper articles, and newsletters. In other instances, practitioners have developed programs to offer assistance in writing proposals for securing funding or joined with the business community to develop economic programs that would create jobs and job training programs (Solomon 1976).

Research on attitudes and preferences concerning ethnic commitment in agencies delivering child welfare services was co-conducted with three sample groups (Jenkins 1981). The samples included NASW child welfare workers, workers in ethnic agencies, and clients (parents). In all cases, the largest number of clients expressed preference for the right to have separate programs, and the alternative of using public funds to run their own programs but were less strong and more divided on whether they themselves would prefer separate services. Thus, it is not at all clear that when such an ethnic agency does exist, it is the structure of choice for everyone.

Moreover, because ethnic agencies, despite their potential for reinforcing the mental health of the individual and community, are unlikely to exist in significant numbers, the pluralistic agency becomes the most realistic possibility. It represents the model toward which most agencies, both public and private, that have been dominated by the melting pot ideology now appear to be headed. Agencies with a pluralistic perspective offer programs that can be reasonably tailored to fit the varying needs of different cultural groups. Clients may be assigned to workers of their own group or they might not depending on the policy. The determining factor as to how much such a "mixing-matching" policy may be pursued is who or what group are the decision makers and wield the power. Very often the decision makers represent the dominant societal group and do not bring the strong commitment needed for creating effective empowerment strategies. The necessary diversity in staff that characterizes the pluralistic agency may be a benefit or a liability. It will result in effectiveness only under certain conditions. First, it must be open to examining policies that disempower and undermine clients, allowing staff to examine together goals and program in order to determine what constitutes effective programming that offers clients real opportunities to develop competence, mastery, and some control over their lives.

Second, in the creation of such policies and programs, ethnic representatives must be valued for the expertise and perspective they bring and their input must be considered in the determination of needs and services that will be effective with individuals and organizations within their community. This is necessary not only because their perspective usually reflects that of the ethnic population and the community but also because failure to facilitate participation from staff in the functioning of the agency as a place of work can result in employee demoralization and burnout (Keefe 1984).

Third, the multicultural staff must be able to engage in dialogue about their difference in perceptions and experiences. Failure to provide the opportunity to understand and process these differences within a multicultural staff will lead to one of two outcomes both of which constitute unhealthy contextual conditions for empowering people:

1. Staff will cover over the conflict in perceptions and orientation and block off the confusion, frustration, and strong feelings, causing an undercurrent of stress, tension, distrust,

and suspicion. People may be unable to take advantage of an opportunity, when offered, to engage in dialogue and learning and may react with rigidity because they feel unsafe or incompetent.

2. Conflict will erupt and staff will become burned out and fatigued if they try to hammer out program and policy before they have an opportunity to understand cultural dynamics and the significance of cultural identity and meaning in relation to themselves, their clients, and their work together. When practitioners do not understand their own and each other's cultural baggage and attempt to plan, organize services, and work together, their differing expectations, experiences, and perspectives will result in polarization and pitched battles over every aspect of service delivery.

The following is an example of what occurred when one agency found itself in such a position. Having committed itself to delivery of services to Afro-American clients, the multicultural staff set about developing policy and program to implement such a goal. Professionals whose traditional training had been anchored in the melting pot ideology felt their competence severely threatened by the different opinions of Afro-American staff, who often expressed with conviction differing positions about client needs, intervention strategies, and program structuring. This is an example of the dialogue that occurred in those meetings when polarization began to develop as Whites sought to close off the dialogue and Blacks pressed to continue the painful engagement.

BLACK: Don't run away from the pain—you have to stand it as we have had to stand it. To get close to Blacks and see your participation is painful. You want us to protect you in a way you didn't protect us.

WHITE: It won't work if you make us so angry and frustrated— we won't hear and understand what you are saying.

WHITE: I'm hurt at the thought I'm incompetent because I'm White. I want to know what it is I need to know to be a therapist for Black children.

BLACK: This is what it's all about. We can't help Black children until we can look together at what they need and Blacks know this better than Whites—therefore, Whites must listen.

WHITE: I feel we Whites will never fully understand the Black experience (gives examples of psychotic patient who is angry when told she is understood; she feels she's been through hell and no one can understand). I feel these confrontations are necessary for us to develop some understanding, and some polarization is inevitable.

BLACK: (a community worker) I was insulted by Dr. X's response to our demands. (Dr. X, though intending to share openly his feelings as a White about the new procedures under discussion, changed his mind at the last minute and, instead, quoted from an article written by a young Black on the stages that Blacks go through in finding identity.) It showed lack of respect for Blacks. All he needed to do was listen to us right here in this room, but Whites haven't learned how to do that—I'm disappointed in all you mental health experts.

BLACK: Whites cannot stand to have Blacks be quicker, more alert, and more knowledgeable than they are, especially about their own behavior.

WHITE: (Dr. X, who quoted from article) I made a terrible mistake. It all came out wrong; this polarization is no good—it only alienates people. I'm a fool to stay here and feel this way. I ought to go out in a suburb and work. But there's no hope of solving it if I and all Whites run. If I stay, there's pain here and fighting with neighbors and friends about all of this.

BLACK: This is what we have put up with all our lives.

WHITE: But you're stronger and you can take it. I thought I could too, but I can't.

BLACK: I don't see how we are ever going to really deal with what we need to know and understand about Blacks and the Black experience unless we go through this.

WHITE: The worst part is my analyst is no damn help.

WHITE: It's hard for us to give up power, to understand how we have institutionalized racism, to change. You must be patient with our slow pace.

BLACK: If you have the right to ask for us to be patient with your slow pace, we have the right to ask you to be patient with our impatience.

Such polarization is inevitable if staff attempt to hammer out a program and strategies without some sense of commonalty and understanding that can transcend their differences in experiences, perceptions, and expectations. This necessary sense of commonalty can only be forged when they have an opportunity to appreciate how the differences in their experiences have created their varying perspectives. Such an opportunity can be provided by training in cultural sensitivity, which facilitates understanding one another's personal experiences in relation to ethnicity, race, and power in a manner that also compels each to understand his own unique responses and *take responsibility for them.*

Such training experiences neutralize polarization, defuse anger, and facilitate transcendence of differences. Even staff that have been fairly sophisticated in these matters have benefited greatly from this process. Even with a high level of self-knowledge, awareness of the experiences and perspectives of colleagues has promoted an increased sense of harmony and healthier working relationships, so that the ordinarily stressful delivery of effective services to culturally different populations can occur within a context that is cohesive and supportive. The collegiality that results enables staff members to use one another as consultants, increasing the effectiveness and competence of all.

Training for cultural self-understanding and for developing the perspectives, capacities, and competencies that are needed with clients facilitates openness to introspection and self-examination. It also enhances the ability to control and even change attitudes one has learned, to use systemic thinking, and to be comfortable with cultural difference.

To achieve these benefits, training must focus not only on ethnicity and race but also on power. The significance of power as an issue in the helping process is only now beginning to receive attention. In reassessing and reevaluating his work, Carl Rogers has asserted that he has felt "compelled to confront openly a subject not often discussed: the issue of power and control in the so-called helping professions" (Rogers 1977, p. 6). The conference brochure of the tenth annual Family Therapy Network Symposium bore these words on a frontispiece: "The illusion that one can unilaterally control other people underlies many problems that bring families to therapy. My dilemma as a therapist is how to free people from this illusion without buying into it myself."[1] The significance of a sense of power, the pervasiveness of powerlessness, and the importance of empowerment as a treatment goal in clinical practice that also has implications for administration in social policy are rapidly gaining recognition.

All practitioners should receive training that will enable them to develop the perspectives and ways of thinking and behaving described here. Programs that promote their development should be offered in educational institutions, service settings, and continuing education programs. They should be requirements for credentialing, certification, hiring, and retention in professional positions. Such training programs must be compulsory because people will *not* take courses or workshops on cultural sensitivity voluntarily. This has been proved over and over again. Hopefully, this book explains why. They are far more likely to take courses that teach facts about cultural values and practices. Some may show interest in ethnic self-awareness, but as these chapters demonstrate, there are often ambivalent and negative feelings about ethnicity that can prompt them to avoid opportunities to develop ethnic self-understanding. For obvious reasons, few will opt voluntarily for racial awareness and the consideration of power as a personal issue that affects one's work and is influenced by cultural role. The issue of identity will likewise be studiously avoided.

It is, in my opinion, a mark of professional incompetence to avoid such training and at the same time continue to treat cross-cultural clients and to offer to them services. We have illustrated the practical importance of exploration and open, liberating discussion in the development of these perspectives, capacities, and competencies that are so critical. Skillfully led workshops and seminars offer one of the better opportunities. Open and honest discussion with other professionals of diverse backgrounds can be helpful. But nothing takes the place of the self-exploration, discussion, and participation provided by the experiential component. While familiarity with the literature is not a substitute, it is hoped that this book will make a beginning for its readers, reinforcing a commitment on the part of practitioners, planners, and administrators toward positive self-definition, appreciation of cultural differences, and development of the perspectives and competencies that are critical in cross-cultural work.

These are attributes needed far beyond the realm of professional activity. The cultural and technological changes ushered in by the Industrial Revolution have led to the movement of people around the world. Multicultural interactions and multicultural communications have become commonplace and have contributed to the rapidly changing nature of all societies. The dynamics, confusion, misunderstanding, and conflict that can occur as a result of these changes therefore are international in scope and likely to pervade our world for the foreseeable future. This book has described the nature of these dynamics and ways of promoting and facilitating constructive outcomes. Using the information and approaches described, more and more people will be prepared to work effectively on the many cross-cultural problems in our societies. They will know how to manage the dynamics of ethnicity, race, and power in ways that celebrate the differences among people while also promoting mutual under-standing, empathy, and respect.

Appendix:

Teaching Methods

Experiential Group Model

Neutralizing the anxiety that is mobilized in interaction with culturally different others; developing awareness of one's own culture, its meaning, its indoctrination concerning others and the psychological benefit of maintaining these cultural biases; recognizing and committing oneself to the changes needed for effective cross-cultural interaction are goals not easily achieved. However, the model described here offers trainees an opportunity for such mastery. Providing an experience for unravelling the multi-faceted complexities involved in cross-cultural interaction, the model teaches participants how cultural identity and issues of power and powerlessness traverse the various levels of human functioning and affect their own behavior as service providers.

This understanding is developed by exploring within a group format the participants' own feelings, perceptions, and experiences vis-à-vis ethnicity, race, and power. As they identify and acknowledge their predispositions and biases in these areas, grappling with them privately and within the group, they discover the origin of the feelings and perceptions that influence their behavior with culturally different others. This in vivo experience gives them an emotional understanding of the differences as well as the similarities between themselves and others. The growth that can occur results in new ways of thinking and behaving. Participants can achieve increased clarity concerning cultural identity, greater respect for differences in people, and greater

211

comfort in cross-cultural interaction. And they come to understand the importance of taking responsibility for their values and biases on both personal and societal levels.

The Technique

This approach may be described as a combination of introspection and experiential involvement marked by personal sharing and interaction, plus discussions that place the evolving content in a conceptual framework.

The assumptions of this approach can briefly be presented as follows:

1. People need to feel predominantly positive about their cultural identity and group connectedness, although some ambivalence is to be expected.
2. Clarity concerning values including value conflicts, even when resolution is impossible, enhances one's functioning.
3. When persons of different cultural backgrounds interact, they need validation and acceptance of their cultural identity. However, this carries a risk, since values may differ and learned perceptions of the other may represent distortions and bias.
4. Distortion and bias take on greater significance when they are used to justify power arrangements that oppress and exploit victims, as in the case of class and racial categorization, discrimination, and other forms of oppression.
5. The significance touches all levels of functioning for both benefactor and victim with enormous implications for every aspect of human behavior.
6. Service providers must transcend distortions and bias, since they are destructive to effective work and undermine the values and goals that undergird service delivery. Transcendence should involve a search for solutions on a societal as well as a personal level.
7. Transcendence is made possible by an understanding of the distortions and preconceptions one has internalized, their etiology and purpose. A commitment to control or change them and the societal structures which they justify is thus possible.

8. An experiential group in which there is trust and support enables the self-examination necessary to clarify ethnic values, to confront racial and other cultural bias, and to understand its etiology, purpose, and benefits, including its costs to benefactor as well as victim.

9. Emotional growth occurs via self-confrontation and interaction within the group. Conflict, if managed with sensitivity and respect, will enhance growth. Resolution of conflict in perceptions between participants is achieved when one or both alter their position.

10. An understanding of one's power gestalt (i.e., feelings and experiences as persons of power and nonpower) deepens the understanding of the self in the social context, offering an opportunity for self-expression in the social context and offering an opportunity to avoid the embracing of power for destructive purposes.

Learning from people's experiences is the basic strategy of this model. It demonstrates that there is a wealth of information within any group and that no group's process is exactly like that of any other. Common elements of every group's process include anxiety and resistance about the work to be done, lifting of resistance and engagement in the sharing experience, the confrontation of self and others that occurs privately and in interaction.

The model promotes comprehension of the systemic nature of culture, which is a perspective that professionals must acquire. The personal experiences that people share and analyze help unravel the complexities involved, teaching them to use complex cognitive process and helping them to see how events take place on various levels of social functioning (i.e., individual, interactional, familial, cultural, group) that affect one another in an ongoing way. Analyzing these experiences illustrates for clinicians how the interaction of variables on any or all of these levels may influence a specific situation. They are thus forced to think systemically. They learn to consider internal *and* external function, generalities *and* specifics, sameness *and* difference in relation to how cultural identity and meaning operate. The emotional nature of culture and the lineality of language make it difficult to convey such cultural dynamics through lectures and reading. A focus on personal identity and meaning requires consideration of internal and external factors in the operation of culture because it forces recognition of the way personal cultural meaning, self-esteem, and sense of self are shaped by interaction with others and by events in the outside world.

Focus on personal identity and meaning forces clinicians to use a way of thinking that considers both specifics and generalities in cultural process. While the focus begins with personal experience and emphasizes the significance of the individual—his or her perspective and experience—these specifics can be placed in the context of general knowledge about a given cultural group. This highlights the way general facts about a cultural group apply or do not apply to oneself and one learns automatically to consider what generalizations about culture must be qualified. Most importantly, there is reinforcement for viewing clients as unique and special within the general context of their cultures. This avoids the traditionally theoretical and oftentimes meaningless approach to culture whereby general ethnic values and cultural practices are the sole emphasis (McGoldrick 1983). Defining a cultural group in terms of ideas, attitudes, traits, and behavior is a static approach to learning. It is useless to clinicians, because it cannot describe the dynamic nature of cultural attributes (Bernal and Gutierrez 1988) and the way such static meaning must be qualified by many intervening factors.

There is a *personal* understanding that the social is a part of the self, that events inside and outside the family influence the specific cultural meaning one attaches to one's own group connections and those of others. There is also an emotional understanding that one's sense of self, one's personal misperceptions, distortions, and defensive behaviors are based on internal and external factors. Moreover as the unfolding of experiences documents the levels, degrees, nuances, and subtleties that can exist in the cultural issues that are examined, this forces people to think in terms of relativity and variability and protects against tendencies to use black-and-white thinking, to generalize, or to overemphasize specifics.

Another dimension of systemic thinking that is enhanced in such training is the ability to consider sameness and difference. One learns about the variations in ethnic and racial identity and meaning that can exist *within* cultural groups, the subtleties that may be present, and how this applies to oneself. One also learns how one may be similar to and different from persons inside one's own group and, at the same time, similar to and different from others who are outside. And very significantly, one develops awareness of how one may define oneself differently from the way one is defined by others both inside and outside the group and how one responds to such a condition. The finding, for example, that responses to differences within one's group can be as strong or stronger than responses to those outside is often surprising. This perspective in relation to oneself facilitates the ability to see others, especially clients, in these multiple ways.

Developing a perspective that considers both sameness and difference is important because a focus on either without attention to the other will lead to distortion. Attention only to similarities, which reinforces the orientation that "all people are the same," invites the ignoring or denial of differences. On the other hand, a focus on difference without attention to commonality can reinforce distancing and barriers between people. At the same time, perceiving oneself as unique and having an identity that is separate from others can make it safer to join and connect with them. Difference in the context of similarity or similarity in the context of difference is the desired perspective. When people are able to acquire this perspective, cultural differences between them and others will not automatically invoke barriers, since commonalities will provide a bridge. Sameness will not inherently mean that one's uniqueness will be denied or identity lost, and difference will not mean "better than" or "less than" but merely "different than."

When there is a focus on power in training for developing cultural self-awareness, many of the dynamics cited above receive even greater clarification and emphasis. Exploring experiences in relation to power reinforces systemic thinking since power (or lack of power) is itself a systemic phenomenon. We have illustrated in the examination of the experiential data how power (and lack of power) exists for everyone but in varying degrees and on varying levels. Understanding the degree, its nuances, and how it differs or is the same for individuals including oneself, can help practitioners be aware that the power which they have and which is a key factor in the clinical relationship must be used effectively and not abused. Their experiences in relation to having (or lacking) power and the "power gestalt" they bring to the helping encounter can compound this power or lack of power, causing high vulnerability to abuse. Moreover compounding of power can be further affected by the status assignment and the value designation of the cultural group of both practitioner and client, creating yet more vulnerability. The reluctance of people to admit to the power they have, the defenses they erect to avoid this knowledge, the pain that is embodied in powerlessness, the compulsion to defend against it, and the problematic behaviors that people, practitioners included, will use to maintain their defenses are all issues that make if difficult for professionals to understand and manage the power dynamics in the cross-cultural encounter. Training must seek to correct this.

Beginning the Process

Each stage in the learning process begins with some basic questions that every participant is asked to consider. The answers to these questions help them identify their own perceptions and feelings about themselves and their cultural identity, to understand these responses cognitively, and to place them in a conceptual framework that can deepen understanding and offer guidelines for effective functioning.

Overview of the Process

After all participants are introduced to one another, they are asked to discuss their goals for participating in the process and to agree on a code of behavior that will (1) enhance trust within the group; (2) guarantee respect for each individual's contributions; and (3) enable everyone to attain his or her personal objectives. Since some participants may have come by choice whereas others may have been required to attend, there is discussion about reactions people have to the existence or nonexistence of choice upon the work to be done. The importance of discussing whether or not people had a choice in the decision to come to the group cannot be underestimated. If people feel forced to participate in a process that involves personal vulnerability, they feel trapped. They need opportunity to express this and to consider how it may hinder the work. Discussing the powerlessness they feel allows them to handle it by choosing whether to open themselves to the process. Unless they examine their feelings about this sense of entrapment, they may allow their resentment to take the form of resistance or sabotage. Nearly everyone has a goal that relates to understanding ethnic issues. Many have clear expectations of confronting their biases and changing them. The examination proceeds with a focus on the following questions.

1. What is your ethnic background? What has it meant to belong to your ethnic group? How has it felt to belong to your ethnic group? What do you like about your ethnic identity? What do you dislike?
2. Where did you grow up, and what other ethnic groups resided there?
3. What are the values of your ethnic group?
4. How did your family see itself, as similar to or different from other ethnic groups?
5. What was your first experience with feeling different?
6. What are your earliest images of race or color? What information were you given about how to deal with racial issues?
7. What are your feelings about being White or a person-of-color? To Whites: How do you think people-of-color feel about their color identity? To people-of-color: How do you think Whites feel about their color identity?
8. Discuss your experiences as a person having or lacking power in relation to the following: ethnic identity; racial identity; within the family; class identity; sexual identity; professional identity.

As the questions indicate, this approach separates ethnicity from race in the examination of feelings, attitudes, and behaviors, and then uses power as a means of integrating them. Social class issues growing out of power dynamics are power phenomena that cut aross both ethnicity and race and are thus discussed in both stages, receiving a final review when participants process power dynamics.

Setting the Contract

Expectations on the part of participants and the leader receive validation in the setting of the contract that affirms the goals and rules guiding the work. Because self-awareness is the desired outcome, articulation of individual goals is critical. Every member must be helped to state as clearly as possible the goals he or she wishes to set. Often goals are vague and people are told they will have an opportunity to redefine or restate them. These goals become the contract that all members make with themselves about the work they wish to do. This contract and the option for revision give leverage to the method of self-confrontation and the expectation of responsibility for growth and change. The contract is reviewed throughout the process. When resistance is high, a review of each person's goals and a consideration of whether satisfactory progress is being made can mobilize flagging motivation or provide an extra push that overcomes resistance. Revision of goals is common as new perspectives and greater comfort is achieved within the group.

In clarifying my expectations as leader, I discuss my goal of enabling members to (1) achieve self-understanding, and (2) reach the specific goals they set, which I hope will include reinforcement of attitudes and behaviors that respect differences among people. I identify my leadership style as that of encouraging self-confrontation through group interaction. The rules to which group members are asked to agree include:

1. Regular prompt attendance
2. Commitment to work towards one's goals
3. Respect for everyone's contribution

The last stipulation may be tested when feelings are heightened and may require reaffirmation, especially when race and power are examined. It is the expectation that all members will participate; nonparticipating members will be encouraged to share but not pressed; however, silence will be taken to mean the group does not feel safe to them.

The following statements are representative of the goals participants have articulated and the questions they have raised:

Become aware of my own prejudices and work on them. Combat ignorance and stereotypes in myself.

Find ways to change racism because it hurts, because it's wasteful, and because people with low self-esteem perpetuate it.

Explore my biases. I know I'm not as free of prejudice as I want to be. Understand how my ethnicity has influenced my relationships with others.

Understand racism and how I, as a Black, and others react to it; also how racism is connected with social class prejudice.

Understand my own ethnicity. I have difficulties dealing with my Jewishness and some prejudices about Jews. I want to understand this and other minorities.

Figure out why I feel anxious in this group.

Understand the culture and values of American Blacks, Hispanics, and Haitians. I understand these groups among our patients the least. Also how does unemployment and lack of insurance coverage affect these people?

Understand my prejudices, but, more important, understand power and how it affects men and women.

Develop empathy with all students in this school and be able to communicate with their parents' anger.

Understand why it's hard to communicate with people who are different and how to express these things to kids.

Raise my consciousness of what I do in the classroom, the terminology I use that touches on people's sensitive areas.

Become aware of the differences in my students, both in and out of the classroom. Be able to recognize strengths and weaknesses, both academic and social, that may be rooted in cultural differences.

Get to know my co-workers. Be able to help myself and my students accept ideas of others. My class is great at minding other people's business; I want to say the right things to encourage tolerance.

Get some balance about my anger and powerlessness as a Black in the majority system and how to stop perpetuating racism.

Get a broader knowledge base so I can deal with my anger about how we Blacks are treated and what's happening to my sons as Black males.

Understand how to handle my anger when, as a White, a guilt trip is run on me. How does sexual identity connect with racial issues? My supervisees are mostly minorities, and I want to deal with them in the most human way, despite the baggage we both bring.

Be able to work more effectively with Black clients and staff. The intense environment I work in exaggerates racial feelings. What are the values I have as a White that are not shared by my clients? What is my role in the behavior of clients who say "yes" but don't do it?

How to deal with the anger I get from Blacks. How I am like or different from other Whites (which I think I am). How to empower the families I work with.

Eliminate personal biases so that I can bring about social change.

Feel more comfortable in cross-cultural groups. As a Jamaican, I feel not only different from Whites, but also American Blacks. I want to understand these differences between people from the Caribbean and American Blacks.

Be better able to handle the onslaught which I, as a Black, have to handle every day.

Understand how to negotiate and discuss differences that exist between therapists and patients. See how transference is affected and how to overcome these barriers. Understand women cross-culturally.

Explore my own intense reactions about my own ethnicity, which is Jewish. Increase my tolerance for differences within my ethnic group.

Understand more about men.

When participants are asked to reexamine goals, they often add more specificity and depth to their intentions, as in these examples:

I am a Native American. I want to understand my own feelings so that I can do this process with my people. We don't know who we are and have great difficulty even approaching the issue.

I want to understand people's perceptions of me as a Black man. People say I'm hostile and prejudiced. That doesn't fit with how I see myself.

Requests are made for feedback from other group members about one's behavior, how one is perceived, the latent messages one gives, and requests to group members for help in the struggle to change attitudes. In one situation, a Black participant felt Whites were trying to avoid coming to grips with their prejudices. When opportunity was offered to add new goals, he amended his statement as follows:

> Understand why White people, who won't face their prejudice and manage it, think they can work with people-of-color and help them.

This comment catalyzed the group, and the effort to manage people's consequent responses led to significant progress in understanding race and power.

Guiding the Group

It helps to begin each session with a summary of what happened the week before. Often group members have difficulty remembering, especially when the content has involved pain and conflict. A brief review also brings any participants who were absent up to date and with little loss of time moves the group to the place where it left off the previous session. This method works best if the leader's style is predominantly facilitating and enabling, rather than confrontative, so that participants feel safe enough to share, compare, and differ with each other. The stance of the leader is at all times empathic, even when confronting participants with their biased, avoiding, or disrespectful behavior. While calling attention to commonalities among participants in the cultural traits they share, the leader also points out differences, ambivalances, and conflicts, encouraging work toward understanding their etiology and purpose.

In this way, the resolution of conflicts is possible and differences can be accepted. Resolution and acceptance may not be immediate but may occur later in the process, since there frequently is a return to issues for reworking. It is not uncommon for an issue that surfaced during the examination of ethnicity or race to receive final understanding and resolution in the stage on power. Resolution may not even occur within the time frame of the process, but the understanding gained and the commitment made can be such that the work will continue. An important insight is that these issues require ongoing attention.

Decreasing Resistance

Leaders must continually take the pulse of the group, bringing to attention resistance, withholding, tension, and dissatisfaction, whether manifest or latent. Asking how the group is going, how others are experiencing it, or sharing their own feelings as a barometer can bring this about and enable everyone to work toward creating a climate that encourages sharing.

In addition to the considerations mentioned above concerning resistance, others deserve mention.

As participants share personal responses, for example, the leader encourages interchange, placing the shared information into a conceptual context. In doing this, he or she must choose among the issues that are raised to push the exploration further providing continuity by linking them with previous insights and summarizing frequently. This is done with the goal that people will eventually get to the point where they are ready to seek resolutions for their discomfort and sense of entrapment. The example below illustrates the many directions a discussion may take and the fact that complete understanding, and therefore resolution, often does not occur until the final stage on examining power. This interchange followed the leader's sharing some historical information about racism and her family:

> That made me aware of the pain and the guilt I feel about how people-of-color have been treated.

> It reminded me that the destruction is still going on for Blacks and other people-of-color. I felt angry.

> Sometimes I think that the guilt I feel as a White is punishment enough and I don't need to do anything to change racism. At other times, I feel guiltier because I don't do anything.

> I don't feel guilty at all—my family was not in this country during slavery.

> That story was so foreign to my experience that I could not relate to it. So I had no reaction.

The speaker above is addressed by another group member:

> How could you possibly not have a reaction when there was so much pain in that story? (Tears)

This exchange could have led to a discussion on any one of the following issues:

1. The variation in attitudes within the group, recognizing how one's reactions are similar to and different from those of others
2. Possible meanings of the "no reaction" of one participant
3. The pervasiveness of guilt, and its cost in terms of energy, pain, and ambivalence, its manifestations in interracial interactions including cross-racial work
4. The need to transcend guilt and other inhibiting reactions
5. Whether the history of one's family's presence in this country has any connection with responsibility for solutions to the dilemma of racism

In guiding the discussion that followed the above interchange, the leader focused on one, three, and four, making a note to bring up two and five later. In a discussion several weeks later, the "no reaction" was clarified as a protective device when the participant, who was a Southerner, shared her intense ambivalence about race. She described her usual reaction as:

I can't afford to feel pain at every little thing. If I do, I would be thoroughly overwhelmed. I know the others are expressing their pain, but I have always had trouble with powerlessness and this subject makes me feel too powerless.

Only during the examination of power when this participant shared information about her background could she and the group understand more clearly her sense of ambivalence. And only at this time, too, could the group tackle the question of whether all Whites, irrespective of arrival time in this country, carry any responsibility for the perpetuation of racism. Again, the significance of the final stage in the consideration of power in deepening understanding, and thus providing clarity about effective cross-cultural interaction, becomes obvious.

Resistance may exist in all phases of the process. Resistance that is manifest in intellectualization and in retreat to tangential issues is handled by a respectful but firm steering of the group back to the emotional plane. Persons who are unclear, ambivalent, in conflict, or predominantly negative about their ethnic background may attempt to protect themselves from the discomfort mobilized by the effort to answer the questions placed before

the group. Recognition of bias can stir up feelings of disappointment in oneself, embarrassment, guilt, and helplessness. People
fear rejection and loss of status as a result of showing vulnerability or making statements that may be considered offensive. The
leader counteracts this by comments that emphasize (1) the
strength that is demonstrated in honestly confronting oneself
and in risking vulnerability, and (2) the comfort and sense of freedom that can result.

Differences in experiences and perceptions are inevitable and
are often manifest in the expression of negative feelings. It is
these differences that offer the greatest opportunity for growth
and understanding. However, they also represent the greatest
hazard since they fuel feelings about differences in cultural identity and experience that are strong and deep. And while the
leader strives to bring them to the fore so that they can be clarified, examined, and understood by all, he or she must also strive
to prevent the process from becoming dominated by negative affect and polarization. Expression of anger frightens participants
and threatens to immobilize the process, but it is, nonetheless, a
necessary step for some individuals before they can begin to listen to others and look at themselves. The leader must work actively to create the sense of safety in the group that will facilitate
this process; here the role of the leader is critical in creating this
ambience of security, since it is only in an atmosphere of safety
that people will attempt to examine, understand, and master
these biases. Modeling of risk taking is all-important. For this
reason, the leader should always begin the go-round with herself.
The leader should also share her own reactions at any time when
it will forward the work of the group (such as to undermine resistance). Adams and Schlesinger (1988) give an example of how
sharing by the leader had a powerful impact upon group members.

At times when resistance is high or conflict is heightened, the
leader, therefore, reaffirms the contract made at the beginning of
the process, whereby participants were asked to agree that each
individual's contributions would be respected despite the fact that
they might arouse discomfort. This necessary stance is characterized by "living with" prejudiced and offensive ideas as a tactic
for accomplishing the goals of the group (Adams and Schlesinger
1988, p. 6). This "living with" stance is facilitated when people
can feel safe enough to express ideas and attitudes of which they
feel ashamed. The leader creates such safety not only in the de-

mand that respect be accorded each participant but also by encouraging people to listen to and support each other. For when people feel support from the group to express themselves without excessive blame or judgment, this not only enables them to clarify and to confront these ideas but to work on changing them.

While leaders must work hard to create this security among participants, they also must be careful that safety does not slip into protection. They must gently prod people to express those ideas for which safety has been so primary, "reaching for" areas of conflict, confusion, and ambivalence and bringing them into focus (Adams and Schlesinger 1988, p. 8). And when, as often occurs, group members resist by intellectualizing or going off on tangents, they bring the focus back to feelings and personal meaning. Filibustering can be managed by adhering to a limit on the time devoted to a single individual's exploration. In the ethnicity examination, anyone's contribution can be used to spark the discussion and interaction that leads to understanding. The leader must be prepared to turn any issue that arises into a topic of exploration that can help reach the goals.

At such times when differences lead to negative exchanges, the leader will find it useful to (1) remind the individuals involved of the personal goals they have set, (2) remind the group of the ground rules that require respect for everyone, (3) clearly articulate the different perspectives while demonstrating empathy and understanding for both, and (4) generalize the position of each so that others in the group also feel involved, thus expanding the discussion and getting people to talk about the issue (Adams and Schlesinger 1988).

The following episode illustrates this strategy. Several weeks before the occurrence of the episode that will be described below, a psychiatric trainee had identified himself as a product of Southern, White, Anglo-Saxon, and Jewish roots. His identification was predominately as a Unitarian and a WASP, and this had angered two Jewish female psychology trainees whose families had suffered greatly in the Holocaust. In this session where the discussion centered on the importance of being clear on one's self-definition, one of the women addressed him:

> It makes me angry when Jews don't want to be Jews. We need all Jews to be unified in order to fight oppression. We can't survive without them.

The other said:

> It's a special outrage that he identifies as a WASP, which is
> *the* power group. It wouldn't be so bad if he were Catholic.
> If Jews don't unify and recognize their oppression,
> they will lose their freedom.

The psychiatric trainee responded angrily that he had a right to decide his own identity and to be Jewish as little or as much as he wished. Several sessions later, in the leader's absence, the group chose to meet, and the two women attacked the male participant again for his disloyalty as a Jew. The attack was serious enough, some group members thought, to precipitate the asthma attack he subsequently had. The leader empathized with the sensitivity and pain behind both positions, the insistence on the right to self-definition, and the need for unity in struggle. She reminded the group of its commitment to respect everyone's contributions. Other group members expressed their reactions to these dynamics and joined the debate:

> I understand how Al feels. Although I identify as Jewish, it's
> never been in the way my family does. They were always
> talking about the Holocaust and how Jews are hated.
> Somehow that distanced me. I think it was because I didn't
> personally feel the hatred my parents taught me to expect.
> Sure I got called kike and asshole by non-Jews, but
> extermination was not my experience.

Another participant said:

> I really think that a continual focus on the hostility
> experienced in the past can get out of hand, prevent Jews
> and any others who do it from understanding that others
> may have been treated as bad or worse.

A third said:

> Al has already told us that his father was not strongly
> Jewish, so his family experience has been totally different
> from yours.

This evidence of support enabled Al to reveal a sense of personal vulnerability that softened the polarization stance. He said:

> I think I have felt a need to identify with strength because of
> a number of things that have happened in my life. The
> precariousness of Jews has been too threatening to me.

Several group members engaged him in questions concerning his father's knowledge of his Jewishness. This had never been discussed. In later sessions Al reported that he had engaged his father in several conversations about the family's Jewish roots. This had improved their relationship and Al was feeling comfortable about acknowledging this part of his heritage. Meanwhile, the two Jewish women whose painful past had impelled their rejection of Al's definition of himself reported at the group's end that although their commitment to the Jewsh cause remained as strong, they recognized the intolerance that they had displayed. One said:

> I can see now that people need to be allowed to define themselves as they wish. But that's real hard when how they do it threatens what I see as our [Jews'] need for preserving the group. We can't afford to lose anyone because there is always the danger that it can happen again if we are not strong enough as a group.

This example illustrates (1) the intensity of feelings attached to the congruity and lack of congruity of people's self-definition; (2) the conflicts it can cause; (3) the pain that usually drives these conflicts; (4) the need for empathy and firm direction from the leader to insure a successful conclusion; and (5) the growth that can occur in terms of self-acceptance and tolerance of others.

It can be expected that full understanding of issues and resolution of conflict occurs only after the group has processed an issue several times. Frequently, it is the exploration of power that brings closure. For example, Gary, a group member of WASP background had been reluctant to speak, but he finally did identify his affluent Yankee heritage. The group members, who included Jews (5), French Canadian (1), and WASPs (2), did not react to his description of affluence and family power or the ambivalence with which it was shared. They became very active, however, when Gary suddenly switched the topic to discuss his confusion upon initial contact with Blacks as an intern in an inner city hospital. In making the point that his upper-middle-class private school upbringing had kept him protected and unknowing about Blacks and their culture, he recalled an incident in which he was threatened by Blacks with robbery. The group immediately focused on their fears of Blacks in the inner city hospital where they were getting their training, and all shared experiences of theirs or others of violent encounters with Blacks. The leader questioned the connection between Gary's exploration of being WASP and the group's focus on violence and Blacks, reminding the group that Gary was explaining his discomfort about power and the elitism associated with his background when the topic suddenly shifted to the fear of dangerous, violent Blacks.

One trainee responded:

I have thought all week about that discussion. I was very uncomfortable when Gary was talking—what I didn't share in the group is that my family is also middle class, and I am uncomfortable about that.

A second said:

Did we really do that [switch the subject]? I can't believe we really did that. It bothers me that we did that.

This episode and the following interchange were returned to again and again as the group moved through the process. In the next session, group members pondered their responses of the previous two weeks.

JOHN: That interpretation of us scapegoating to avoid dealing with feelings about Gary was very powerful.

LEADER: How did you feel about that?

MORRIS: Well, I first denied it. I thought, "Well, that's the way it is," but then I had to admit that we really did avoid our feelings about Gary by scapegoating Blacks.

GARY: I really did not hear what you said at all. It took me 20 seconds to hear it and then I thought "So what?" Later, I could see I really didn't want to hear it.

HELEN: I couldn't see the group scapegoating Blacks to avoid feelings about Gary, because I identified so much with him.

HARRIETT: Well, there were other things going on when the group's anxiety about Blacks got raised. It got dark an hour earlier [a time switch from daylight saving time to eastern standard time] and Lou [Canadian member] had mentioned several times his fear of American crime.

JOHN: Is it possible you [leader] are overreacting?

GARY: There we go again trying to avoid the issue. Now we're accusing her of what we did.

LEADER: It is hard, isn't it, to take responsibility for our biases and to understand the need they serve. Of course, we have to check out all the possibilities, and that takes energy, but we have to face our biases, too. It is important to consider how this tendency to scapegoat Blacks affects your work with them.

It remained for the exploration of power several months later to validate the dynamics that had occurred in this incident. Group members returned to it again and again before the final resolution.

The following episode illustrates the leader's role in expanding the discussion, appropriately identifying the underlying issue of difference that changes the emotional tone, deferring the final resolution until the examination on power. The group was developing a real appreciation for (1) the complexities involved in understanding the responses of people-of-color, and (2) the way of thinking and the flexibility required for cross-racial interaction. The interaction that produces learning sometimes involves confrontation as in an episode which began with the following dialogue between a White psychiatric resident and the Black administrator of a neighborhood health center:

I want to know why you think Whites cannot treat people-of-color?

Many of the problems at my center are a result of Whites who think they know best how to work with people-of-color and they don't. They don't want input regarding issues about child abuse, refuse to understand that forcing an 18-year-old to return to school where he's in a class with 14-year-olds with teachers who don't care is destructive. We have a mechanism for input to professional staff about the needs of clients. It happens that this mechanism consists of White professionals, people-of-color [Black, Latino] nonprofessionals, and representatives of the client group. The professionals, and especially the physicians, will not listen to the opinion of others about what clients need. They think their training has prepared them and there's no need to translate it into ethnic issues. For example, a patient needs a dietary change. There's no way you can make them stop eating rice and beans—you need to examine what in the diet is nutritious and supplement it rather than demand they stop. The patient doesn't come back because the professionals don't respect the culture.

Well, that sounds very logical when you explain it. But you said Whites can't learn what they need to know and that angers me.

I'm pessimistic about them doing it.

Then what am I here for. I feel like picking up my marbles and leaving.

Other White participants commented:

Why are you so angry about what he says. I feel I can learn what I need to know and I have something to offer.

I do too. I feel I try hard and I do a good job. If the patient doesn't return, it may not only be due to lack of respect. The patient could be resistant to working with Whites, period.

I understand where he's coming from. Watching how women were treated in an inpatient service I was on, I asked the same question about men, especially White men.

I can see how in the beginning of the work, such a question might be asked, but if a clinician is a good person and caring, he can do the work. If there's a problem, it may be the patient.

What does he think we take the Hippocratic Oath for? Physicians give equal treatment to everyone. We work hard to learn to help people; we are ready to help everyone.

Two Black participants then said:

That is precisely what is being said—that equal treatment may *not* be what is needed but rather specific treatment based on people's differences.

Sometimes clinicians may work hard and think they're helping, but aren't. What they're doing is helping patients according to their own need, making themselves rather than the patient feel better.

And received this response:

Well, I don't think it's any different for Whites working with Blacks than for Blacks working with Whites.

The Blacks responded:

Do you know what Blacks need? Yes, it is different. People-of-color live in a White world—we know what you're about and how to cope with you, but you can get away with not knowing about us. You don't have to think about us, and there's a lot you don't know that you may have to learn.

It's like when I worked in an all-White agency. I had to think about the meaning of my being Black to the client. And I constantly kept it in mind even though I knew White people—I live in their world. I didn't have to learn how they function.

These remarks angered some of the Whites, one of whom said:

No one is going to tell me what I have to do. That's your perception.

Another responded:

It's hopeless—we will never get beyond this anger.

At this point, the leader pointed out that while Whites were feeling angry, attacked, and put-down, people-of-color were feeling misunderstood and their pain ignored. She then asked how each would have wanted the other to respond. A White said:

Not attack us, but let us say what our response is, express *his* feelings of how he found it painful.

Another White said:

It doesn't matter what we say; it's never enough.

To which a Black responded:

What would be enough would be your being honest and expressing your feelings and not intellectualizing.

And received this response:

When I'm angry, I get defensive and that only makes for more anger—and more trouble. So I intellectualize.

The leader then commented:

Hearing that it may be different for Blacks than it is for Whites stirs up a lot of anger in you. It's important for you to know that. Patients may think this too. Why do you think this bothers you so much?

Silence. The leader asked:

What's going on?

The trainee responded, somewhat sadly:

I am thinking that if I can't use my experience to understand another's pain, how can I help?

The group could plainly see that there were feelings of pain and anger on both sides, with each wanting the other to express the pain instead of anger. For expression of anger by one party *tends to make the other feel like a victim*. At the same time, when one does express pain instead of anger, one feels vulnerable and can then feel like a victim. These dynamics become much clearer in the exploration of power.

Leader Qualifications

Leader style and qualifications are critical to the effectiveness of this approach. Paramount are skill in group process; relative comfort with conflict; flexibility, creativity, patience, and openness; and willingness to share one's own feelings and prejudices, thus modeling risk taking while at the same time maintaining control of the group. Also mandatory are a secure sense of ethnic and racial identity and the ability to interact with others in a non-power-oriented manner (Adams and Schlesinger 1988). Critical also is appreciation of differences in people, which is the primary desired outcome of the process. The leader demonstrates this in the use of the individual contract and in the respect shown for each participant in terms of purpose, depth of self-awareness, and capacity for growth (Adams and Schlesinger 1988).

While ready to share and model risk taking, the leader must also exercise care not to interfere when the work is going well, allowing participants to carry on the process as much as they can. Comfort and appreciation of differences in people imply a high tolerance for tension and conflict, which are often present when differences exist. Being able to encourage articulation of differences among participants and supporting the group while it works toward a comfortable stance require a leader skilled in managing tension and conflict.

Also key are conceptual clarity about the transactional nature of culture, power and systemic process, family dynamics, and coping strengths, since placing the content that members share in the context of concepts related to these issues is the key to the effectiveness of the process.

Composition of the Group

I have worked with groups in which there was heterogeneity of ethnicity, race, religion, educational background, and occupation and with groups that were much more homogeneous. In my opinion, groups in which members are from a variety of backgrounds are characterized by greater interaction and vividly demonstrate the multifaceted complexities involved in cross-cultural interaction. Although heterogeneous groups are more likely to involve conflict and require more attention to the complexities that arise, the experience is, in my opinion, far richer. The ultimate goal of appreciation for difference is forwarded by the aspect of heterogeneity which, if handled well, supplies us in vivo experience with difference. When the training group mirrors the cultural diversity of the client population and such persons are able to share personal and professional experiences, the experience can have special value, and all participants achieve greater depth and breadth of cultural understanding (Gaw 1982). On the other hand, Brislin and Pedersen (1976) suggest that homogeneous groups facilitate separating cultural from interpersonal differences better than do heterogeneous groups. Some experts on interracial groups advocate homogeneity because they believe resistance by majority persons and discomfort for minorities can be minimized (Katz 1978; Echols, Gabel, Landerman, and Reyes 1988).

> The most basic characteristic of the educational format is that it is an all-white group. This is essential to creating the atmosphere of security, safety and trust needed for participants to feel able to express, recognize and change racist attitudes and behaviors. In addition to fostering trust, the all-white group encourages the white students' racial identification. One of the important steps that whites must go through in learning about racism and their role in combatting it is to recognize themselves as white. While . . . ethnic minorities are forced by their racial oppression to be

aware of themselves as members of racial groups, whites generally have the luxury to feel "normal," not aware of their whiteness. (Echols et al. 1988, p. 18)

Some experts who work with heterogeneous groups separate them into smaller homogeneous subgroups for a brief period to attend to a specific task.

Homogeneous groups that are all White have presented an additional problem for me as an Afro-American. As the only person-of-color in the group, I am required to share information and provide the type of stimulus to interaction that usually occurs when other persons-of-color are present. Without this input, the group will fail to achieve certain insights. However, to function consistently as both a member and a leader creates confusion for group members as to which role I am taking at a given time. Moreover, it appears to mobilize more than the expectable degree of anger when the leader role is overexercised, causing increased resistance to the process. I no longer work with all-White groups and will recruit, if necessary, persons-of-color to participate.

Frequency, Duration, and Size of Group

The significance of enough time to do the work cannot be overestimated (Adams and Schlesinger 1988; Brislin 1981). In the groups I have conducted, the variation has ranged from one session to 30 sessions (8.5 months). Much of the data presented here has been taken from sessions spanning six to eight and a half months. When the time frame is short, only a superficial level can be reached. This, nonetheless, is beneficial for developing a beginning awareness. The percentage of sessions devoted to each stage may vary according to the needs of the group. In general, the range is as follows: ethnicity, 25 percent; difference 10 to 15 percent; race, 30 percent, and power, 30 percent.

External Factors

Many factors outside the group itself can influence its process. Key factors include sanctioning of the program by the administrator(s), whether or not group members work together closely outside of the group, and, if so, the kinds of relationships they have. Endorsement of the group by the decision-maker of the agency can be critical to its success (Brislin and Pedersen 1976). In my experience, when such sanction has been ambivalent, instructions by administrators about the group relative to its significance and to expectations such as regular attendance, have been unclear. This has interfered with the work of the group, requiring time and energy to obtain clarification and institutional commitment as a context for the work. When conflict and polarization exist in the work situation of group members, they tend to bring the associated anger, frustration, and feelings of powerlessness into the group. It is important to clarify these feelings and their sources, getting agreement to control their interference with the group process. This often lends emphasis to the importance of context in systemic process. It is particularly important to resolve, if possible, negative feelings that exist among group members who work together closely outside of the group. Otherwise, the threat of spillover into the work environment may cause withholding and defensive behavior within the group.

Caveat

It is important to point out that the process is *not* a therapeutic but rather an educational one. While it identifies roots of feelings and mobilizes early memories, the goal centers on growth in terms of self-understanding and development of attitudes and ways of thinking that will enhance functioning as a service-provider.

The process does tap significant psychological conflict, creating greater insight. Thus it facilitates increased self-acceptance and greater tolerance of ambivalence. Such changes may also be accompanied by diminished tendency toward bias. For some persons, conflicts connected with ethnic identity, racial, or power issues that are mobilized by the process may be so entrenched that mere identification and understanding of their dynamics are not enough to achieve comfort and control. In my opinion, such persons are better off having awareness of themselves and the dangers that exist for them in cross-cultural work. They can then make a choice in terms of whether to avoid such interaction altogether or whether to seek assistance in order to work further on these conflicts so that better functioning in cross-cultural work becomes possible.

Not to be overlooked is the fact that while this process seeks to reveal and clarify one's values, beliefs, assumptions, expectancies, and biases, it has an inbuilt value orientation of its own. This is validated by the fact that it values self-confrontation, openness, and sharing thoughts and feelings. These are all consistent with American cultural values, being essentially the values that guide most of the activity in mental health. However, these values may be incongruent with those of certain cultural groups whose members may find the process extraordinarily stressful. In several instances, for example, Asian participants have had such reactions.

Outline of Process

Introduction

- Explanation of the complexity of culture in human functioning covering the following parts:
- Definition of culture, ethnicity, race
- The transactional, systemic nature of culture and its existence at all levels of the social system
- The significance of power in cultural dynamics; cultural group status assignment and its effects
- The significance of culture on the individual level: effect on identity
- The significance of a clear and positive sense of cultural identity
- Relevance for practitioners as well as clients
- Description of the process
- Conducting the process
  —Goal setting
  —Contract

Exploring Ethnicity

Begin with questions.[1]
Use the participants' sharing to illustrate the following points:

- Significance of ethnicity is reflected in the strong reactions that people manifest when examining ethnic meaning

- The positive integrated sense of self necessary for sound functioning can be strongly influenced by ethnic meaning
- The universality of ambivalence
- The complexity of ethnicity
  —Ethnic meaning can come from multiple sources
  —In the absence of strong ethnic identity, other group connections may assume primacy, for example professional, gay, and so forth
  —People's definitions of themselves ethnically depend on definitions by others *but also on definition by themselves*
- American identity as the essence of the melting pot and the context for everyone
- Complexities cause inconsistency, confusion, ambiguity, identity conflict
  —Identity conflict as a major hazard
- Group status assignment as a key factor in cultural meaning: power becomes an issue
  —can cause negative identity or identity conflict
  —consequences of negative identity or identity conflict
- Significance for practice

Examining Difference

Begin with questions.
Use the participants' responses to illustrate the following points:

- Difference touches on powerful psychological issues; perceptions and feelings related to psychological separateness
- Responses have been internalized and are automatic when in the presence of difference
- Experiences predominantly negative
- Difference is usually perceived as "better than" rather than merely different from: a power-related issue.

As people respond to the questions, clarify the source of the experience, the context, and the feelings. Chart these on a chalkboard or flipchart.

Examining Race

Introduce this stage with comments that suggest:

- Understanding of own responses and consequences
- Taking responsibility for control over destructive responses
- Commitment to action that facilitates clinical effectiveness
- Acknowledgement of heightened anxiety of the stage
- Reaffirmation of goals and ground rules

Begin with questions.[2] (It is better to hold the question of collusion until all participants have grappled with the other questions and with the definition of racism.)
Use participants' sharing to illustrate the following points:

- Race is a biological term that has acquired social meaning through institutionalization of power differential
- Human service deliverers are trapped, like others, in biases that affect their work
- Freedom from entrapment is critical for effectiveness and requires awareness of racial meaning and control of responses
- Responses to experiences based on race are strong
  —Content is characterized by confusion, ambivalence, and pain that is well-defended against. These responses need to be understood
- There is less resistance to examining early experience and how one was taught bias
- People-of-color use a variety of mechanisms to cope with their racial experiences. These must be understood: effective coping mechanisms are critical
- The definition of racism demonstrates its systemic nature and the saliency of institutional racism
- The collusion of everyone in the perpetuation of racism must be understood
- Taking responsibility for collusion is critical for practitioners
  —Whites must acknowledge its benefit (see Ordway 1973)
  —People-of-color must acknowledge their internalization
- To assist clients who are victims of racism, practitioners need to be flexible, clear thinkers who are able to cope with

ambiguity and confusion, and comfortable with their own racial identity

- The significance for Whites and people-of-color that each individual becomes able to experience racial identity as a valued identity.
  —Significance for individual functioning
  —Significance for clinical work
  —Consideration of effort by each individual that is needed to attain this sense of value in relation to racial identity

Exploring Power

Summarize the connections made so far between ethnicity and power, difference and power, race and power.

- Define power on individual, interactional, cultural group levels
- Note the significance of power in clinical work that is compounded by the cultural status group assignment of practitioner and client
  —Vigilance is needed to guard against vulnerability to exploration of power on these two levels

Begin with questions. (As participants respond to the questions, record feelings and responses on a chalk board or flipchart so that a picture emerges similar to the chart on pp. 130–133.) Use the sharing of participants to illustrate the following points:

- Everyone has experiences having and lacking power on the various levels of human functioning
- Context is critical to this understanding and experiences related to power stemming from family experience and identity related to ethnicity, race, sex, and other identities must be understood
- Full understanding of everyone's own experiences with having power requires identifying feelings and behaviors, benefits, and costs
- Full understanding of everyone's own experiences with lacking power requires identifying feelings and behaviors and the consequences of powerlessness

- When understanding is applied to clinical work, practitioners must consider:
  —How much is gratification in the practitioner's role related to power inherent in clinical or cultural group status role?
  —How much are treatment goals and process dependent on the practitioner's personal need for power?
  —The dilemma of the practitioner:
  A sense of power is critical to mental health
  Power in the clinical and aggrandized cultural group role is gratifying
- Effective clinical outcome requires a shift in client's perception of self as victim and perception of practitioner as aggrandized
- A shift in power can be experienced as a psychological loss that will not be risked if personal need for power is great
- The solution: to perceive the shift not as a loss but a gain— to be capable of vulnerability in sharing power
- The benefit: freedom from entrapment and appreciation of differences in people.

Classroom Model

Cultural self-understanding can also be acquired in a classroom format despite the fact that the emphasis may be primarily conceptual rather than experiential. While some exploration can occur through class discussions, the emotional work usually executed in the experiential group occurs primarily in the written assignment which requires students to analyze their own cultural identity and that of their client(s) and to consider the significance of these for their work at the clinical interface.

Assignment

Paper on the Significance for the Cultural Interface in Treatment
Select two clients (one from a majority cultural group and one from a minority cultural group).
Discuss briefly

- Your own cultural group in terms of
  —Values, norms, and beliefs including race, class, and power determinants. Consider the significance of economic, social, and political realities and their effect on the group's definition of itself.
  —Your family's adaptation to these values, norms, and beliefs
  —Your own individual cultural sense of identity and meaning
- The cultural identity of each of your clients in terms of values, norms, and beliefs, including race, class, and power determinants; and
- The significance of the interfacing of these two identities in treatment, with a focus on goals, relationship, and process.

The assignment is constructed to give students an opportunity to struggle with the complexities of cross-cultural work in an orderly fashion. It presses them to think generally about a given cultural group and then specifically about individuals. Thus they learn to consider a client's uniqueness within that context. When they are required to conduct this analysis with a minority and a majority group client, the issue of race also becomes the subject of analysis.

Students will become anxious about the assignment since at the outset they are unable to anticipate how it will come together. If their sense of cultural identity is extremely fragmented and ambivalent and they cannot deal with the confusion and anxiety that the paper mobilizes, they may become blocked and be unable to complete the paper. In such cases, they may require support from the instructor and extra time to complete the assignment.

Notes

CHAPTER 3

1. The idea of specialness, as examined by Erikson (1968), serves as a mechanism for reinforcing a positive sense of cultural identity. This illusion of being chosen uses other groups "as a screen of projection for negative identities." While enhancing group cohesiveness through the mechanism of shared illusion and the promotion of self-esteem, this mechanism also encourages conflict between groups. The issue of power is readily apparent in the use of such a mechanism, which suggests one group is superior to others (p. 40).

CHAPTER 4

1. Ko-Yung Tung, "Census Puzzle," *The New York Times,* April 13, 1980, p. 18-E.

2. Comment made by Chet Curtis on "World of Difference," WCVB-TV, Boston, 1980.

3. McGill and Pearce (1983) state:

> The acronym WASP—White Anglo-Saxon Protestant—has been used in loose reference to Americans who are White, Protestant, and primarily of early British immigrant origins. In addition, the terms WASP and Anglo-American have been used to refer to American families who have been in the United States a long time, to those participating in what Margaret Mead has described as the "American Culture" . . . and to refer to White Protestant Americans of vague or mixed national origins, as distinguished from a single, ethnic designation.

243

CHAPTER 5

1. This behavior is consistent with Bowen's (1978) theory of the societal projection process through which victims, for example minorities, perform a function in the social system whereby they provide a sense of stability and relative freedom from anxiety and tension for benefactor–beneficiaries, i.e., Whites (E. Pinderhughes 1983). Kovel (1970) also cites White racism as a stabilizing force in American culture, because it serves as a source of gratification, defines social meaning, absorbs aggression, and facilitates a sense of virtue.

2. Louise Sparks and Carole Phillips used the following definition in *Becoming Anti-Racist*, a paper presented at the annual meeting of the American Orthopsychiatric Association, Boston, April 1983:

   Racism involves more than prejudice (prejudging, projecting attributes onto another). It is concerned with power arrangements whereby individuals of one group are maintained in a subordinate position (victim) by another (benefactor) because of biological origin. This subordination is maintained via institutional structures, ideology (attitudes, belief) and interpersonal behavior. These interactions produce outcomes which tend in all cases to be beneficial to Whites economically, politically and psychologically. There are three main assumptions:

   1. Racism is the product of culture and of certain historical, political, economic arrangements. People are *socialized* to think and behave in racist ways.
   2. Racism is created and maintained by the actions of people.
   3. Both Whites and people-of-color maintain racism.

3. See Sparks and Phillips in *Becoming Anti-Racist* (1983) for definition of collusion. People-of-color maintain their oppressed position when they adopt ways of managing racism that accept society as it is but do not attempt to resolve it or change the oppressor–oppressed relationship. They may:

   a. Identify with the aggressor—attribute the major problems to people's life-styles although they don't openly believe in their group's innate inferiority.

   b. Focus on culture, seeing the stereotype of the group as the main issue. In refusing to fit in with the society's stereotype, romanticizing beauty and specialness of culture, they do not challenge the institutional arrangements.

   c. Avoid focus on race and attempt to achieve individual success.

4. Annual Conference on Mental Health, sponsored by the Black Task Force, San Francisco General Hospital, October 1984.

CHAPTER 8

1. Spiegel (1975) identifies this as the role of cultural broker.

CHAPTER 9

1. Lynn Hoffman, quoted in the inscription of the Tenth Annual Family Therapy Network Symposium (1987) Conference Brochure.

APPENDIX

1. For additional ideas, see DeVore and Schlesinger (1981b), Green (1982), and McGoldrick et al. (1983).
2. See Katz (1978) for supplementary materials that can facilitate this exploration.

References

ADAMS, A., & SCHLESINGER, S. (1988). Group approach to training ethnic sensitive practitioners. In C. Jacobs & D. Bowles (Eds.), *Ethnicity and race: Critical concepts in social work.* Silver Spring: NASW Publication.

ANDERSON, R. & CARTER, I. (1984). *Human behavior in the social environment.* New York: Aldine Publishers.

ARCE, A. (1982). Cultural aspects of mental health care for Hispanic Americans. In A. Gaw (Ed.), *Cross cultural psychiatry* (137–148). Littleton, MA: Wright-PSG.

ATTNEAVE, C. (1983). American Indians and Alaska Native families; Emigrants in their own homeland. In M. McGoldrick, J. Pearce, & J. Giordano (Eds.), *Ethnicity and family therapy* (55–83). New York: Guilford Press.

BASCH, M. (1975). Toward a theory that encompasses depression: A revision of existing causal hypotheses in psychoanalysis. In J. Anthony & T. Benedek (Eds.), *Depression and human existence.* Boston: Brown.

BASS, B., WYATT, G. & POWELL, G. (1982). *The Afro-American family: Assessment, treatment and research issues.* New York: Grune & Stratton.

BELL, C., BLAND, I., HOUSTON, E., & JONES, K. (1983). Enhancement of knowledge and skill for the psychiatric treatment of black populations. In J. C. Chunn II, S. J. Dunston, & J. Ross-Sheriff (Eds.), *Mental health and people-of-color: Curriculum development and changes.* Washington, DC: Howard University Press.

BERGER, R. & FEDERICO, R. (1985). *Human behavior: A perspective for the helping professions.* New York: Longman.

BERNAL, G. & GUTIERREZ, M. (1988). Cubans. In L. Comas-Diaz, & E. Griffith (Eds.), *Cross-cultural mental health*. New York: Wiley.

BLANCHARD, E. B. (1981). Observations on social work with American Indian women. In A. Weick & S. Vandiver (Eds.), *Women, power and change* (96–103). Washington, DC: National Association of Social Workers.

BOCHNER, S. (1982). *Culture in contact*. New York: Pergamon Press.

BOWEN, M. (1978). *Family therapy in clinical practice*. New York: Jason Aronson.

BRADSHAW, W. (1978, December). Training psychiatrists for working with blacks in basic residency programs. *American Journal of Psychiatry, 135* (12), 1520–1524.

BRAGG, R. (1982). Cultural aspects of mental health care for black Americans. In A. Gaw (Ed.), *Cross-cultural psychiatry*. Littleton, MA: Wright-PSG.

BRICE, J. (1983). West Indian families. In M. McGoldrick, J. Pearce, & J. Giordano (Eds.), *Ethnicity and family therapy*. New York: Guilford Press.

BRISLIN, R. (1981). *Cross cultural encounters*. New York: Pergamon Press.

BRISLIN, R. & PEDERSEN, P. (1976). *Cross cultural orientation programs*. New York: Gardner Press.

BROWN, C. (1984, September 16). Manchild in Harlem. *New York Times Magazine*, p. 40.

CAFFERTY, P. & CHESTANG, L. (1976). *The diverse society: Implications for social policy*. Washington, DC: NASW.

CHARLES, C. (1986). Mental health services for Haitians. In H. Lefley & P. Pedersen (Eds.), *Cross-cultural training for mental health professionals*. Springfield, IL: Charles C Thomas.

CHESTANG, L. (1972). *Character development in a hostile environment* (Occasional Paper No. 3). Chicago: University of Chicago School of Social Service Administration.

_____. (1976). Environmental influences on social functioning: The black experience. In P. Cafferty & L. Chestang (Eds.), *The diverse society: Implications for social policy*. Washington, DC: NASW.

COMAS-DIAZ, L. (1988). Cross-cultural mental health treatment. In L. Comas-Diaz & E. Griffith (Eds.), *Clinical guidelines in cross-cultural mental health* (335–362). New York: Wiley.

COMAS-DIAZ, L. & GRIFFITH, E. (1988). *Clinical guidelines in cross-cultural mental health*. New York: Wiley.

DE LA CANCELA, V. (1983). An analysis of culturalism in Latino mental health: Folk medicine as a case in point. *Hispanic Journal of Behavioral Sciences, 5*(3), 251–274.

_____. (1985). Toward a socio-cultural psychotherapy for low-income ethnic minorities. *Psychotherapy, 22*(25), 427–435.

DE VORE, W., & SCHLESINGER, E. (1981a). *Ethnic sensitive social work practice.* St. Louis: C. V. Mosby.

_____. (1981b). Instructor's manual to accompany *Ethnic sensitive social work practice.* St. Louis: C. V. Mosby.

_____. (1987). *Ethnic sensitive social work practice.* Columbus, OH: Merrill Publishing.

DRAGUNS, J. (1981). Cross-cultural counseling and psychotherapy: History, issues, current states. In A. Marsella & P. Pedersen (Ed.), *Cross-cultural counseling and psychotherapy.* New York: Pergamon.

DRAPER, B. (1979). Black language as an adaptive response to a hostile environment. In Germain, C. (Ed.), *Social work practice: People and environments* (276). New York: Columbia University Press.

ECHOLS, I., GABEL, C., LANDERMAN, D., & REYES, M. (1988). An approach for addressing racism, ethnocentrism, and sexism in the curriculum. In C. Jacobs & D. Bowles (Eds.), *Ethnicity and race.* Silver Spring, MD: National Association of Social Workers.

ERIKSON, E. (1968). *Identity: Youth and culture.* New York: Norton.

EVANS, D. (1985, Summer). Psychotherapy and black patients. *Psychotherapy, 22*(2), 457–460.

FALICOV, C. J. (1983). Mexican families. In M. McGoldrick, J. Pearce, & J. Giordano (Eds.), *Ethnicity and family therapy.* New York: Guilford Press.

FIELDSTEIN, D. & GIORDANO, J. (1976, March). *The new pluralism and social work education.* Paper presented at the annual meeting of the Council of Social Work Education.

FERGUSON, Y. (1982). Improving intervention strategies with minority group adolescents. In B. Bass, G. Wyatt, & Powell, G. (Eds.), *The Afro-American family: Assessment treatment and research* (203–210). New York: Grune & Stratton.

GANTER, G., & YEAKEL, M. (1980). *Human behavior and the social environment.* New York: Columbia University Press.

GARCIA, E., GIBSON, G. & MALDONANDO, D. (1978). *A model course syllabi compendium: Social work and Chicano content.* Houston: Chicano Training Center.

GARCIA-PRETO, N. (1983). Puerto Rican families. In M. McGoldrick, J. Pearce, & J. Giordano (Eds.), *Ethnicity and family therapy.* New York: Guilford Press.

_____. (1988). Institute on Ethnicity and Family Therapy. Annual Meeting, American Orthopsychiatric Association, San Francisco.

GARY, L. (1981). *Black men.* Beverly Hills: Sage Publications.

———. (1978). *Mental health: A challenge to the black community.* Philadelphia: Dorrance.

GAW, A. (1982). Chinese Americans. In A. Gaw (Ed.) *Cross-cultural psychiatry.* Littleton, MA: Wright-PSG.

GEHRIE, M. (1976). Aspects of the dynamics of prejudice. *Annual of Psychoanalysis, 4,* 423–446.

———. (1979, May). Culture as internal representation. *Psychiatry,* 42(5), 165–170.

GELLER, J. (1988). *Racial bias: The evaluation of patients for psychotherapy in clinical guidelines in cross-cultural mental health.* New York: Wiley.

GERMAIN, C. (1979). *Social work practice: People and environment.* New York: Columbia University Press.

GIBBS, J. T. (1980). The interpersonal orientation in mental health consultation: Toward a model of ethnic variations in consultation. *Journal of Community Psychiatry, 8,* 195–207.

GILLIAM, D. (1982, October 2). "Black-White: Lawsuit points out current state of race relations." *The Washington Post.*

GILLIGAN, C. (1982). *In a different voice.* Cambridge: Harvard University Press.

GIORDANO, J. (1975, Winter). Servicing and organizing the white ethnic working class community. *Journal of Education for Social Work,* 11(1), 37–43.

———. (1988, March). *Workshop on ethnicity and family therapy.* Annual Conference American Orthopsychiatric Association, San Francisco.

GIORDANO, J., & LEVINE, M. (1975). *Mental health and middle America: A group identity approach,* (Working Paper Series No. 14). New York Institute on Pluralism and Group Identity.

GLAZER, N., & MOYNIHAN, D. (1963). *Beyond the melting pot.* Cambridge: M.I.T. Press.

GOMEZ, A. (1982). Puerto Rican Americans. In A. Gaw (Ed.), *Cross-cultural psychiatry* (109–136). Littleton, MA: Wright-PSG.

GORDON, M. (1981, March). Models of pluralism: The new American dilemma. *Annals of the American Academy of Political and Social Science,* 178–188.

GREELEY, A. (1976). Why study ethnicity? In J. Cafferty & L. Chestang (Eds.), *The diverse society: Implications for social policy.* Washington, DC: NASW.

GREEN, J. (1982). *Cultural awareness in the human services.* Englewood Cliffs, NJ: Prentice-Hall.

GREENSON, R., TONEY, E., LIM, P., & ROMERO, A. (1982). Transference and countertransference in interracial psychotherapy. In Bass, Wyatt, & Powell (Eds.), *The Afro-American family: Assessment, treatment and research issues.* New York: Grune & Stratton.

HALE, J. (1980). The black woman and child rearing. In L. F. Rodgers-Rose (Ed.), *The black woman.* Beverly Hills, CA: Sage.

HARRIS, O., & Balgopal, P. (1980). Intervening with the black family. In C. Janzen & O. Harris (Eds.), *Family treatment and social work practice.* Itasca, IL: Peacock Publishers.

HELLER, D. (1985). *Power in psychotherapeutic practice.* New York: Human Services Press.

HO, M. K. (1987). *Family therapy with ethnic minorities.* Beverly Hills, CA: Sage.

HOPPS, J. (1982, June). Oppression based on color (editorial). *Social Work, 27*(1), 3–5.

HOWARD, J., & HAMMOND, R. (1985, September 9). Rumors of inferiority: Barriers to black success in America. *The New Republic,* pp. 17–21.

IVEY, A. (1981). Counseling and psychotherapy: Toward a new perspective. In A. J. Marsella & P. Pedersen (Eds.), *Cross-cultural counseling and psychotherapy* (279–311). New York: Pergamon Press.

JACKSON, A. (1981, Winter). Education for multiracial practice in Great Britain. *Journal of Education for Social Work. 17*(1), 102–110.

JACKSON, G. (1985). Cross-cultural counseling with Afro-Americans. In *Handbook of cross-cultural counseling and therapy.* Westport, CT: Greenwood Press.

———. (1987, April). Institute on cultural sensitivity. Annual Meeting Washington, DC: American Orthopsychiatric Association.

JACOBSEN, F. (1988). Ethnocultural assessment. In L. Comas-Diaz & E. Griffith (Eds.), *Cross-cultural mental health.* New York: Wiley.

JALALI, B. (1988). Ethnicity, cultural adjustment and behavior: Implications for family therapy. In L. Comas-Diaz & E. Griffith (Eds.), *Cross-cultural mental health.* New York: Wiley.

JENKINS, A. (1985). Attending to self-activity in the Afro-American client. *Psychotherapy 22*(2S), 338–340.

JENKINS, S. (1981). *The ethnic dilemma in the human services.* New York: Free Press.

———. (1988). Ethnicity: Theory base and practice link. In *Ethnicity and race: Critical concepts in social work.* Washington, DC: NASW.

JOLOPINTO, J. (1983, May–June). Guess who's coming to therapy. *Networker, 7*(3).

KATZ, J. (1978). *White awareness: Handbook for antiracism training.* Norman: University of Oklahoma Press.

KEEFE, T. (1984). Alienation and social work practice. *Social Casework: The Journal of Contemporary Social Work, 63*(3), 145–153.

KLEIN, J. (1980). *Jewish identity and self-esteem.* New York: Institute on Pluralism & Group Identity, American Jewish Committee.

_____. (1976A). *Theory and application of ethno therapy to Jews.* New York: Institute on Pluralism and Group Identity, American Jewish Committee.

_____ (1976B) Ethnotherapy with Jews. *International Journal of Mental Health, 5*(2).

KLINE, H. K. (1970). An exploration of racism. In *Ego ideal formation.* Smith College Studies in Social Work, 40 (3), 211–235.

KLINEBERG, O. (1982). Contact between ethnic groups: A historical perspective of some aspects of theory and research. In Bochner, S. (Ed.) *Cultures in contact.* New York: Pergamon Press.

KNOWLES, L., & PREWITT, K. (1969). *Institutional racism in America.* Englewood Cliffs, NJ: Prentice-Hall.

KOVEL, J. (1970). *White racism: A psychohistory.* New York: Pantheon Books.

LEE, E. (1983). A social systems approach to assessment and treatment for Chinese-American families. In M. McGoldrick, J. Pearce, & J. Giordano (Eds.), *Ethnicity and family therapy.* New York: Guilford Press.

LEFLEY, H. (1986). Introduction to cross-cultural training. In H. Lefley & P. Pedersen (Eds.), *Cross-cultural training for mental health professionals.* Springfield, IL: Charles C Thomas.

LEFLEY, H., & PEDERSEN, P. (Eds.). (1986). *Cross-cultural training for mental health professionals.* Springfield, IL: Charles C Thomas.

LEIGHTON, A. (1982). Relevant generic issues. In A. Gaw (Ed.), *Cross-cultural psychiatry.* Littleton, MA: Wright-PSG.

LEVINE, I., & Giordano, J. (1978, March). Ethnicity as social ecology. (Working paper series no. 19.) New York: Institute on Pluralism and Group Identity.

LICHTENBERG, P., REINERT, C., & LEVINE, S. (1983, April 6). *Psychological contributions to social struggle.* Paper presented at annual meeting of the American Orthopsychiatric Association, Boston.

LONGRES, J. (1982, January). Minority groups: An interest group perspective. *Social work, 27*(1), 7–14.

LUM, D. (1986). *Social work practice and people of color.* Monterey, CA: Brooks-Cole.

MAHLER, M. (1975). *The psychological birth of the human infant.* New York: Basic Books.

MARTINEZ, C. (1988). Mexican-Americans. In L. Comas-Diaz & E. Griffith (Eds.), *Cross-cultural mental health.* New York: Wiley.

MAY, G. (1976). Personality development and ethnic identity. In *The diverse society: Implications for social policy*. Washington, DC: NASW.

McCLELLAND, D. (1975). *Power: The inner experience*. New York: Wiley.

McGILL, D., & PEARCE, J. (1983). British families. In J. McGoldrick, J. Pearce, & J. Giordano (Eds.), *Ethnicity and family therapy*. New York: Guilford Press.

McGOLDRICK, M. (1983). Ethnicity and family therapy: An overview. In M. McGoldrick, J. Pearce, & J Giordano (Eds.), *Ethnicity and family therapy*. New York: Guilford Press.

_____. (1984, January 18). *Fourth Annual Prominent Family Therapy Workshop*. Sponsored by Coastal Community Counseling Center, Copley Plaza, Boston.

McGOWAN, B. (1988). Helping Puerto Rican families at risk: Responsive use of time, space and relationships. In *Ethnicity and race: Critical concepts in social work*. Silver Spring, MD: NASW.

MEDICINE, B. (1981). American Indian family: Cultural change and adaptive strategies. *Journal of Ethnic Studies, 8*, 13–23.

MENDES, H. (1982). The role of religion in psychotherapy with Afro-Americans. In B. Bass, G. Wyatt & G. Powell (Eds.), *The Afro-American family: Assessment, treatment, and research issues*. New York: Grune & Stratton.

MILLER, J. B. (1982, May). Evil women: A consideration of the origins of destructiveness in women and men. *Distinguished Psychiatrist Lecture Series*. Annual Conference, American Psychiatric Association, Toronto.

MONTEIL, M., & WONG, P. (1983, February). A theoretical critique of the minority perspective. *Social Casework, 64*(2), 112–117.

MYERS, H. (1982). Research on the Afro-American family: A critical review. In B. Bass, G. Wyatt, & G. Powell (Eds.), *The Afro-American family: Assessment, treatment, and research issues* (35–68). New York: Grune and Stratton.

NAVARRO, V. (1980, November). Panel on culture and health. *Symposium on Cross-cultural and Transcultural Issues in Family Health Care*. University of California, San Francisco.

News from the Committee. (1980). New York: Institute on Pluralism and Group Identity.

NORTHERN, H. (1987). Assessment in direct practice. *Encyclopedia of social work* (18th ed.) (212–222). Silver Spring, MD: National Association of Social Workers.

NORTON, D. (1976). Residential environment and black self-image. In S. Pastora, J. Cafferty, & L. Chestang (Eds.), *The diverse society: Implications for social policy*. Washington, DC: NASW.

ORDWAY, J. (1973). Some consequences of racism for whites. In C. Willie, B. Brown, & B. Kramer (Eds.), *Racism and mental health*. Pittsburgh: University of Pittsburgh Press.

PADILLA, A. (1981). Pluralistic counseling and psychotherapy for Hispanic Americans. In A. Marsella & P. Pedersen (Eds.), *Cross-cultural counseling and psychotherapy*. New York: Pergamon Press.

PALMER, S. (1983, March). Authority: An essential part of practice. *Social Work, 28*(2).

PAPAJOHN, J., & SPIEGEL, J. (1976). *Transactions in families*. San Francisco: Jossey-Bass.

PASTER, V. (1985, Summer). Adapting psychotherapy for the depressed, unacculturated, acting out, black male adolescent. *Psychotherapy, 22*(5), 408–416.

_____. (1986, October). A social action model of intervention for difficult-to-reach populations. *American Journal of Orthopsychiatry, 56*(4), 625–629.

PEDERSEN, P., & LEFLEY, L. (1986). Introduction to cross-cultural training. In P. Pedersen & L. Lefley (Eds.), *Cross-cultural training for mental health professionals*. Springfield, IL: Charles C Thomas.

PIERCE, C. (1970). Offensive mechanisms. In F. Barbour (Ed.), *The black seventies*. Boston: Sargent Publishers.

PINDERHUGHES, C. (1973). Racism in psychotherapy. In C. Willie, B. Brown, & B. Kramer (Eds.), *Racism and mental health*. Pittsburgh: University of Pittsburgh Press.

_____. (1974). Ego development and cultural differences. *American Journal of Psychiatry, 131*(2), 171–175.

_____. (1986, Spring). The American racial dilemma: A social psychiatric formulation. *American Journal of Social Psychiatry, 6*(2), 107–113.

PINDERHUGHES, C., & PINDERHUGHES, E. (1982). Perspective of the training directors. In A. Gaw (Ed.), *Cross-cultural psychiatry*. Littleton, MA: Wright-PSG.

PINDERHUGHES, E. (1979, July). Teaching empathy in cross-cultural social work. *Social Work, 24*(4), 312–316.

_____. (1982, January). Family functioning of Afro Americans. *Social Work, 27*(1), 91–6.

_____. (1982, March). Black genealogy: Self-liberator and therapeutic tool. *Smith College Studies for Social Work, 52*(2), 93–106.

_____. (1983, June). Empowerment for our clients and for ourselves. *Social Casework, 64*(6), 331–338.

_____. (1984). Teaching empathy: Ethnicity, race and power at the cross-cultural treatment interface. *American Journal of Social Psychiatry, 4*(1), 5–12.

PINDERHUGHES, E. (1986). Minority woman: A nodal point in the functioning of the social system. In M. Ault-Riche (Ed.), *Women and family therapy*. Rockville, MD Aspen Systems Corp.

PINDERHUGHES, E., KIRKPATRICK, W., PANESWICH, K., SALANDES, N., & WELTS, D. (1979, April). The effect of ethnicity on the psychological task of separation–individuation. Paper presented at annual conference of American Orthopsychiatric Association.

POWELL, G. (1982). Six-city study of school desegregation and self-concept among Afro-American junior high school students: A preliminary study with implications for mental health. In B. Bass, G. Wyatt, & G. Powell (Eds.), *Afro-American family: Assessment, treatment and research issues*. New York: Grune & Stratton.

RAMOS-MCKAY, J., & COMAS-DIAZ, L., & RIVERA, L. (1988). Puerto Ricans. In L. Comas-Diaz & E. Griffith (Eds.), *Cross-cultural mental health*. New York: Wiley.

ROGERS, C. (1977). *Carl Rogers on personal power*. New York: Dell Publishing.

RUBIN, A. (1987). Case management. *Encyclopedia of social work* (18th ed.) (212–222). Silver Spring, MD: National Association of Social Workers.

RUIZ, R. A., & PADILLA, A. B. (1977). *Personnel and Guidance Journal*, 55, 401–408.

RYAN, A. S. (1985). Cultural factors in casework with Chinese Americans. *Social Casework, 66*(6), 333–340.

SANDERS, D. (1975). Dynamics of ethnic and cultural pluralism. *Journal of Social Work Education, 11*(3), 95–100.

SATA, L. (1982). Discussion: Cultural issues in psychiatric training: Perspectives of training directors and residents. In A. Gaw (Ed.), *Cross-cultural psychiatry*. Littleton, MA: Wright-PSG.

SCHOFIELD, W. (1964). *Psychotherapy: The purchase of friendship*. Englewood Cliffs, NJ: Prentice-Hall.

SHON, S., & JA, D. Y. (1983). Asian families. In. M. McGoldrick, J. Pearce, & J. Giordano (Eds.), *Ethnicity and family therapy*. New York: Guilford Press.

SEIDENBERG, R. (1984, October). *Know something, do something*. Presentation at the Annual Conference and Training Institute, American Academy of Psychotherapists, Chicago.

SIU, R. G. H. (1979). *The craft of power*. New York: John Wiley & Sons.

SOLOMON, B. (1982). The delivery of mental health services to Afro-American individuals and families: Translating theory into practice. In. B. Bass, G. Wyatt, & G. Powell (Eds.), *The Afro-American family: Assessment treatment and research issues*. New York: Grune & Stratton.

SOLOMON, B. (1976). Social work in multiethnic society. In M. Sotomayor (Ed.), *Cross-cultural perspectives in social work practice and education* (pp. 165–176). Council on Social Work Education.

SPARKS, L., & Phillips, C. (1983, April). *Becoming anti-racist*. Paper presented at annual meeting of the American Orthopsychiatric Association, Boston.

SPIEGEL, J. (1984, Winter). Ethnic issues in family therapy. *Newsletter of the American Family Therapy Association*, Number 18, p. 2.

_____. (1975). Cultural aspects of transference and countertransference revisited. *Journal of the American Academy of Psychoanalysis*, 4(4), 447–467.

SPURLOCK, J. (1973). Some consequences of racism for children. *Racism and mental health*. Pittsburgh: University of Pittsburgh Press.

_____. (1982). Black Americans. In A. Gaw (Ed.), *Cross-cultural psychiatry*. Littleton, MA: Wright-PSG.

STEMPLER, B. (1975, October). Effects of aversive racism on white social work students. *Social Casework*, 56(8), 460–467.

SUE, D. (1978, April). World views and counseling. *Personnel and Guidance Journal*, 458–62.

_____. (1980). *Cross-cultural counseling position paper*. Position paper from the Education and Training Committee. Washington, DC: American Psychological Association.

SUNDBERG, N. (1981). Cross-cultural counseling and psychotherapy: A research overview. In A. Marsella & P. Pedersen (Eds.), *Cross-cultural counseling and psychotherapy*. New York: Pergamon Press.

TENTH ANNUAL FAMILY SYMPOSIUM. (1987). Conference Brochure, "Who's responsible for change." Washington, DC.

THOMAS, P. (1967). *Down these mean streets*. New York: Vintage Books.

THOMPSON, J., BLUEYE, H., SMITH, C., & WALKER, R. D. (1983). Cross-cultural curriculum content in psychiatric residency training: An American Indian and Alaska Native perspective. In J. Chunn, P. Dunston, & F. Ross-Sherrif (Eds.), *Mental health and people of color* (269–288). Washington, D.C.: Howard University Press.

VALDEZ, T., & GALLEGOS, G. (1982). The Chicano familia in social work. In J. Green (Ed.), *Cultural awareness in the human services*, Englewood-Cliffs: Prentice-Hall.

WARNER, J. (1987, April). *Clinical practice with biracial families*. Paper presented at the Annual Conference of the American Orthopsychiatric Association, Washington, DC.

WEAVER, D. (1982). Empowering treatment skills for helping black families. *Social Casework*, 63(2), 100–105.

WILKESON, A. (1982). Mexican Americans. In A. Gaw (Ed.), *Cross-cultural psychiatry*. Littleton, MA: Wright-PSG.

WINICOTT, D. (1971). *Playing as reality.* London: Tavistock Publications.

WRONG, D. (1980). *Power: Its forms, bases and uses.* New York: Harper & Row.

WYATT, G. (1982). Sociocultural assessment of home and school visits in psychiatric evaluations of Afro-American children and families. In B. Bass, G. Wyatt, & G. Powell (Eds.), *The Afro-American family: Assessment treatment and research issues* (35–68). New York: Grune and Stratton.

WYATT, G., BASS, B., & POWELL, G. (1980). *A cognitive and affective assessment of mental health professionals' attitude towards Afro-Americans: A preliminary study.* Prepublication manuscript. Department of Psychiatry, Neuropsychiatric Institute, UCLA Center for the Health Sciences.

ZUNIGA-MARTINEZ, M. (1988). Chicano self-concept: A practice stance. In C. Jacobs and D. Boules (Eds.), *Ethnicity and race: Critical concepts in social work.* Washington, DC: NASW.

Index